Yale Russian and East European Studies, 10

Andrew D. Kalmykow (Andrei Dmitrievich Kalmykov)
(1870–1941), taken around 1902.

Memoirs of a Russian Diplomat

OUTPOSTS OF THE EMPIRE, 1893–1917

by Andrew D. Kalmykow

Edited by Alexandra Kalmykow

New Haven and London, Yale University Press, 1971

B
Kalmykov,
A.D.

Designed by John O. C. McCrillis
and set in Baskerville type.
Printed in the United States of America by
The Vail-Ballou Press, Binghamton, New York.

Distributed in Great Britain, Europe, and Africa by
Yale University Press, Ltd., London; in Canada by
McGill-Queen's University Press, Montreal; in Mexico
by Centro Interamericano de Libros Académicos,
Mexico City; in Central and South America by Kaiman
& Polon, Inc., New York City; in Australasia by
Australia and New Zealand Book Co., Pty., Ltd.,,
Artarmon, New South Wales; in India by UBS Publishers'
Distributors Pvt., Ltd., Delhi; in Japan by John
Weatherhill, Inc., Tokyo.

M. Kalmikoff, jeune diplomate d'une intelligence et d'un esprit politique remarquables.

PAUL DOUMER, President of France (1931–32),
L'Indo-Chine Française

Contents

Illustrations

Foreword

Diplomats are not the best writers of memoirs. Professional caution and habitual reticence tend to prevent them from revealing official secrets; good manners make it difficult to indulge in personal gossip. If the temptation to write becomes too great, a diplomat will usually put together a string of stories about travels, receptions, dinners, conversations, and a hunting party or two. A reader who expects to be given a close look at the inner workings of international politics races avidly through the book only to be disappointed in the end.

Russian diplomats wrote even less than their German, French, or English colleagues. However, the Bolshevik Revolution, which broke up and scattered the personnel of the old ministry of foreign affairs, freed all the stranded ambassadors, consuls, and attachés of the necessity to keep the secrets of a vanished regime. A number of them, including S. D. Sazonov, former minister of foreign affairs, rushed to tell the public of their experiences. A few waited many years to gain the proper perspective and achieve some detachment before setting pen to paper. A. D. Kalmykow spent almost a quarter of a century working for the imperial government. He is unique among Russian diplomatic memorialists in having been trained in Oriental studies and having served in such posts as Tabriz, Astarābād, Bangkok, Ashkhabad, and Uskub. His *Memoirs of a Russian Diplomat* is not a detailed autobiography. It provides only glimpses of a past which has already become incredibly distant: childhood in Simferopol and the sight of Turkish prisoners of the war of 1877–78; grandfather

telling the boy one March morning that Tsar Alexander II had just
been assassinated; Mendeleiev lecturing at the University of St.
Petersburg; Tolstoy chasing a dog out of his study . . . The main
subject matter of the book is, of course, the author's diplomatic
career, for which the foundation was laid in the Asiatic Department
of the Ministry of Foreign Affairs.

Perhaps the most fascinating pages of the book are those dealing
with Persia in 1896, the year Nāser ed-Din Shah was assassinated and
his inept son, Mozaffar ed-Din, mounted the throne. For several
decades Russia and Britain had been fighting a silent battle for
predominance in the empire of the shah. When young Kalmykow
arrived in Tehran, Russia's influence was in the ascendant. He has
nothing to say about his country's policies, preferring to chronicle
the social life of Tehran's tiny foreign colony. Yet he provides bits
and pieces of valuable information. Where else would one find a
characterization of E. K. Biutsov (Bützow), the Russian minister, and
A. N. Shcheglov, his counselor, both capable and highly influential
men? The only comparable Russian source, the diary of Colonel
V. O. Kosogovskii, commander of the Persian Cossack Brigade, has
not been published in full. Where else would one find an expression
of Russian private views of Amin os-Soltān and Amin od-Dowleh,
the two Persian statesmen who dominated the scene after the death
of Nāser ed-Din Shah?

During his service in Tehran, Bangkok, Ashkhabad, Tashkent, and
St. Petersburg, Kalmykow met and dealt with a large number of
history makers of the early twentieth century, among them the future president of France, Paul Doumer; General A. N. Kuropatkin,
who would lead Russian armies to defeat in the Japanese war; Sir
Charles Hardinge, one of the architects of the entente; General N. I.
Grodekov, a participant in and historian of the conquest of Transcaspia; the archimperialist N. H. Hartwig, of whom Kalmykow preserved the kindest memories; A. P. Izvolskii and S. D. Sazonov, in
succession ministers of foreign affairs. Each appears for a moment,
participates in a minor event, is briefly sketched, but acquires a
reality he had not had before.

Kalmykow's memoirs will not lead to the revision of our views on
great historical events and figures. However, they do add a dimension of immediacy and intimacy which cold official dispatches seldom
convey. When A. D. Kalmykow in the years of exile fairly and hon-
estly recorded his memories of people and places he had known, he

performed a service for which students of Russian diplomatic history as well as all those who cherish the ephemeral past will be grateful.

FIRUZ KAZEMZADEH

Yale University
January 1971

Preface

The eve of the Russian Revolution is one of the most intriguing and significant phases of Russian history, yet it is but imperfectly understood, largely because of the various biases so noticeable in sources relating to this period. My father's memoirs, covering some three decades preceding the revolution, have the rare merit of scholarly objectivity. His purpose in relating his life in Russia and on diplomatic service in the Far, Middle, and Near East and in the Balkans is to make this intricate period more comprehensible to the American reader.

A man of tremendous erudition—he knew fourteen languages and took part in the excavations conducted by the Imperial Russian Archaeological Society—my father was a learned student of the past as well as a keen observer of current events. His comments on Russian internal affairs and foreign policy are evidence of both the competence and firsthand knowledge of a participant in the events described and the impartiality of an outside observer, which he gained from his years abroad. In 1893, upon completing with distinction his studies in the School of Oriental Languages of the University of St. Petersburg, where he formed a lifelong friendship with Russia's most outstanding orientalists—the president of the Russian Academy of Science, S. F. Oldenburg, and Academician V. V. Barthold—he joined the Ministry of Foreign Affairs. Keenly alive to the changing role of the Orient in world politics, he asked to be sent to Persia, a country he considered important for Russian diplomacy, though it rated lowest as far as career advancement was concerned. In the era of rampant Anglo- and Russophobia, my father was among the very few who saw the rationale of an Anglo-Russian rapprochement; and, to the extent of his power he contributed to it. His observations on Persia during the three years he spent there shed new light on the background of the 1907 Anglo-Russian entente.

In his memoirs my father modestly underplays his role when, as the Russian chargé d'affaires in Bangkok, he originated and implemented a territorial exchange between Siam and Indochina which served to maintain peace in Southeast Asia until World War II and helped preserve the independence of Siam, now Thailand. Paul Doumer, later president of France and at that time head of France's Far Eastern interests as governor general of Indochina, was greatly impressed by my father's diplomatic talent.

During the First Balkan War, as Russian consul general in Uskub, Turkey, my father, entirely at his own initiative and without outside authority, took over for three days the dangerous burden of administering a city abandoned by the Turkish civil and military authorities and prey to complete anarchy. For his self-forgetful courage in preventing a massacre of the Christian population by the aroused Moslems, the Russian government made him commander of the order of St. Anne, and the French conferred on him the order of the Legion of Honor. Upon his return to Russia, he was lionized in Moscow, where his admirers presented him with a bejeweled silver cigarette case bearing the inscription: "To the Hero Consul, A. D. Kalmykow." The leading newspapers published his picture, a tribute the Russian press very seldom bestows.

During World War I my father was stationed in the Aegean as an observer of the Dardanelles operations. His brilliant diplomatic career was cut off in midstream by the Russian Revolution, and he came to the United States to enter the academic profession. He was a member of the American Oriental Society and a contributor to its journal. He continued to maintain a keen interest in and objective observation of world events, and he did considerable writing. At the time of his sudden death in 1941, my father was putting the finishing touches on his splendidly integrated memoirs. My devotion to my father and to the preservation of authentic records of the past prompted me to insert in the manuscript additional material painstakingly collected from his drafts. Though not devoid of value, these additions somewhat altered the harmonious balance and sui generis style of the original, and they delayed its publication. I am very grateful to two editors at the Yale Press: Mrs. Marian Neal Ash, for her kindness and patience in accepting the additional material; and Mrs. Merle Spiegel, for her wonderful skill in preparing the printer's copy. My warm thanks to to Professors G. V. Vernadsky and F. Kazemzadeh of Yale University for reading the manuscript and recommending it for publication. I am further obliged to Professor Kazemzadeh for supplying the modern transliteration of the Iranian terms and citations and for several footnotes, which are duly identified by his initials. The remaining footnotes were supplied by my father and myself. My Russian transliterations are not entirely consistent, as a uniformly accepted standard is yet to be worked out. My grateful appreciation also goes to Professor F. C. Shipley of the City University of New York for his excellent comments and criticisms in the early stages of the writing of the memoirs, and to my brothers, Vladimir and Andrew, for their most valuable help and advice throughout the long years when the manuscript was in preparation. The index was compiled by Miss Delight Ansley.

Alexandra Kalmykow

Long Branch, N.J.
June 1971

1 Early Life in Russia

Life in Russia ran smoothly and swiftly in the 1870s, when I was born. The whole country, invigorated by the great reforms of Alexander II in the sixties, was moving forward at an accelerated pace without precedent in the past. Gigantic railway lines crept forward across the endless expanses of the empire; private banks were opened for the first time. Capital appeared. Great works were produced by famous writers. Russia became in fact a progressive country. And then came the absurd adventure of the Russo-Turkish war of 1877–78. Turkey had no quarrel with Russia. Turkey was actually the only neighbor who was, at the time, friendly and respectful to Russia. The war ended in a hollow victory, without gains and with considerable losses of men, money, and prestige. A new and much worse war with Japan, in 1904–05, which could not be called victorious by any stretch of patriotic exaggeration, was followed by the first revolution. A few years of respite, and then came the war with Germany and the great revolution, which destroyed all.

My life ran parallel to the growing discontent in Russia until I was finally washed away by a splash of the flood. How it happened is the content of this book.

Childhood

I was born in the south of Russia in 1870. From an early age I often had the sensation that I did not fit in, and all my life I strove to accommodate myself to the conditions around me. Frequently I felt uneasy. Whether it was my fault or the fault of my surroundings I cannot tell. I can only say that discontent with their fate and longing for a better one have become a common trait of all Russians in and out of their native land.

I was brought up as a lone and only child. That meant that I was surrounded by older persons, very kind but infinitely wiser, stronger, and superior to me, and I perceived it at every step. My father, a keen sportsman, kept dogs, and these dogs became my friends and playmates. My old nurse, a very religious woman, told me that dogs had no souls—just breath. That seemed strange to me, but I accepted the explanation.

My connected recollections date from the age of seven, when I was suddenly confronted with political and diplomatic questions. We were then living in Simferopol, chief town of the Crimea. One day I saw boys running like mad in the streets, selling newspaper extras and shouting: "War with Turkey!"

"We have declared war on Turkey, or rather the government has," said my father.

"War?" I asked.

"Yes, to help the Serbs and the Bulgarians. Russian diplomacy has raised the Balkan question."

All that was very obscure to me. I saw that my parents looked grave; I knew also from previous conversations and pictures in the illustrated magazines that the Bulgarians, good Christians and Slavs like ourselves, were being massacred by the Turks. But the following conversation was more illuminating.

"It's thirty miles to the seacoast," continued my father. "If the Turks land in the Crimea, they will be but two days' march from Simferopol."

"They won't come here," said my mother resolutely.

"Of course not," acquiesced my father. "We have a few troops here, and now that war is declared the government may think about sending some more."

For several days I felt disturbed. I did not relish the idea of sharing the fate of the unfortunate Bulgarians at the hands of invading Turks. One night I even dreamed that the Turks were entering our town: I heard shots and cries and awoke in a cold perspiration. It was my first experience of being really frightened.

Some time passed before we heard the rumbling of field batteries on our quiet residential street, and regiments of infantry and cavalry passed by. Soldiers were quartered in our house—huge fellows with enormous, heavy rifles, so different from the shining English guns of my father. Our house stood at the end of the street, and the ground rose immediately beyond. The heights were occupied by the troops. The sight of the soldiers made me and the other children bellicose and impatient for victory. The atmosphere of the city became highly patriotic.

Because of the war we did not go to our estate in the summer. My father stayed in town and sent my mother and me to a bathing resort on the sea. There was a small battery on the coast, which I was not allowed to visit, but I could go to the cape where a tall signal mast stood. I was greatly impressed by the sight of the mast. It looked so grand and efficient with its collection of flags and big empty black balls for signaling.

Turkish ironclads were cruising in the Black Sea. The money for building the Russian Black Sea fleet had been stolen by high officials in St. Petersburg, and the Turks were masters of the sea. However, Turkish warships had fired only a few shots at our resort before our arrival and did no damage. Possibly their ammunition had been stolen also.

At the end of the season we returned to Simferopol. Many wounded soldiers had been brought there from Turkey. My father was indignant at the progress of the war. He had a collection of arms, and he showed me a British rifle taken during the Crimean War.

"Look at it," he said. "It's a rifle. But our soldiers in 1854 had only smoothbore muskets with a short range of fire. Their bullets could not reach the enemy trenches. The same is happening now. The Turks have magazine rifles, and we are armed with worthless Krinka guns which often jam and become useless."

I also saw a pistol taken from rebel mountaineers and sent to us by my uncle, who was an officer in the Caucasus and had been wounded there. On the barrel was engraved the word *Birmingham*. It was my first acquaintance with the respectable trade of the arms merchants.

My father had contempt for military men and diplomats and spoke about them in terms of biting sarcasm which it was strange to hear from this mild and usually reticent man. By an irony of fate his only brother was a general, and I, his only child, was to become a diplomat.

I do not remember all the military callers at our home in Simferopol, but my mother spoke with sympathy about a young and modest officer who looked, as she said, very shy at that time. His name was N. V. Ruzskii. He was to become one of the best Russian generals commanding on the German front during World War I.

Once I was taken to the railway station. Soldiers with bayonets stood in front of the platform, for a train was due to arrive with Turkish prisoners captured on a transport at sea, chiefly raw recruits from Asia Minor, who had no uniforms and were still wearing their national garb. All the town was agog at the news of the arrival of the enemies, imprisoned and disarmed but still enemies. The station was crowded with people eager to see them. I had heard much talk about the Turks, but the prospect of seeing them alive seemed somehow incredible. I stood with other children, all tense and awed by the presence of armed soldiers. We were not exactly frightened but extremely curious and excited. The train appeared, slackened its speed, and stood still with its long line of freight cars. The sliding doors were opened, and a lot of extraordinary people emerged in Oriental dress and headgear, looking theatrical and rather nice, not at all frightful. As the freight cars had no steps, the Turks had to jump out—quite a performance, which brought our astonishment to its climax. One man had a cat on his shoulder. We children roared with delight.

Up to the age of eight my life was limited by the unruffled horizon of Simferopol. Now came the first contact with suffering and a change of surroundings. My mother took me to the Red Cross hospital, and I saw convalescent soldiers lying on their cots; others were sitting or moving around, some on crutches, some with an empty sleeve pinned to their breast—the rising generation of Russia mutilated for the sake of the Balkan Slavs.

Death seemed to claim its victims everywhere. My little brother, born recently, died. My father tried vainly to alleviate my mother's grief and then decided to send her on a trip to St. Petersburg. My grandfather and Mrs. Stasova, a childhood friend of my mother's, lived there. My mother took me with her, and we crossed all Russia in a shaky train with bad springs. Pullman cars had not yet made their appearance in Russia. I was very tired by the journey, which lasted four days, and quite bewildered, when we arrived, by the noise and bustle of the horse carriages on the stone-paved streets of the capital.

We stayed with Mrs. Stasova, whose husband, Dmitrii Vasilievich, was the president of the Bar Association of St. Petersburg. Their apartment was twice as large and lofty as ours, but it had no garden. None of the houses seemed to have gardens, and the yards looked desolate and were forbidden to me. There was no place where children could play—and that was called a capital! Walks with my mother, who was always in a hurry and held me firmly by the hand, offered little consolation.

Mrs. Stasova gave me a large box of tin soldiers. I played with her son, who had an enormous collection of the same toys. We shot with peas, and the soldiers fell from the table and broke. We had as many casualties as the Russian army. People around us talked chiefly about war. I grew sick of it and acquired a dislike for war which lasted all my life.

We often went to visit my grandfather, who was very kind to me, his first grandson. But I was surprised to see that he was a short, heavy man with a white beard, not at all like the slim cavalry officer of the Guards, as he was represented in the oil painting in our old country house.

My mother was cheered by the affection shown by her relatives and friends, but I longed to be back at Simferopol. We returned there, but not for long. My father was called to St. Petersburg, and I was again alone with my mother.

Father had taught me to read, with the help of wooden alphabet blocks. It was easy and pleasant. I soon progressed to a book and told my mother every story in it innumerable times. I became a lover of books.

But now I had a teacher of arithmetic, a very impatient and disagreeable one, and I acquired an aversion to the man and a lifelong dislike of mathematics. On the day of my father's arrival, I showed an exemplary industry, which brought an expression of unpleasant surprise to the face of my teacher. I asked him to write in my copybook that he was pleased with me. He agreed and wrote a few lines in an impossible handwriting, which I could not decipher. When father came, I showed him my attestation with modest pride, but he did not seem to be pleased with it. It appeared that my teacher wrote that I could be a good pupil but was rarely so. From that time I positively loathed the man and could never forgive him his treachery.

Boyhood

Soon after the Russo-Turkish war of 1877–78, my father was promoted to the supreme court at Kharkov in the Ukraine. We left

neat, sunny, little Simferopol, surrounded by gardens and with a blue
mountain range in the distance, and came to Kharkov—an important, large, prosperous city of rather vulgar appearance but boasting
a university, several millionaires, and a considerable commercial and
intellectual activity already disturbed by terroristic attempts.

One evening as the closed carriage of the governor, Prince D. N.
Kropotkin, returned home, the porter opened its door and saw the
governor's body in a pool of blood. The coachman had not heard
the report of the gun, drowned in the thunder of the iron-bound
wheels and the clatter of the horses on the stone pavement, and the
assassin escaped detection.

More was to come. Early in the morning of March 1 (old style)
1881, my grandfather entered my room with a newspaper shaking
in his hands and told me that Emperor Alexander II had been killed
by a bomb in broad daylight on the streets of St. Petersburg. My
parents looked sad and perturbed.

"It was bound to come," said my father, "since the emperor delayed granting a constitution. Now everything will go from bad to
worse." In answer to my queries—I was already eleven—father told
me in a few words the meaning of representative government, which,
in his opinion, was an absolute necessity for Russia. I never again
raised this question with him, but for the rest of my life I was a confirmed liberal.

But I had no time to think much about politics. I was preparing
for high school and had met several boys and girls with whom I
entered into a lifelong friendship. In summer we went to our estate
as usual, and I made the acquaintance of peasant boys. They were
very strong, clever, and enterprising. A nine-year-old boy could ride
a barebacked horse with a cord around its neck instead of a bridle. I
tried the same without success and with considerable risk to my person. My parents intervened and provided me with a saddle and regular riding lessons. I received a shotgun, and the fishing and hunting
expeditions with my father made life in the country a real paradise
for me.

But the existence of the peasants was far from happy. They had
already put most of their land to the plough and lacked pastures.
They began to graze their cattle on our meadows. The steward came
and said that it was necessary to hire mounted and armed night-
watchmen, as other landowners had done, to prevent trespassing.

"No," answered my father curtly. The steward looked puzzled,
bowed, and went out. "The peasants need pastureland," said my

father as we remained alone. "It is only just, and I shall give it to them, but don't talk about it." My father's tone was categorical. On serious occasions he spoke briefly, like the judge he was, and never reversed his decisions.

Horse thieves appeared in our province; they were caught by some peasants and killed on the spot. The guilty peasants were arrested and brought to trial at the criminal court at Kharkov. My father was head of the civil court and had nothing to do with the case. One evening several judges happened to meet at a private party and talked indignantly about the killing of the horse thieves and the savagery of the peasants.

"What is your opinion?" they asked my father, a very kind and quiet man.

"The peasants were right," he answered. "The police are few and powerless to protect the herds on our vast plains. Cattle and horse stealing means destitution for the peasants and their families, and they had to protect their property; there was no other way out left for them." The judges remained aghast but were deeply impressed by this point of view.

My father had a large law library, including practically everything that concerned civil cases. He was also interested in the works of Russian writers. He read short stories aloud to me and brought me up in an atmosphere of deep, almost religious reverence for the great Russian literature which had reached its zenith in the late 1870s.

The stay in Kharkov also played an important role in the life of my mother, who became deeply interested in popular education.

The society of Kharkov was personified in its business and intellectual aspects by the family of the Alchevskie. Aleksei Alchevskii and his wife Khristina Danilovna Alchevskaia were a perfectly matched and happy pair, although nothing was more different than their tastes and outward appearance. Alchevskii, a powerful banker, creator, and promoter of the financial enterprises in the city, was an extremely busy man, always in a hurry and rarely seen in society. His wife insisted that he wear a tall silk hat, since he was short and stooped, and she obliged him to make a round of social calls twice a year. The rest of the time he was left free to spend in the presidential recesses of his bank. Mrs. Alchevskaia reigned supreme in her beautiful apartment. She supplied whatever her husband lacked in appearance. She was imposing, majestic, stately, with a gracious smile or an irate frown. But like her husband she possessed an iron will, indomitable energy, and relentless efficiency in her own sphere of action. Her vocation was social work; and her specialty, primary education for children and illiterate adults. She founded a free school, formed a society of women teachers, and fought the illiteracy of the Russian Empire.

Alchevskii was slightly ironical but secretly proud of the achievements of his wife. One day P. I. Biriukov, friend and biographer of Count L. N. Tolstoy, called on Mrs. Alchevskaia. During the course of the conversation he referred to her fine handwriting.

"Oh, no," she said. "All my letters are written by my secretary. I have so much mail. I would go blind were I to attend to it myself."

"And now your secretary will go blind," observed her husband. But Mrs. Alchevskaia paid no heed and kept her Olympian smile.

Mrs. Alchevskaia was despotic, but she had a warm heart and plenty of tact and was devoted to her work of social welfare. When she met my mother, she understood her at first sight. My mother had a very kind but strong character. They became great friends and worked together. My mother devoted herself entirely to the promotion of free elementary education. Mrs. Alchevskaia, my mother, and several teachers wrote a big volume called *Chto chitat' narodu? (What's to Be Read by the People?).* It was an exhaustive, critical survey of Russian popular literature, a standard work which received the highest award at the Paris Fair of 1889. Mrs. Alchevskaia went there herself, and the French papers spoke about the venerable white-haired lady enthroned in the Russian section.

Youth

I was fifteen when the minister of justice, D. N. Nabokov, the only liberal minister of Alexander II to keep a portfolio under Alexander III, came to Kharkov, had a long talk with my father, and appointed him to the senate of the empire, which was the supreme court of all Russia. My father went to St. Petersburg to be presented to the new emperor, Alexander III, with other recently appointed judges.

"What did the tsar say to you?" I asked my father on his return.

* *Chto chitat' narodu. Kriticheskii ukazatel' knig dlia narodnogo i detskogo chtenia sostavlen uchitel'nitsami Kharkovskoi chastnoi zhenskoi voskresnoi shkoly (What's to Be Read by the People: A Critical Bibliography of Popular and Children's Books Prepared by Teachers of the Kharkov Private Sunday Primary Education Girls' School)*, Kh. D. Alchevskaia, E. D. Grodeieva, A. P. Grishenko, Z. I. Dashkevich, L. I. Dashkevich, L. E. Efimovich, A. D. Ivanova, M. A. Ivanova, A. M. Kalmykova, N. P. Pengo, O. S. Rudniova, E. I. Tsvetaieva, vol. 1 (St. Petersburg, 1884; rev. ed. St. Petersburg, 1888). This book is written almost exclusively by Kalmykova and Alchevskaia. *Ed.*

"Nothing. He came in abruptly, shook hands with us and went out. That was about all." My father shrugged his shoulders.

We settled in the capital, and I entered the Third High School, or Gymnasium, as such schools were called in Russia. The course comprised eight years. I had already passed the first four in Kharkov and had four more ahead of me—equivalent to the American college education. Like all good schools, it had its traditions; unfortunately they were mostly classical—Greek and Latin. Natural science, considered subversive to religion and good citizenship, was not offered.

The teachers were mainly Germans from the Baltic provinces, who spoke broken Russian, to the intense delight of their pupils. The teachers would get red and threatening, while we tried to suppress our laughter. The program was quite medieval, but the mental training was excellent, the teachers were good, and we were well prepared by them for the university, which was to follow.

History was taught only up to the beginning of the nineteenth century. We sat tense with attention while the teacher with a wry face skimmed over the French Revolution in a few phrases, and then with evident relief and a sudden outburst of eloquence spoke about the downfall of Napoleon, the victorious advance of the monarchical armies, and the reestablishment of the legitimate monarchs on their thrones. He stopped short at that. What more did we need to know?

I was received into a company of six boys, and once a week we met in turn at each other's houses. The purpose of our society had nothing to do with political or radical ideas. It was simply a struggle with Latin syntax, which was ruthlessly impressed upon the brains of the young generation to prevent its interest in other fields.

Our leader was Peter Struve, the future prominent professor of economics and Social Democrat. He belonged to a talented family which had produced astronomers, governors, and diplomats. His uncle, K. V. Struve, was at that time the Russian minister in Washington. Struve's knowledge of classical languages seemed superhuman to us: he could read fluently any Latin or Greek text and sat at lessons with a superb indifference. When the teacher called on him, he would slowly rise, asking his neighbors: "What the devil have we to translate today?" The teacher would grin and wait patiently while Struve fumbled in his book and finally started a faultless translation amid the silence of a spellbound class.

Another schoolmate, Kulomzin, was the exact opposite of Struve, who always looked serious and even as a schoolboy had a professorial appearance. Kulomzin was gay, alert, and full of wit. He was very practical and mocked abstract ideas. "The tsar is the first man in Russia," he said to me once, "and that's that." He had already planned his future life while still a student. He told me that he would be a marshal of nobility in his native province, a gentleman-in-waiting of the emperor, then a vice-governor and governor. He carried out his program in full, until the Revolution put a stop to it.

His father, A. N. Kulomzin, was a typical bureaucrat of the old school, benevolent, patriotic, and imposing—a big, heavy man with a large bodily expanse suitable for his many decorations and the gold braid of his uniform. He was in charge of the proceedings of the Committee of Ministers, a laborious and influential office that required a good memory but no special talents that might have offended the susceptibilities of the ministers. The position of Kulomzin was safe and dignified. Ministers and cabinets could rise and fall, but Kulomzin continued his ascent undisturbed till he became the leader of the Upper Chamber.

Then came the greatest moment in the life of the old bureaucrat. He had to speak to the tsar in the name of the nation. Emperor Nicholas II had addressed the Russian representatives only twice during his reign. The first time was at the opening of the first Duma. The tsar called the members of both chambers to the palace and read his speech himself. He expected no answer and received none. The deputies listened and dispersed in silence.

The second time, the emperor spoke to the chambers on the occasion of the declaration of war on Germany. The tsar asked the help of the representatives. It fell to Kulomzin to reply to the royal request. This time he forgot all his pomposity. He spoke with sincerity and emotion as a man deeply affected. I can quote from memory only his first phrase: "The words of Your Majesty have penetrated into the innermost depths of our hearts." He swore the loyalty of the nation to its monarch and remained true to his word until his last breath. I hope the younger Kulomzin, if he is still alive, will forgive me these details about his father.

My third friend was Verevkin, son of the commander of the fortress of St. Peter and Paul in St. Petersburg. It was both the Tower and the Bastille of monarchical Russia, with the difference that the Tower of London had become a museum and the Bastille had been razed to the ground a hundred years before. But the St. Peter and Paul fortress was still full of prisoners of state.

General V. N. Verevkin was a stern, silent military man, slightly deaf. When asked at his appointment if this infirmity would hamper him in the exercise of his duties, he answered: "Not at all. I am accustomed to give orders and not to hear answers." A widower, he was very fond of his children and devoted much care to them. I saw a tapestry in the room of his son and asked him if he had put it there himself. "No," he answered, "Father did."

It was with an involuntary feeling of apprehension that I approached the grim walls of the fortress for the first time, crossed the bridge over the moat, and entered the gloomy gate with sentinels whose bayonets shone in the moonlight. In the dim shadows cast by a few flickering lanterns I crossed a second bridge and a wall with deep cannon embrasures and came out on a plaza with the old church in the center and the commandant's house on the left. The door was brightly lighted. I followed an orderly through several rooms with severe antique furniture and, with a sense of relief, reached a door behind which I heard the boisterous laughter and cheerful voices of my friends.

Later I was shown the whole fortress, except for the political prison. In the far western end stood the ravelin of Alexis, a separate enclosure with a low square building in the middle. It had large barred windows. Through them I could see empty whitewashed rooms and a small garden with a few trees. It looked like a military barracks. In these rooms prisoners of state had been confined, tortured, and strangled, beginning with Prince Alexis, son and heir of Peter the Great. I have been told that the graves of some of the prisoners were under the trees. Prince Alexis was buried under the staircase of the church.

"You see there is nobody there now," said my friend. "There is another jail, quite comfortable, just back of our house." I shuddered as he continued to speak about the comforts enjoyed by the prisoners. I must add that the fortress, situated on the bank of the Neva and facing the imperial palace across the large spread of the river, is certainly one of the most picturesque sights of St. Petersburg, but its beauty left me cold.

I never spoke with my father about my future. It was tacitly supposed that I should become a lawyer like him. The senate long ago had been deprived of legislative power, but it still remained the supreme court of the empire and was the most highly respected institution of monarchical Russia. The autocratic rule of Alexander III brought about the final decline of the senate.

A senator—a nice, slightly epicurean and egotistical sportsman, a friend of my father's—talked about the decrees of the Ministry of Justice and said: "Well, what remains now of the great liberal reforms of Alexander II and the independence of judges from arbitrary removal? Nothing, nothing at all." He broke into a good-humored, unconcerned laughter, but my father did not laugh.

I saw that my father was far from being satisfied with the changed position of the judges, and I became hesitant about entering this profession. As the end of the course in the gymnasium was nearing and I had to make a decision, my father died, and I was left without his guidance at a critical period of my life. There were no colleges in Russia; the universities consisted of special schools. I decided to enter the School of Oriental Languages of the University of St. Petersburg; that would give me an opportunity to travel and to join the Foreign Service. My mother was surprised but made no objections.

I registered in the School of Oriental Languages, but as the hours were few and the students were free to attend in their spare time any courses they wished, I went to hear Mendeleiev, who occupied the chair of chemistry and started his course by speaking about his newly discovered periodic law of the atomic weights of elements. I also heard the academician N. P. Kondakov lecture on Leonardo da Vinci and his painting of the Mona Lisa, the Gioconda of the Louvre. The University of St. Petersburg was brilliant in 1889, and a lifetime would not have been enough to listen to the exposition of scientific facts and ideas of genius so lavishly showered upon us. But what a contrast between the freedom of university halls and the strict discipline prevailing outside them, with the army of uniformed policemen and secret spies guarding the inviolability of an autocratic monarchy on the threshold of the twentieth century.

The students were young, liberal, and excitable; trouble arose often. At times cossacks were massed before the university, but they did not invade the sanctum of our alma mater. Courses were suspended, students arrested and released afterward. This was not a revolutionary movement but only a scattering of little squalls announcing the future storm.

2 The Foreign Office

I considered that diplomacy in Asia was the right thing for me, since I had a diploma in Oriental languages. I was greatly interested in Persia, had studied its language and literature, and had even taken private lessons from a native Persian. The more I learned about Persia, the more I liked it. It seemed a wondrous land of beautiful poetry and works of art, of roses and nightingales. Full of hope, I called on the only diplomat I knew, P. M. Lessar, political agent in Bokhara, who happened to be in St. Petersburg in 1893. A splendid type of fighting diplomat, Lessar was amicably disposed toward me and was a straightforward, sarcastic, fearless man, with an iron will in his lame and sickly body. He once mentioned to me that he had an irresistible desire to enter a lion's cage and had offered a hundred rubles to the famous lion tamer, Julius Seth, to let him do it. Seth answered that he himself could enter the cage only once a day after feeding time, during the evening performance, and Lessar declined to make a public exhibition of himself.

When I spoke to him about my academic credentials and my desire to become a diplomat, Lessar laughed with his usual quiet, bitter, and sympathetic laughter. "You happen to know Asian languages and have graduated from the Oriental School—that is enough to spoil all your future career in the Foreign Office. Any other diploma would be better, even one from the Academy of Music. Then at least you would not be treated as an interpreter fit only for minor positions."

Thoroughly upset, I sadly returned home and reported to my mother, like Achilles wronged by the Greeks. My mother looked affectionately at me and said: "Lessar is right, but don't worry. All you need is a proper recommendation. I shall get you one." It appeared in the form of an oblong letter signed by a well-known titled name and worked like a charm.

I took it and with a fast-beating heart directed my steps to the Palace Square, on which stood the Foreign Office. I opened the brass-grilled door and entered an old-fashioned, dark, low vestibule, the gloomy, mean entrance to the bureaus of our diplomacy. The minister had another, much more dignified entrance to his apartment and private office. A uniformed doorkeeper in a long cloak slowly approached me and took my overcoat. As I had occasion to observe later, he gauged his speed according to the rank of the visitors, and sometimes showed a remarkable celerity.

I mounted a staircase—there were no elevators as yet—and walked down a corridor until I met an usher. I gave him my letter, which I fingered with my cold, awkward hands, and said that I wanted to see Count D. A. Kapnist, the head of the Asian Department. The usher silently bowed his head and invited me to follow him. We entered a large reception room, with a glossy floor and furniture which stuck to the walls and seemed to invite one to remain standing. I stood silent and alone, depressed by the solitude. The usher vanished. In the distance I saw a grandfather's clock and next to it another usher, just as wooden-faced and expressionless.

I did not know how long I had been waiting when a door opened, and a small man with a short neck and a head that seemed to touch his shoulders briskly walked in holding my letter in his hands. It was the count. He confronted me, and spoke in a high-pitched voice, in broken sentences. "You desire to serve in my department, Mr. . . . Mr. K." He succeeded in remembering my name and again started to speak quickly, with interruptions of inarticulate mumbling and rapid soundless quivering of his lips. "All right . . . go to the registrar." He made an indefinite gesture in a vague direction. "Goodbye." He projected a little hand in a semblance of a farewell and hurried back to his room.

I walked out, filled out an application, and called on a senior officer with a thick face and hanging moustache, nicknamed "the Walrus," a stout man who lifted his shoulders but not the bulk of his body as he gave me his hand and offered me a seat: "Your appointment will be listed in the *Official Gazette* in July. Report in September. You will have three months of vacation and, of course, no pay in the beginning. Do you speak English besides French?"

I again called on Lessar, vainly trying to conceal an overflowing sense of triumph. He pretended not to notice it and quietly looked at me with his steel-gray, knowing eyes. "You want to go to Persia, that means the Middle East. I must warn you that advancement there is very slow. Constantinople and the Near East offer better chances for promotion, and life there is much more pleasant for a young man." Lessar grinned.

"What would you prefer for yourself?" I asked bluntly.

Lessar became serious and suddenly seemed to look older, with deep furrows on his hollow cheeks. He remained silent for a while, twisting his long, drooping moustache. "Middle East is my specialty," he said with grim determination. "I consider it the most interesting part of Asia. But make your own choice. I do not want to influence you."

"Then I shall go to Persia," I said. Lessar smiled, and a pleased expression appeared on his emaciated face.

"It will be a hard life for you," he said. "All is not rosy in the East, and there is plenty of monotonous work to do." He continued speaking, and I hung on his words. At that time he was the leading Russian authority on Asia.* Lessar never wrote anything except his diplomatic reports and a few articles in geographic magazines, but he traced the Russian frontier with Afghanistan, making the surveys himself, since he was a railway engineer by education, and he framed the Russian policy in Central Asia, incidentally affecting that of England as well. The policies of both nations were interdependent in the East, and one reacted on the other. Lessar was often summoned to assist the Russian Embassy in London, since the aged ambassadors there were entirely innocent of the intricacies of the map of Asia and stared at it with a blank look which was interpreted by the irate representatives of Downing Street as the acme of perfidy and diplomatic conceit.

Lessar was the chief mainstay of Russian diplomacy on Eastern questions when, in the 1880s, our Foreign Office got into a dreadful entanglement with England which almost dragged us into a war with that country. There was a great deal of irritation against England

---

* Three men were then considered in Russia as leading authorities on Asia: Lessar, G. N. Curzon, and Sven Hedin. Hedin mentions Lessar with great praise in his books.

in Russia, when the pitiful results of the Berlin Congress of 1878 were made known. The Russian government consequently resolved to give a gentle warning to the British lion. Troops were moved in the direction of India into the vast deserts of central Asia, a virtual no-man's-land inhabited by only a few wandering nomad tribes of predatory habits. The move succeeded beyond expectations. After the first stupor had passed, a loud outcry arose in England—the Anglo-Indian government became seriously alarmed; violent interpellations took place in the British Parliament; and there was a deluge of fiery articles, pamphlets, travel books, and heavy treatises. The treatises no one read and everyone quoted, using them as ponderous missiles to hurl at the heads of obstinate opponents. Russia was violently assailed by the English press.

Our embassy in London was the first to suffer. The diplomats were hopelessly ignorant about everything relating to Asia and asked St. Petersburg for instructions. Our Foreign Office was in no better position to give a coherent answer and inquired of the military authorities. They, in turn, invoked strategic considerations—a vague reply, as the land in question was unmapped and practically unknown.

The roar of the British lion became stentorian, with a menacing tone. In 1885, a partially decoded English telegram was brought to Alexander III by the minister of foreign affairs, N. K. Giers. The meaning of the telegram was not clear, but it seemed that a declaration of war by England was imminent. The next day a new version of the same telegram was submitted to His Majesty, conveying opposite information. The emperor was annoyed; he said squarely that we would not recede an inch but that any further advance must be stopped and a final frontier with Afghanistan established. The Ministry of Foreign Affairs was made responsible for tracing it. Mr. Giers, who was mortally afraid of the tsar—a rude man with a good deal of common sense—was sorely pressed. In this extremity he applied to Lessar, constructing engineer of the Central Asian Railway, who had made an extensive study of the country and happened to speak English fluently. Our foreign minister clung to him as to the last plank of salvation. Lessar was transferred to the diplomatic service and sent to London.

The crux of the controversy was Hodja Saleh, the furthest point of the Russian sphere of influence, according to a communication made in 1872 by the Russian minister of foreign affairs, Prince A. M. Gorchakov. This point, however, could not be located with any degree of precision by either government, and Lessar simply dropped it. The English insisted on the existence of an impassable mountain range to the north of the Afghan town of Herāt. Lessar declared that he was ready to lay tracks across it in no time and run a locomotive straight into Herāt. The English opposition collapsed, and the frontier was accepted in principle. The rest was easy.

Lessar felt that Russia and England could and should live in peace and on good terms. He expressed his views freely, not only in St. Petersburg but also in London, where the popularity of this extraordinary man is attested by numerous cartoons in the London newspapers of 1885. Lessar had a whole collection of them, and showed them to me with keen delight.

He was not allowed to continue his work in central Asia. Grave complications arose in China, and our London Embassy again ran aground and clamored for help. Lessar was appointed counselor of the embassy in London and ordered to study Chinese affairs. He was sent to Peking as Russian minister and died there at an early age during the Russo-Japanese war, serving his country to his last breath.

A Diplomat at Large

Still in high spirits and full of glee, I declared to my mother that I should take advantage of the first opening to go to the East, preferably to Persia. These tidings did not produce at all the impression I expected. My mother clasped her hands on her knees, sighed sadly, and said: "Have your vacation first. Go to visit your grandmother in Ekaterinoslav. Take a good rest; you need it after your university examinations. We shall talk it over when you come back and start working in the Foreign Office."

On my way south I stopped at Kharkov, where I had lived as a boy while my father was president of the Court of Appeals there. I was surrounded by my old schoolmates and became the center of general curiosity: a diplomat is a rare bird in a provincial town. To my extreme confusion, my young friends scrutinized every detail of my attire. My light English suit of bluish gray with a checkered effect produced by the weave of the solid-color fabric met with universal approval. I was also fortunate with my crepe de chine necktie.

In the meantime I tried to direct the conversation to another topic and was fairly successful when an assertion was made which turned into an argument.

"I tell you, the latest fashion in St. Petersburg is to have the lining of the hat of the same color as the suit."

"How do you know?"

"Listen. Here is our diplomat straight from there; ask him. Please show your hat." The last words were directed at me.

I felt embarrassed. I had never thought about the lining of my hat and had not the slightest idea of what color it was. My reputation was at stake, and there was no way out. Reluctantly I took off my hat. The lining flashed; it was pale blue. For the rest of my stay in Kharkov, I was the arbiter of elegance.

Elderly people, friends of my father, also showed interest in me. But to my astonishment some persons whom I had never met before looked at me with ill-disguised coolness. For them a diplomat was the symbol of pretense, vanity, and sheer stupidity. They thought that diplomats prevented the declaration of patriotic and, in their opinion, righteous wars, which was partly true, and were solely responsible for the outcome of unlucky campaigns, which was obviously unjust. The memory of the Congress of Berlin, which consecrated the hegemony of Germany over Europe, was far from obliterated in Russia. I found that diplomacy itself was not popular, and even people well disposed toward me personally were dubious about the utility of the diplomatic profession in general.

"Slightly better than vaudeville," my mother once said about our Foreign Office.

I firmly believed in the importance and necessity of diplomacy, but there was the fact that people distrusted it, and there must be some reason for that. But Kharkov was not the place to solve this problem any more than the other provincial cities I visited that summer. Before my vacation was over I became impatient to return to St. Petersburg and to begin my work among new and fascinating surroundings.

The day I was longing for arrived. I walked up the staircase of the Asian Department, was introduced to my new colleagues, and took my seat at a mahogany desk in a lofty room with filing cabinets full of secrets of state. I looked around. Well-groomed clerks were copying letters in careful handwriting; there were no typewriters yet. The chief of the section and his two assistants, one for the

Middle and the other for the Far East, were busy with dispatches and telegrams.

A consul on leave, who had come to see Count Kapnist, sat on a chair in a corner with his hands in his pockets and gazed at the ceiling with assumed indifference, although we knew that he expected a promotion to be offered him during this interview. He was soon called, and returned looking flushed and contented. The chief of the section shook hands with him. He laughed nervously, glanced at his watch, and hurriedly left the room.

"Try this," said a quiet, even voice behind me. I looked around and saw a clerk who laid before me a large code book and sheets of coded telegrams. He pointed out the decoding instructions and explained them in a calm undertone. His manner was very polite and the expression of his eyes serenely innocent, but I felt a slight touch of irony in them. The offered work was already a test for me. I started to work feverishly. I felt perspiration gathering on my brow as I ran into impossible Chinese names. My neighbor threw a side glance at me, choked, and rapidly put a handkerchief to his lips. I felt my ears burning.

"Something wrong with the cable?" he asked.

"Yes, there is a nine, and it ought to be a seven."

"Well, try a seven," he answered, and grinned.

I tried, and the meaning became clear. It was evidently a mistake in the text. I finished the decoding and took it to my chief. He read it, stopping at Chinese names, thinking a little, and quietly separating them. The incongruous maze of unpronounceable letters was thus reduced to two or three very short words. My chief reread the text and nodded approvingly. I breathed freely and wiped my forehead.

At three o'clock the room emptied. It was time for tea in the messroom. My newly acquired friend took me there. We walked through the next room, much larger than ours, occupied by the Turkish and Balkan section. People there considered themselves part of European diplomacy and looked down on us who transacted the correspondence with the faraway regions of Asia.

When we entered the messroom it was already full of people. On the table stood a large cake presented by Consul M. M. Bakunin on the occasion of his appointment to Batavia, capital of the Dutch East Indies. People began to tease him: "You know, instead of servants they keep big apes in Java."

"How shall I speak to them?"

"In Dutch, of course; they understand it."

A secretary of legation was leaving for a distant state. "Beware of Prince X.," said a diplomat to him. "He is a rare scoundrel."

"Who said so?"

"The tsar." A discreet silence ensued, interrupted only by the tinkling of glasses. According to the Russian fashion, tea was served in tumblers with silver holders.

When I returned to my desk, a new batch of telegrams was awaiting me. I took them with self-assured complacency. Codes were no longer a terror to me. I felt quite at ease and lit a cigarette. I was launched.

My existence now assumed a regulated course. In conformity with the leisurely mode of life in St. Petersburg, work in government offices began about noon. I started out after eleven and walked down the long and beautiful Nevskii Prospekt. Our Foreign Office stood on the large plaza on the right side of the semicircle facing the Winter Palace, next to the ministries of Finance and War. All the buildings were of the same severe empire style; only the palace itself was eighteenth-century baroque, the last phase of Italian Renaissance.

From the windows of the Asian Department I could see the gigantic monolithic column of Alexander I in the middle of the plaza, and farther away, above the trees of the park, the long façade of the Admiralty building. It was a monumental view of imperial Russia.

On the first floor of the Ministry of Foreign Affairs were located the State Archives, since published in part by the Soviets, and the Chancellery in charge of the correspondence with Europe and America. The second floor was occupied by the Asian Department and the minister's apartment, his official reception rooms, his study, and the office of his private secretary.

When Winston Churchill wrote that Sazonov, instead of going home to bed after the meeting of the Council of Ministers, drove by chance to the Foreign Office late in the evening and found there the Austrian ultimatum,* the distinguished author labored under a misapprehension. Sazonov's bedroom and his study and the Chancellery of the Foreign Office were in the same building and on the same staircase. Whatever Sazonov's other mistakes might have been, he did not go away on a weekend when Europe was going ablaze.

* W. S. Churchill, *The World Crisis. The Eastern Front* (London, 1931), p. 107. *Ed.*

I was attached to the Persian Bureau, but I had to help my colleagues for the Far East in the same room. Often after finishing with a telegram from China I had to copy an answer to Persia. With what a thrill I took into my hands for the first time the authentic letters of the ambassadors, stating in courteous but firm tones the views of their respective governments. They wrote in French, with the exception of the British and American representatives, who used English. The Japanese minister wrote in perfect Russian and even signed his name in Russian: Nissi. The Japanese knew Russia—how little we knew Japan.

I saw a treaty written on a large sheet and signed in thick black Chinese characters drawn with a brush. It was the signature of Li Hung Chang, called the greatest (and greediest) Chinese of his day. Like Talleyrand, he counted in millions the fees for his good offices. Li Hung Chang, or Count Li as he styled himself, died in 1901, after receiving a million dollars from the Russian government. His death made this grant useless. But nothing could be done without bribes in China, and military pressure would have cost more.

The correspondence of the Asian Department was chiefly with the Russian legations in the Eastern countries and with Great Britain on Asian affairs, the latter often strained and always unpleasant. With the United States we exchanged letters mostly about fur seals on the Aleutian Islands. These beautiful and perfectly harmless animals were being exterminated because of their costly fur and needed the protection of international law.

We had to read Russian and English newspapers. How often their articles were in complete contradiction to the telegrams we decoded. The work of a confidential clerk is very interesting—I was able to get a glimpse of the trend of Russian politics at the end of the reign of Alexander III.

The first impression was a sense of enormous strength and absolute security. How far this was warranted is a different question. Russia apprehended nothing and feared nobody. This was the general opinion, and to doubt it would have meant to expose oneself to a charge of lack of patriotism. Only in the inner circle of Russian diplomats did there exist, from the time of the Congress of Berlin in 1878, a real dread of a collision with a foreign power or powers. Carefully guarded as this sentiment was, it leaked out; and both the press and public opinion often accused Russian diplomats of timidity and lack of nerve. Of course the military establishment and the old conservatives were the first to accuse. They considered Russia as safe as the United States, although Russia's continental position in Europe and Asia exposed her much more to attack. Great Britain displayed a similar confidence in her own strength at that time and often defied France and Russia on African and Asian questions.

The two chief currents I encountered in the Russian Foreign Office were the recent alliance with France and the chronic enmity with England. Of course I was very patriotic and felt incensed against the British diplomats, the archenemies of Russia. It was Bismarck who, by his alliance with Austria and Italy, created a kind of Frankenstein monster in the center of Europe. This stirred France and Russia and brought a military understanding between them. A military convention with France was made by Alexander III as a precaution against an attack by Germany. A second German victory over France, similar to that of 1870, would have been highly dangerous to Russia—Russia would not have been able to withstand alone a subsequent joint attack by Germany, Austria, and Italy, with England unfriendly and possibly hostile. In the opinion of the Russian Foreign Office, the carefully planned and executed series of agreements between the Russian and French governments constituted a warning to Germany, restraining her warlike disposition and temporarily checking the probability of war.

If the relations of France and Russia with England could have been improved and a united front presented against Germany, the outbreak of World War I would have been delayed if not altogether prevented. But after 1870 England could never make up her mind whether it was more advantageous to consider Germany a friend or a foe. Only the building of a powerful German fleet a few hours away from the shores of England made the statesmen of Great Britain realize that "splendid isolation" free from foreign entanglements was no longer advisable. It was Lessar, then counselor of the Russian Embassy in London, who was the first to demonstrate to the English statesmen that there was no valid reason for war between England and Russia.

Second to Lessar as the authority on Asia was Pokotilov, secretary for Chinese affairs, who sat next to me and transacted the correspondence with the Far East. A young, genial, talented man, Pokotilov had a real knowledge of and interest in Asia. He had been in China, spoke Chinese perfectly, and accordingly was looked down on in the Foreign Office. He did not stay there long. The minister of finance, S. Iu. Witte, offered him a much better position and soon after sent him to Peking as president of the Russo-Chinese Bank. Our ministry made honorable but tardy amends—after Lessar's death, Pokotilov was appointed minister to China, remaining at the same time head of the Russo-Chinese Bank. He died from overwork soon after the Russo-Japanese war.

Lessar and Pokotilov were practically the only men in the Russian Foreign Office in St. Petersburg who knew and understood the East. Count Kapnist, head of the Asian Department, was a refined gentleman speaking to perfection several European languages but unable to retain correctly in his memory a single Oriental name. After all, I was not so very wrong in trying to go to Asia to get firsthand knowledge of it. Life in one's own country makes a person impervious to the different concepts of a foreign people. A diplomat, like a sailor, requires long experience with the storms and hidden dangers of an unknown sea. Many of my colleagues had never been abroad on an official mission. After years of quiet, subordinate work in the Foreign Office, people were suddenly appointed ministers to distant lands. They have never been successful. With the passing of Lessar and Pokotilov, Russian policy in China became a hopeless muddle and remains one to this day.

Usually we were far from being overworked in our department, but this happy existence was interrupted by political crises, and every crisis in Russian foreign policies originated precisely in the sphere of action of the Asian Department. It seemed that no war could be waged by Russia without the Balkans or the Far East being the cause of it, and our Asian Department being involved and held responsible.

Serious crises recurred every ten years with the regularity of solar eclipses. When I joined the Foreign Office, a crisis was just ahead, but nobody had the least inkling of it. The Trans-Siberian Railway was near completion and touched the sensitive shore of the Pacific. Japan felt the shock and started to act.

One Sunday morning in the summer of 1894, it was my turn to be on duty. I rose early, had a nice walk, and came to the Foreign Office in the best of spirits. After several hours spent alone doing nothing, as there was nothing to do, I intended to go out for lunch

when a long cable was brought to me. I started to work on it, when
G. A. Plançon, the chief of the Far Eastern Bureau, dropped in.

"Nothing serious, I hope," he said.

"One moment," I answered, rapidly decoding the cable. I finished
and showed it to him. It was the declaration of war between China
and Japan. Telephones began to ring; people were summoned; and
copies were sent to the Emperor and to the ministers of Navy, War,
Finance, and Communications. Only late in the afternoon did
several hungry and harassed diplomats leave the Foreign Office.
The next day cables started to pour in from everywhere. Things
grew worse. Japan trod for the first time on the soil of Manchuria
and spread out toward China proper. Count Kapnist came to our
room holding a cablegram, and the chief of the section showed him
different points on the map hanging on the wall.

"Where are they going?" murmured the Count. Nobody could
tell him, and the question still remains unanswered.

The opinion of the Foreign Office, accepted by the government,
was that Japan must never be allowed to take root on the continent
of Asia and that it would be preferable to fight her while she was
still confined to her islands. In accordance with this policy, a special
fleet was to be built for the Far Eastern station, Port Arthur fortified,
and a strategic railway line constructed. In short, everything was to
be done to make the war inevitable, its outbreak nearer, and its
declaration easy.

Count Kapnist, a hesitant and cautious man, resigned. There was
a general shuffling of personnel, and I was placed temporarily in
charge of the Persian Bureau.

Japan retreated for the time being but resolved to become a
strong naval and military power and to support her expansion by
force of arms. England favored the newly formed constitutional
government of Japan and was against autocratic and reactionary
Russia. Only after the Russian defeat in the war with Japan and
the opening of the Russian Duma did English public opinion, and
some British statesmen, swerve toward an entente with Russia,
without breaking with Japan. But that was to come later. In the
meantime the Asian Department entered into a new period of
false security and sham success. All became quiet in the Far Eastern
Bureau. I was busy with the correspondence with Persia and planned
to go there.

The Persian Bureau

As my attention became concentrated on Persian affairs, I was confronted at once by the acute hostility between England and Russia. Obsessed by the idea of a Russian threat to India, England tried to counter Russian influence wherever she could discover it—from Constantinople to the Far East.

Promising English statesmen—mostly under forty—assure us that British policy has always been concerned with peace and sea trade. Possibly this has been so; I cannot judge the inner thoughts of British diplomats, but their correspondence with Russia in the last quarter of the past century hardly supports this assertion. At least, such was the impression of the Russian Asian Department, which was in a continuous state of irritation. Although Germany was the only danger to Russia, as well as an increasing threat to the commerce and sea power of the British Empire, both England and Russia were extremely conciliatory to Germany and glared at each other.

In the early nineties Persia was one of the main sources of conflict, and my work was immediately concerned with it. I did not feel sure that the Russian policy adopted in regard to Persia was the right one. Was it worthwhile to incur the enmity of England for the sake of problematic influence in Persia? Could not England and Russia define their needs by mutual agreement? As a last resort, could not Persia be left alone, as was undoubtedly her sole desire? In 1885 Great Britain and Russia had been very near to war over a frontier dispute in central Asia. Could it happen again? The problem was of utmost importance, but to find a solution was beyond me. I addressed myself to Lessar.

"Will England attack Russia?" I asked. Lessar looked at me and smiled: "Let her try," he said, "she will be the worse for it."

"And we? Are we not to attack first?"

"No reason to," he answered. We remained silent. He stroked his long, hanging moustache with its thin twisted ends, which were faithfully reproduced by English cartoonists of the time.

Lessar, with his calm, powerful, ironical mind, was the only man in the Russian Foreign Office to scoff at the idea that an armed conflict between Russia and England was inevitable. His opinion carried weight with Count Kapnist; with the aged foreign minister, N. K. Giers; and with Emperor Alexander III. He succeeded in shelving the Afghan question, the most dangerous one, but the bickering over Persia still continued.

Persia constituted a land passage south of the Caspian Sea between the Near East and India and was also an approach to India from Russia. England wanted to have all Persia under her control, and Russia opposed this. Both policies pushed to extremes were wrong. Persia had neither railways nor highways, and hence her strategic and economic importance was next to nothing. That did not diminish in the least the sharpness of the diplomatic conflict between Russia and England; the relations of the two nations became envenomed. I found the Asian Department extremely anti-British, for the rivalry with England extended from Constantinople to the Far East, and the Persian Bureau was a particularly acute center of this enmity. The other Great Powers took no interest in Persia, leaving England and Russia free to quarrel over her.

I saw deep distrust and thinly veiled hostility. Was this the only foundation of diplomacy, and where would it lead? Only a small corner of the curtain over the vast scene of international relations was lifted for me, and the spectacle was not an edifying one. I felt instinctively that the game was not worth the candle. Was it possible that other questions, much more serious and involving the very existence of nations, were treated in the same haphazard, cantankerous, and drifting way? I was perfectly certain that England and Russia would not go to war over Persia, that they could not divide it, and that its annexation by either one of the contending parties was out of the question. Persia was a perfectly unpalatable apple of discord: neither of the contesting parties would have liked to take it, but neither would concede it to the other.

As I was soon to see myself, Anglo-Russian relations in Persia differed somewhat from those in the cabinets of London and St. Petersburg. Outside Tehran, there were only two points of friction —Meshed in the northeast and Tabriz in the northwest; there were no other Persian towns at that time with both British and Russian consulates. The conflicts in Tehran were so serious at times that they affected the acts of the Persian government, were mentioned in the English and Russian press, and usually ended in the recall of the losing minister. But gradually both sides got tired of the game. Nāser ed-Din Shah kept the same grand vizier, who assumed a neutral position. The Russian diplomats were by nature inclined to be passive and to remain on the defensive. On the other hand the British Foreign Office adopted the practice of promoting the English minister in Tehran to the post of ambassador at St. Petersburg. This prospect made them more cautious about picking useless quarrels with the Russians in Persia. An atmosphere of moderate goodwill spread in both legations. The consulates in Tabriz and Meshed were still fighting with each other, but their complaints were received coldly by their chiefs in Tehran, who considered them as mere parochial quarrels, devoid of interest and political importance.

In the wider field of international politics, Russian and English diplomacies moved on almost parallel lines. When Russia entered into a military convention with France, England tried to make an agreement with Germany, limiting the increase of their respective navies. The offer did not suit Germany, and she declined it. But England was more successful in signing a treaty of alliance with Japan, which finally brought the Japanese onto the continent of Asia. Russia and England with their respective allies formed two hostile groups, leaving a free hand for the expansion of Germany. The latter turned her attention to the acquisition of colonies, which constituted no danger for Russia.

Late in the fall of 1894, we heard that Tsar Alexander III was leaving for the Crimea. Shortly after, we were suddenly summoned to our chapel on the upper floor. Work ceased, and people streamed from their offices to the big staircase. The service for the restoration of the Emperor's health was short and impressive. We understood at once that his condition was desperate and that we should soon be called to a funeral mass.

The news came. Again we went to church, this time in uniform, with black bands on our left sleeves. The Emperor Alexander III was dead, and his son, Nicholas II, was sovereign of Russia. We dispersed after the service and resumed our work. The heavy asthmatic breathing of our chief was the only sound in the dull silence of the room.

The death of Alexander III was indeed a blow to Russia. He had been a bulwark of strength. Too much depended on him. Now he was replaced by his young son. All that we knew about Nicholas II was that he was small, weak, and could never make a decision, not even about his marriage.

To grasp the situation it is necessary to remember that Russia was an autocratic monarchy. This meant that she was governed by a hereditary dictator who owed unlimited power not to a popular election or to outstanding qualifications but to a mere chance of birth. Alexander III had one essential quality: he was a born ruler of men. Kind, honest, and brave, he was always true to his word. He assumed a heavy responsibility in not granting a constitution when he ascended the throne. But after this initial and fatal mistake, which brought his dynasty to ruin, he performed his duties to the best of his understanding.

I risk being taxed with partiality when I say that among the various departments of the Russian government the Foreign Office was one of the best and that foreign policy as shaped by Alexander III was the most successful Russia ever had. As a sovereign he was not quarrelsome; rather accommodating in his relations with his neighbors, he was highly respected by them.

When a French squadron was to visit St. Petersburg for the first time, some ministers objected that the "Marseillaise," the revolutionary anthem of the French republic, could not be played by a Russian military band. "Why not?" said the Tsar. "Do you expect me to compose a new anthem for them?"

Alexander III had received a rather limited and strictly military education, had mastered well the simple duties of a commander, and was very kind to the privates. I myself heard how amiably he greeted the two sentries who stood at the gate of the palace. But he was not a militarist and was averse to war, as it would result in the deaths of his soldiers, something he would not agree to except in case of dire necessity.

Giers, the foreign minister, was shocked by the little attention the tsar gave to international affairs. A defensive alliance with France and no useless wars with anyone were the only instructions Giers could get from him. The rest did not concern the emperor. That was not enough for the foreign minister, who despaired of ever initiating the tsar into the delicate web of diplomatic negotiations. Giers considered the tsar a brusque and rough soldier who did not at all appreciate the political perspicacity and talents of his adviser. But the tsar was not as bad as that. He liked his foreign minister and helped him with plain common sense when Giers was faltering under the hailstorm pouring from Downing Street.

"I am only the tsar's pen," explained Giers when he was pressed too closely. The explanation held good, for few ambassadors dared to treat directly with the tsar, who did not mince matters.

The nervous, anxious Giers, who was mortally afraid of Germany and only slightly less of Great Britain, and the sturdy, good-humored tsar, who was afraid of nothing, were well matched and made Europe safe for monarchy and even for democracy as far as France was concerned. The white-hot English notes cooled down as they were deposited on the desk of Alexander III by the unsteady hands of Giers.

The United States could enjoy an unprecedented prosperity, France the safety of her frontiers, Great Britain an unchallenged sway over her colonial empire. The rule of the tsar weighed heavily on Russia but assured political and economical stability for all nations. The huge, reactionary, ignorant, immobile Russia was the ballast which stabilized the equilibrium of the world. All that came to an end with the death of Alexander III. His demise was hardly noticed outside Russia. Who cared about the person of the tsar? Cabinets were assured that politics would remain unchanged under his successor. Russia was to be forever the same Russia. What an illusion!

3 Persia

After staying a year and a half in the Persian Bureau of the Foreign Office, I decided to see with my own eyes and to investigate myself the land which had sorely tried the patience of English and Russian statesmen. I made a decisive move and asked to be sent to Persia. From the point of view of service, it was a mistake. Only a small position in a consulate was open at that time, and I accepted it. Countries were rated according to the comforts of life and the prospects for advancement, and Persia was at the bottom of the list. It was considered a "hole," a place to be avoided by all means. "At least reasonable people think so," said a diplomat to me, intimating by the icy intonation of his voice his doubts that I belonged in that category.

I was attached to the staff of the consulate general at Tabriz, the chief city of northwestern Persia, and began my preparations for departure. It appeared that I needed complete traveling equipment.

"Don't forget a camping bed," said the chief of the section. "You will need it."

"Can't I buy one in Tabriz?"

"Of course not. Persians do not use beds; they sleep on the floor. They have no furniture at all—just carpets."

It developed further that Persians take off their shoes when they come in for a visit and walk in their socks right into the reception rooms of a European lady, keeping their hats on their heads as compensation. But this was only a matter of manners. There were other more serious differences from our ideas. To keep several wives in one's house seemed monstrous to a European but was considered desirable in Persia and other Moslem lands.

I began to understand that the general aversion to going to Persia had a real foundation after all. I felt the necessity of seeing a real Persian and called on the Persian minister. I saw a small, dark man. He did wear a round cap indoors, but for the rest he looked quite European and spoke French fluently. We sat on chairs with our shoes safely on our feet. He was very polite and grew eloquent when he heard that I was going to Tabriz, his native city.

"A fine town," he said. "Its air and water are excellent. What more do you need?" I needed many more things, but I tried to look satisfied and nodded my agreement.

I became reconciled to the idea of a certain lack of conveniences which I was sure to find in Persia. After all, I was not going there for the sake of comfort but to see Persia and study Persian life. That is what mattered; all the rest was secondary. Once this point was clearly established in my mind, everything looked radiant again. At the same time, I felt an increased attachment for the people and even the buildings I was going to leave, and I well realized that by accepting a consular position I severed my direct connection with the diplomatic activity of the capital of Russia. But my wings were open, and I could not stop my flight. With the recklessness of youth I was exultant at the prospect of starting on my first adventure in the East. On the last day, however, this heroic disposition dropped at the sight of the tears streaming down my mother's face. With a heavy heart I boarded the train that was to take me away from her and from Russia.

A Winter Journey to Persia

I felt sad and lonely in the sleeping car as the thundering express rolled on relentlessly, still full of the rush and glamour of the great capital we had just left. For a while I gazed blankly at the red velvet sofa in the compartment and the box of chocolates on it that my mother had given me with her last recommendations about luggage, health, and drafts of air. But my thoughts were soon distracted by the thrill and expectations which my journey held in store for me. It was not as a mere tourist that I was traveling but as an officer sent by the government to the outposts of the Empire on a responsible and patriotic errand in a distant and fascinating land. I was also anxious about the safety of the codes, entrusted to me at the last minute for the viceroy of the Caucasus, General S. A. Sheremetiev.

At Kharkov the train stopped for a few minutes, and I jumped out of the car right into a crowd of boys and girls who had come to bid me farewell. We were all talking and laughing when I heard behind me a voice that sounded familiar. I turned and saw Count Kapnist, my former chief. He had an estate in the province and lived there. His beard shone silver white on the dark brown fur of his expensive winter coat. He asked me for news about the old place, his lips quivering. He wanted to add something but changed his mind, grasped my hand, and moved away, a sad, broken, finished man among this clamorous, buoyant youth.

I crossed the stupendous Caucasian mountains in an excellent mail coach and reached Tiflis, the capital of Caucasus and the last civilized stage of my journey. I called on the viceroy, a tall, lean, affable, aristocratic old gentleman, who managed to rule the turbulent Caucasian population with the least possible amount of interference with their customs, creeds, and racial prejudices. His political secretary, A. N. Shcheglov, a merry, energetic fellow, whom I was to meet again in Tehran, came to bid me goodbye.

I had to continue my trip across snow-covered Transcaucasia in a primitive horse carriage without springs, jolting on a frozen road swept by a cold wind, on an elevated tableland that looked extremely unattractive in winter. It was January 1895, and the further south I proceeded, the colder it was, because of a constant rise in altitude.

Finally I arrived at the Russian frontier post of Julfa, the end of the empire. Across the River Aras, which formed the boundary, I had my first view of Persia. It looked like the South Pole, with Tabriz a good hundred miles away in the icy desert beyond the snowclad hills.

I realized with horror that I had to cross a frozen barrier and that there were no roads in Persia and no wheeled traffic—nothing but paths for mules and horses. The carriage deposited me at the post house. I sat down in deep dejection as the sound of the wheels slowly died away, leaving me to my melancholy fate.

There was nothing to gain by sitting there. I rose and walked dismally down the street. Julfa consisted of a few dwellings. If there were any inhabitants, they kept well inside their houses. The street led to a big customhouse on the shore of the river. I entered a large, well-heated room. Several officers in uniforms with green trimmings sat at their desks and talked in loud voices. The talk stopped abruptly at my appearance, and a tall, broad-shouldered man rose and moved toward me. It was the chief of the customhouse.

I introduced myself and said in a depressed voice that I wanted to cross the Aras and go to Persia. My voice faltered with the last words. The giant looked at me and broke into a stentorian laugh that shook the windows. "Impossible," he said. "There are ice floes in the river. Your qolām [native servant of the consulate] has been on the other side since yesterday and cannot cross. You will have to wait till the ice passes."

"How long?" I asked at this culmination of my misfortunes.

"The longer, the better," he answered, grinning. "Stay with us. Cheer up. I promise we'll make you comfortable. Come along."

I followed this amiable man to his quarters. In the evening all the local society gathered there to hear the news I brought from St. Petersburg. After supper I was conducted into a cheerful room with a fine bed and fell soundly asleep, forgetting my troubles, Julfa, Persia, and the dreadful road that awaited me.

In the morning I went out and shivered at the difference between the cozy room and the bleak, deserted street and the desolation around. I met no men, only two large eagles walking on the snow. They looked at me with resentment and reluctantly took flight. I found the customhouse animated and full of people writing, talking, and moving about, rubbing their hands.

The chief greeted me and said gaily: "There is less ice on the river. The Aras is going to be gentle again." But to me the Aras did not look gentle. Big circles swirled on its dark surface, and floes heaved, turned, and sank again.

In the afternoon camel caravans came from Persia. The camels were hairy, monstrous beasts, with two humps, not at all like the lean creatures we see in our zoos. The qolām crossed also. "Too late now," he said. "Tomorrow, Enshāollāh [if God wills]." You have to rely on Providence if you travel in Persia. He left early next morning to prepare horses. I wanted to go with him but was detained for lunch. The hospitality of Julfa knew no limit.

The qolām did not return after lunch, and I decided to take the ferry without waiting for him. We crossed safely. Sometimes the ferry is carried away; what becomes of the passengers may be read in the local newspapers. The ferry stopped a short distance from the bank. I stepped on crackling ice and leaped to the shore. The boat moved away; I was left alone in Persia.

I climbed a steep, slippery bank and saw before me a strange vil-

lage of square mud houses with flat roofs. The houses stood on both
sides of a large expanse of frozen mud, the great highway of northwestern Persia. I walked halfway up the street and stopped; the road,
stretching like a ribbon, led straight into the interior of the country.
I could not cross all Persia on foot and alone.

A man peeped out of a door and disappeared before I could call
him. I went to what seemed to be the only inhabited dwelling, and
opened the door. It was the post house; my qolām was inside.

"Horses," I shouted, as I had begun to get impatient with this
dead place.

"This minute," said the qolām. "Befarmāid [Bring in your honored
presence]!" I entered a room with an earthen floor partly covered
with felt rugs. A Persian, smiling, offered me his hand. It was the
stationmaster, customhouse chief, administrator, everything combined, welcoming me to Persia. He wore a black lambskin hat and a
jacket adorned with brass buttons bearing the image of the sun and
lion, the emblem of Persia. I was invited to sit down and take tea
with him. The tea was very sweet, with the peculiar taste of the kind
used in Persia, and was served in small glasses. This little ceremony
finished, I could start with my caravan of loaded horses carrying my
luggage and the mail for the consulate.

I had traveled before, but in lands that were fit for traveling. I
mean that there were hotels or accommodations of some other kind
where one could always get a dinner and a bed, and in most cases
a bath. But Persia was not a travelers' land in this sense. There were
posthouses, which supplied riding horses from one station to the
other, but that was all; the traveler had to look to his own comfort
as best he could. The first thing was to collect information about the
chapar khaneh (post stations) and the distances between them, since
most of the glorious country is a waste—not inhabited, not cultivated, and for long stretches waterless. One must ride without stops
from one station to the other, a matter of thirty miles or more, rarely
less. Mountains are the worst part of the journey. Progress is slow,
and a blizzard in winter, with no shelter within reach, is a serious
consideration. Nobody had told me about all this, and I mounted my
horse as unconcernedly as if I were to travel in a Pullman car with
the railway ticket in my pocket.

Our way led through a plain toward a chain of hills separated by
a gorge called Derei Diz, whose end disappeared in the clouds. As
we entered the pass, it narrowed; the road was nothing more than

the slippery bed of a frozen torrent. The rocky walls drew nearer; the sun, hidden by the mountains, was setting, and the air became distinctly colder. I felt apprehensive and called to the qolām: "Is the station near?"

"Yes, yes," answered he, a brazen lie. I wonder why people lie so easily about distance. Night came in due time, and no station was in sight, only rocks and steep cliffs on both sides. It became piercingly cold. I was riding as if in a dream; things were too ghastly to be real. I had no idea how much time had passed; I felt stiff, stunned, and stupid and realized only that I had to move or freeze. I ceased to believe in southern latitudes.

At last a light appeared. Merciful Providence, it was the station! I was conducted into a stable with an earthen platform at the end.

"What does this mean?" Where is the guest room?" I asked.

"It is better here," answered the qolām. "It's warmer."

That was a mighty consideration. To get warm was the essential thing; all the rest did not matter. And besides, the qolām brought me tea. What a wonderful man! I lay down, was covered with something and immediately fell asleep.

In the morning, as soon as I awoke, I felt that things around me were not as they should be. A small lamp fastened to a wooden pillar gave a reddish light through its blackened chimney. Horses were chewing, stamping their feet. How cold, dear me, and what a smell! Where was I? Oh, yes, in Persia. Something began to stir; it was my qolām, sitting on the ground and making a fire with brushwood. I hastily put my head under the blanket and closed my eyes. Too late —he had seen me.

"Sahib," he said, "time to rise." I was too depressed to have a will of my own and got up. It was still dark, and the stars were glimmering in the sky when we started. After some time the pale light of dawn appeared, but snow began to fall, whirling in the air and beclouding everything. I could hardly see my way. I was soon covered with snow, which continued to fall with pitiless insistence. I felt despair creeping into my heart. The country seemed to be more open now, but the outline of the hills was blunted when seen through the curtain of falling snow. No trace of road was visible, but the qolām in front of me seemed sure of his way and rode without hesitation.

A slight wind began to blow, making the snowflakes twirl and dance. My horse pricked up his ears and hastened his steps so as not to lose sight of the guide. I became almost indifferent to my fate; anything could happen in a land like this. But the wind died as swiftly as it had risen. The air cleared, and the sun shone; at once everything glistened under its rays. The sky appeared beautifully blue. I saw a mud building, a miserable hovel, but what delight it brought to my heart! The horse sped to it and stopped. It was the post house—a room with an earthen floor and a door perpetually ajar. I did not mind it, as I did not expect anything better. The qolām tried to make me comfortable. He brought a thornbush, put it on the ground before me, and lit it with a match. A flame rose, spreading over the crackling branches. A Ritz-Carlton in Persia! I took off my gloves and warmed my hands at the fire.

Food and tea appeared as if by magic. I ate contentedly, and the qolām looked at me with a slight smile on his hard, manly face. Fresh horses, and out again. I laughed as we started cantering. There were partridges on the road and wolves barely a hundred yards away. The air was pure and bracing. "What more do you need?" as the Persian minister had said to me in St. Petersburg.

The road was splendid, and we advanced rapidly. Then the guide drew the reins of his horse and looked ahead attentively. I joined him and saw the reason. A tremendous descent was before us, with a trail hardly marked in the snow, zigzagging along the slopes of the mountain. Trees could be seen far below in the plain, not bigger than tufts of grass at this distance. The sun was low; not a moment was left for hesitation, as darkness would soon set in. Besides, I wanted to get out of the mountains at any price. I had had enough of this kind of Switzerland.

We began the descent. The scenery was splendid, but I was glad when we were down. The trail turned and ended in a frozen stream. The guide in front of me fell with his horse on a sheet of ice; fortunately neither was hurt. The shoes of my horse shrieked on the ice, but I crossed safely; one victim was enough.

The village we reached looked prosperous, with plenty of orchards —an unmistakable sign of prosperity in Persia. The post house was large. I was invited into a room, of which the entire wall facing outside consisted of a large Persian-style window. It was composed of small squares of transparent paper, all torn, with the wind freely blowing in. The qolām quietly started to prepare my bed.

But now I had recovered part of my spirits, and I reacted for the first time since I had entered Persia. I told the qolām firmly that the window must be repaired at once. To my astonishment I was obeyed. In a few minutes an old Persian appeared, with a long beard, a long dress, and the dignity of Zoroaster. He worked solemnly but efficiently. The huge window was put in a perfect state of repair, and the old magician retired as silently as he had come.

A regular Persian dinner was served: chicken with rice, roast lamb, and dried fruits; the rest of the dessert was inedible. All the dishes were served at once on a big wooden tray. No table and no chairs. I sat on the carpet with the poise of an experienced Oriental traveler. In the morning I saw blue hills to the south. Tabriz lay on this side of them, thank God, not more than a thirty-mile ride on a level plain. That could be negotiated before noon.

Tabriz

We reached the blessed city at the appointed time. To the northeast a steep reddish hill with the tomb of a Moslem saint offers to the town the protection of nature and of the deceased divine. On the other sides Tabriz is surrounded by extensive gardens, mostly of almond trees.

I entered the city through a crumbling suburb and penetrated into a labyrinth of crooked streets lined with blank mud walls. All the windows in Persia face the interior court in order to protect the modesty of the women from the gaze of strangers. I soon lost all sense of direction and followed the qolām, turning right and left according to the windings of the street. And this was one of the principal arteries of the town! The others were worse.

Our way led us into a narrow blind alley ending in a dark vault, a fitting finish to my hazardous journey. Two Persian soldiers guarded the entrance. The qolām dismounted; the soldiers stood at attention with their sticks (they had no other arms), and I realized that the gaping door led into my home in Tabriz.

I followed the qolām into an inner court surrounded by low buildings which constituted the quarters allocated to me. The rooms were whitewashed, and the brick floor was covered with carpets. That was all—no furniture. I sat on the windowsill while my camping bed was brought in and opened and my luggage deposited in the empty apartment. After that the qolām, considering that he had completed his task of bringing me to Tabriz, told me he was going to inform the consul of my arrival. I was left with the soldiers. They were artillerymen, gay and likable fellows. In all armies, artillery is re-

cruited from among the cleverest chaps. For infantry service the
intelligence requirements are considerably reduced.

The soldiers tried to be helpful. I followed their movements with
amused eyes. My very bags, sunk on the floor, seemed to look at me
with mute reproach. This was to be my residence! Between these
blank walls I was expected to spend the best years of my life! My
friends in the Foreign Office were right—I was caught in a hole.

But I was not to be left alone to indulge in tardy regrets. From the
moment I crossed the threshold of my house, which was the property
of the consulate, I became its property also. Already my person belonged to the consulate as much as—or rather more than—to myself.
Things began to move at once. A qolām came and said that the consul
inquired about my health after the strain of the journey. Another
qolām asked on behalf of the consul's wife if I needed anything. I
expressed my thanks for the inquiries and said that I would report to
the consulate immediately.

Life in Tabriz

I was nervous. What kind of man would my chief be? Everything
depended on him. In Russia I had my mother, my home, and my
friends. Here in Persia I was alone. The icy mountains I had just
traversed, the forbidding city, and my desolate quarters all produced
a depressing impression, increased by the discomfort of a two-day
ride in heavy winter clothes.

The consulate was a few houses away. It was built in the same
style as my house, flat-roofed, with a courtyard inside, only much
larger and with many more Persian soldiers, qolāms, and some
cossacks at the entrance. Collecting my courage, I entered. I was met
by a short, bespectacled man who warmly shook my hand. It was
A. A. Petrov, the consul general, who was to be my chief, my host,
and my providence in Tabriz.

We took a liking to each other at first sight. I liked the kind look
of his eyes, his smile, the quiet sound of his voice. It was lunchtime,
and he took me straight to his excellently furnished, well-heated
private apartment. Mrs. Petrova, welcomed me very hospitably. We
all sat down at a large table. Petrov, surrounded by his numerous
family, looked like a country squire, happy in his home and wishing
for nothing else. The children chirped merrily, glancing at me. The
two elder girls were more reserved: one was serious, the other had a
mocking expression.

"How long have you been in Persia?" I asked the consul.

"Thirty years," he answered.

A slight shiver ran down my back. No, that would not do for me. I instinctively changed the subject of conversation and started to speak about St. Petersburg. That proved interesting to all, particularly to the girls.

"Take only a house servant," said Petrov, "and dine with us. You won't need a cook. You'll feel lonesome in your house if you eat alone. Now let's go to work." He rose from his place, and I followed him into his office.

The first experience in a new job is a serious matter in the life of any man. I decided to succeed in my work at the consulate or leave Persia altogether. I felt almost like a clergyman entering his first church. The room was not very large, but it was official and imposing. The consul's table was covered with a green cloth edged with gold fringe. On the wall, high above his chair, hung a portrait of the tsar and other objects of national importance, among them an obsolete table of consular fees.

Two safes added to the impressive appearance of the room. One—modern, shining, varnished—contained codes, documents, and bags of gold; the other—antiquated, grim, square, covered with big, round nailheads—was full of Persian silver coins, the currency of the country. To open the old safe was quite a problem, requiring the patience and ingenuity of at least three men. Keys would be tried and advice exchanged without avail. Then suddenly a bang would be heard, people would jump in their seats, and with a loud complaint the door would open by itself, without apparent reason.

As soon as we came in, work started to move with the relentless activity of a conveyor. It was not in vain that the consulate at Tabriz had the reputation of being the busiest one in Persia. I heard the hum of voices and the shuffling of feet from the next two rooms, which were noisy and crowded in comparison with the solemn tranquillity of the consul's office.

One room was occupied by two Persian *mirzās* (native clerks), since most of the correspondence was in Persian, and by a Russian clerk—a silent, almost automatic man, a kind of robot. But when the consul's wife brought in a Russian housemaid, the robot married her at once in our little chapel, much to the disappointment of the consul's family, which remained without a servant.

The last room was the domain of an Armenian clerk in charge of passports, who sat in his chair all day, without moving, crouched like a racing cyclist. Eighteen thousand passports were visaed each year for Persians going to work in the Caucasus.

In came a mirzā with a bundle of papers, which he started to read rapidly in Persian. It was the correspondence with the authorities of Tabriz and our numerous native agents. The mirzā received instructions, retired, returned again with the prepared answers, read them to the consul, licked the end of the paper with his tongue, breathed on a blackened seal, and applied it to the wet spot. The entire performance was executed with extraordinary rapidity. I was completely bewildered and understood nothing.

"Don't be alarmed," said the consul. "You'll get onto it by and by."

The vice-consul, O. Cherkavskii, a jolly young fellow, laughed and rubbed his hands. I felt helpless, and my confusion grew worse when I took the papers and looked at them. They were covered with queer small signs that looked like shorthand, and were in fact shorthand, the Persian *shekasteh*, the only writing used for official and private purposes. The elegant manuscripts exhibited in our museums are costly productions of refined workmanship. Those swanlike curves, those little rows running like ripples on the surface of water, those snakelike coils and daring dashes flying like arrows, are artistic writing created for the delight of the eye—not for daily use.

I doubted that I would ever be able to understand the elusive signs and sounds with which I had to deal. I almost despaired of making any progress. "Take it easy," said Petrov. He took me in his gentle but firm hands, and I was broken in like a young horse trained for harness. I could not have had a better chief; he was competent, experienced, and rarely upset by anything. Once he took his seat in his office, he never stirred from it—something I could never do. He knew his Persians, took them as they were, felt comfortable in Tabriz, and made other people feel comfortable also.

After several months of persistent labor—usually a year is needed —I became master of my work instead of its indignant slave. With what superb pretended indifference I read aloud to my chief for the first time the impossible scrawl of an urgent Persian message and rolled in an uninterrupted sequence, without catching my breath, the high-sounding syllables. The consul could not contain himself and broke into laughter. A mastery of the spoken and written vernacular was an absolute necessity, as neither of our mirzās knew a single word of any European language and both the consul general and the vice-consul were planning to go on leave.

I was in Persia, the land of my dreams, paid by my government, and provided with a private house and interesting work. In short, I had everything I had longed for; yet I was not happy. I was keenly aware of being in a foreign land, a land of fanatical Moslems not altogether friendly toward Europeans and deeply distrustful of one another. The dreary streets with their endless windowless walls; the veiled women invariably dressed in black, furtively and silently walking along the sidewalks; the men looking all alike in their lamb-skin hats and flowing clothes—all this produced an uncanny, night-marish impression. It was impossible to participate in native exis-tence; the only thing I could do was observe from a distance the strange life of this strange people.

Every morning after breakfast I went up to the flat roof of my house for a few moments to breathe some fresh, pure air. The sky was uniformly blue. There is very little rain in Persia and vir-tually only two seasons—summer and winter. Both are cloudless. Summer is long and very oppressive, except in the hills, but winter is delightful. The flat roof is a very useful addition to a Persian home and, as each family lives in a separate house, is thoroughly private.

I watched the raising of flags on the four consulates of Tabriz. Across the street, the French consul was hurrying through the large veranda to his office, where he filled innumerable lists of consular accounts imposed by a merciless bureaucracy. I think the French budget could be cut in half if they had less red tape. But then what would become of the *budgetivorous* (the expression is French) func-tionaries? I do not know what the British and Turkish consuls did in the mornings, as I saw them only in the afternoons when they were on horseback.

The Russian consulate general opened at ten with the ceremonious appearance of the two Persian mirzās. They bowed, salaamed, and shook hands with us. This was obligatory, as a consular mirzā was a socially prominent person and had to be treated as such. After that the second mirzā retired, and we had to listen with special attention to the daily verbal reports of our chief mirzā. He was, in fact, a living newspaper, and a very interesting one. Everything from the health of the crown prince, who was governor general of Tabriz, to last night's scramble was faithfully related. I had a suspicion that this same mirzā reported with the same accuracy to the Persian authorities, with whom he was in constant communication, all that was going on at the consulate.

In the meantime the mail was delivered and opened. Persian correspondence is both profuse and short at the same time. Only the last two lines of a long letter really matter and must be studied carefully; all the rest is Oriental eloquence. We had to answer in the same style. Telegrams had to be composed and written in Persian, except those coded or sent to Russia.

There were also two heads of the Russian merchant community in Tabriz—one for the Russian Moslems and one for the Armenians. These were highly respected and coveted positions, usually held for life. If a new head had to be elected by the merchants, to be confirmed afterward by the consul, the entire community involved was aroused, and the many requests, complaints, appeals, suggestions, personal visits, deputations' visits, and invasions in full strength by each party converted our consulate into the hotbed of an election battle.

After lunch we usually examined judicial cases, a complicated and wearisome procedure. The Koran was considered the source of all laws, or rather customs, of Persia—for there were no written laws, only judicial commentaries on the Koran written in Arabic. We actually had nothing to do with law, since Christians were considered unfit to speak about the Koran or even mention its name. The customs, of course, were also unwritten. We had to have recourse chiefly to precedents and cite pertinent old cases from the consular archives. There were no books of international law at the consulate except those I had brought, among other souvenirs, in remembrance of the days of my innocent childhood at my alma mater, the University of St. Petersburg.

If the defendants were Persians, a special judge—the *karguzar*—examined the complaints of the foreigners in the presence of a consular delegate. The decision was usually postponed until both parties, after much delay, agreed on some settlement based on mutual concessions. If after several months no agreement was reached, the case was transferred to the legation at Tehran, and it was the end of the matter as far as our consulate was concerned.

A very important argument was a written legal opinion of some renowned mullah, who did not mention the parties involved in the case, replacing them by fictitious names. In general this opinion assumed a disinterested aloofness similar to that of an English barrister or a Roman praetor with his jus judicii.

We rarely had to rely on treaties composed in very general terms. There was only one juridical convention, of 1843, in which it was stated that all land in Persia belonged to three persons: the shah, the landlord, and the peasant. These three persons could be combined into one or two units. The shah was sole proprietor of his private pleasure grounds and coproprietor with the peasants settled on his land. A landlord was sometimes exempt from paying taxes to the shah but received dues from the peasants who cultivated his land. In some instances the peasant had no landlord but, of course, had to pay taxes to the shah. Poor as they were, the Persian peasants were better off than the peasants of India, who hold the world record for wretchedness. The semi-independent tribes seemed to be the happiest of all, possibly because they carried arms and could defend their rights.

The person of a Persian was easily exposed to violence; his house less so, because of the presence of women; and his shop was the safest of all, as the whole bazaar would rise in protest.

A married woman remained in full possession of her property, something which was not achieved in France until late in the nineteenth century. This can be explained by the fact that, since men were permitted to have several wives, the parents of each girl wanted to ensure her the possession of her dowry. It may also be traced to the influence of Khadija, the rich widow who married Mohammed. Since her husband had nothing but a fine appearance and prophetic gifts, she probably wanted to keep the purse strings in her own hands. There was also the *sigeh* (semilegal wife), whose modest position gave her the right to a fixed compensation in case of divorce or death of the husband.

Some afternoons I had to go to the Persian court for foreign complaints. The sessions were often protracted. Witnesses were heard and depositions taken. There were no lawyers in Persia, and each man had to present his case himself, which he did with great zest. There is a truly remarkable capacity for talking in a Persian who is directly interested in the matter under discussion. The *karguzar* listened with admirable patience, which I tried vainly to imitate. Finally the voice of a *muezzin* was heard, calling for the evening prayer. The session was over for the day. All the court lay prostrate on the floor, immersed in devotion, and I respectfully retreated. Shadows were

falling on the narrow street which resounded with the hoofs of the
horses, as I rode home comforted by the thought that justice had
been rendered according to the precepts of the Koran, and that a cup
of tea was waiting for me in my little dining room.

After tea a cossack of the consular escort came in, and I prepared
him for the noncommissioned officer's examination. He brought
with him a little cyclopedia containing everything from duties toward God and the tsar to cavalry maneuvers. We diligently studied
it, the cossack with all his heart. He was astonished when I told him
that I had seen the emperor and heard his voice. The cossack could
hardly believe that the tsar had something human in him, in common with ordinary mortals; he insisted that a monarch must have
some superhuman qualities. I agreed, although I had failed to perceive any such traits when I met this exalted being.

I took heartily to my consular work, but after all it was only
a necessary detail in my life. My primary aim was to study Persia,
and above all I needed to make friends. The Persians, like all Orientals, proved to be elusive and secretive. I found it impossible to
call on a Tabrizian except on formal occasions or by special invitation. The European colony, on the contrary, welcomed me very
hospitably. The Russian consulate general closed at 3 P.M., and then
I was generally free to make calls or use the short hours of a winter
afternoon for horseback riding—the chief pleasure that Persia af-
fords.

After my first round of afternoon calls, I decided to make calls
after the late dinner at the consulate, as there was nothing else to do
in the evenings. When for the first time I hammered at the heavy
doors of the closed houses and the medieval silence of a Persian
street resounded with my knocking, it produced quite a commotion.
My unexpected appearance was contrary to all Oriental and, I dare
say, European habits. However, people recovered from their amazement and genially accepted my visits and my clumsy explanations—
they even insisted that I come to see them again.

My first friend outside my consulate was the French consul, Léon
Hugonnet, a slow, near-sighted, studious old bachelor, with hesitant
movements and a surprised expression which sometimes changed to
one of sad resignation. He had published several little-known but
well-written books of travel and felt out of his element in a city with
no printing press and only inferior lithographic productions. Hugonnet was deprived of any solace; he was single, did not care for dogs,

and frankly distrusted horses. He was an excellent and gifted man, but fate had been unmerciful to him from the very beginning.

"I was a small boy when my mother died," Hugonnet told me once. "My father placed me in a religious educational institution. A short time later the priests called me when the class was over, took me out, and spoke at great length, till I understood that my father had just died also, and I was left alone in this world. I still remember the great kindness they showed me. I finished my education, took to journalism, then joined the Foreign Office, and here I am in Tabriz." He smiled.

I also became intimate with the British consul general, C. G. Wood, who came from an old consular family. He was a man of rare charm of character, with nothing of the conceit or reserve which makes Britishers difficult for foreigners to approach. He was jovial, sanguine, stout, and still elegant and active. He had a wife, a family, a home, and he led the life of a sportsman. We often went hunting, and, notwithstanding the difference in age, we could sit together for hours, talking and cracking jokes. I remember a conversation we had one winter evening in 1896.

We were sitting in his small cozy living room, all done in Syrian silk. It was bitterly cold outside, but the little room was snug and warm. We used to assemble there, because in the big official drawing room the temperature was freezing. We had been out on horseback all day, and were now enjoying a well-earned rest, taking hot grog.

"Here's luck," said Wood, lifting his glass. Nothing contributes more to mutual understanding than a good hunt on a frosty day. If the delegates to the world conferences had been jumping hedges together they would have found no difficulty in signing treaties.

"A rotten state, my dear sir, and a rotten government. Nothing to do here, and nothing to hope for."

Strange as it may seem, it was the English consul general who was speaking thus to me about Persia, when our governments were at loggerheads. His statement was true. A country with considerable natural wealth and a people with many good qualities, Persia was experiencing at that time a period of complete decay under the Qājār dynasty.

"Look at the crown prince," continued the consul. "Good for nothing, and his son is much worse, a budding despot."

Such were the views of Wood, and I thoroughly shared them. I am not entitled to express any opinion concerning Wood's official

activity; I can only say that it is to men like him that England and
Russia owe much of the success of their alliance, which lasted
through the strenuous years of World War I.

The crown prince, Mozaffar ed-Din, was governor general of
Tabriz. He and his son, Mohammad Ali, were heirs of the reigning
Nāser ed-Din Shah. Both were old fashioned Orientals who were
utterly unfit to govern; they lacked education and had not yet been
to Europe. But the likeness stopped there. Mozaffar ed-Din was a
kind, open, simple man; his son had a reputation of being false, greedy,
and cruel. Mozaffar ed-Din showed a childish interest in European in-
ventions and wanted to stay at peace with his own people and with
the rest of the world. Mohammad Ali was a born despot, and all his
sympathies were with autocratic Russia.

I saw Mohammad Ali first, shortly after my arrival in Tabriz. The
Armenian community had arranged a theatrical performance, and
the eldest son of the crown prince agreed to honor it with his presence. An officer of the consulate offered to present me to His Highness before the beginning of the play. We left the theater and walked
through a small, snow-filled court, bareheaded and in evening dress.
However, the climate in Persia is dry and wholesome in winter, and
we did not mind. We entered a room with European furniture. On a
sofa opposite the door sat a corpulent young man with a fat, round,
solemn face, small eyes, and a little mouth with a tiny moustache,
wearing a plain black Persian coat. It was Prince Itizad os-Saltaneh,
the future Mohammad Ali Shah, grandson of Nāser ed-Din Shah.
He had a haughty, disagreeable appearance and would have seemed
ridiculously pompous but for a sinister gleam in his eyes. I was presented. The prince nodded to me and murmured "*Ahvol* [How are
you]?" My companion said a few insignificant phrases to the prince,
and we bowed out.

It was bad policy on the part of Nāser ed-Din Shah to keep his
son and grandson far away in Tabriz, without proper European
education and in complete ignorance of affairs of state. Their only
European teacher was an aged Frenchwoman, Mme Limousin, who
taught French to the younger children of the crown prince. She was
a bright, gay, energetic old lady, who often visited the Russian consulate and became a great friend of us all. Later, in Tehran, she met
a dreadful fate—she was robbed, murdered, and thrown into a pit.
The old princes, whom I met occasionally, spoke nothing but Per-

sian. They represented the last generation, which considered their land the best in the universe, with no need of change or reform.

I was very curious to see the crown prince, Mozaffar ed-Din, but had to wait for the festivity of Now Ruz, when all the Persian grandees are obliged to appear in public. Now Ruz, literally the New Day, falls on the eighth of March (old style). In ancient times it was the beginning of the solar year, and, though it has nothing to do with the Moslem religion and its calendar, it is still the most important national holiday in Persia and Bokhara. The adoration of the sun goes back to the dawn of civilization. The name of Mithra, the sun god, appears in Persia in late Achaemenian inscriptions; and during the Parthian revival of Persia, the religion of Zoroaster was known to the Romans as the cult of Mithra.

As the festival of Now Ruz coincides with the beginning of spring, all the people go out of town, after a few days of obligatory visiting, and rejoice in the open fields covered with fresh grass and the first flowers of the year. It is the only time when Persia is green and throbbing with life. Later the earth becomes parched and dry under a burning sun and no rain at all. Only artificial irrigation maintains the patches of cultivated fields and planted gardens; the rest is a dead desert.

The consuls received a formal invitation and drove in full uniform to the palace of the Valiahd (Heir Apparent) to take part in this pleasant holiday of pagan origin. As the carriages drove to the open place before the old citadel, they looked very picturesque surrounded by galloping qolāms with various insignias on their caps—the Russian double-headed eagle, the French tricolor cockade, and the proud crown of England.

We were ushered into a great hall with a large carpet, but otherwise perfectly bare. The prince stood at its far end. Mozaffar ed-Din, stout, middle aged, with a pale face and pockets under his eyes, listened to the speech of congratulation made in French. He nodded to signify that he understood and approved it, started to answer in French, but he broke down and finished in Persian. Mozaffar ed-Din was not a bad man, but he was weakness personified—weakness of health, weakness of character, weakness of opinion, if any. It was said that his father, Nāser ed-Din Shah, characterized him as the most helpless man in the kingdom. Utterly unable to manage his household and his province, he was surrounded by a greedy crowd of courtiers who stole everything. It was the party of Tabrizians, reactionaries of the worst type, who ruined the monarchy after Mozaffar ed-Din mounted the throne. As things stood in 1895, the central government would not receive a cent of revenue from the province of Tabriz, the wealthiest and largest in Persia, if the shah did not send a *pishkar* (vice-governor) to virtually rule Tabriz and administer it in what the Persians called an efficient way.

We were invited to take tea and sweets. There was no attempt to serve lunch, as on the last occasion the butter was so rancid it had proved too much even for the Persians. We returned home, and the next day we received the visit of a dignitary, who conveyed to us the thanks of the prince. He presented us with a little purse from the prince, filled with very small silver coins minted for the occasion and a few gold ones wrapped in a separate paper. I regret to state that the number of gold pieces marked on the wrapper did not correspond to the contents. A remark about this was made to a high Persian functionary, who laughed and said, "I know who stole it," and he mentioned the name of the official. It was a perfectly natural occurrence—a sum sent by the prince never reached its destination in full.

According to Persian concepts, the government of Persia was an absolute monarchy, which meant that the will of the monarch was unlimited and supreme. Translated into Western terms this would signify a dictatorial executive unhampered by a legislative assembly or independent judges. But to accept these definitions literally would be a fallacy. There existed, according to the ideas of the Persian people, a power infinitely above the will of the monarch and a complex set of rules superior to his laws. This power was God, and these rules were contained in the Koran, the sacred book with the revelations of Mohammed, the prophet of Islam.

The Koran was written in Arabic and could be properly understood, explained, and expressed in vernacular Persian only by the clergy. The power of the priests would have been overwhelming had they been able to organize and agree among themselves. But this never happened in Persia; thus the rule of the Shah and his ministers was made possible. The Moslem priests themselves were bound by time-honored traditions, concepts, and customs; as long as these remained immutable, rulers and dynasties could change, but the monarchical system would remain intact.

In the second half of the nineteenth century, when European influence began to penetrate into Persia, contact was established with a new civilization and with Western ideas, entirely free and independent of the spirit of Islam and of the old habits of Persia. Since European nations were infidels in the eyes of the Persians, a shah who introduced Western innovations was open to the accusation of being an infidel himself, which meant a general upheaval of the people, with the threat of deposition to the ruler and ruin to his supporters.

Such was the situation I had to face—a situation in complete opposition to my previous theories about Persia. In the Russian Foreign Office I had studied the reports of the consulate general of Tabriz and the diplomatic dispatches from the legation at Tehran and had accordingly formed my idea of Persian politics and internal affairs. Persia was depicted as a strongly conservative land, far away from the disturbing influences of restless European life and jealously guarded by the firmly established traditions of a time-honored religion and monarchical rule. Nothing could be farther from reality. Persia was a volcano seething with discontent, and the venerable Moslem priests were at the very head of the revolutionary movement.

When I arrived in Persia, revolutionary movements had begun to be a feature of the land. They remained so for twenty years, causing increasing complications for the Persian, Russian, and English governments. In Persia there are two kinds of revolutions: the provincial, local in character; and the general, aimed at the authority of the central government and even at the person of the shah. I witnessed the former in the first year of my stay in Tabriz.

"*Shulug* [revolt]," said the consul, entering the office where I was busy translating some Persian papers.

"What does it mean?" I asked. Revolt was the last thing I expected in Persia.

"Scarcity of flour on the market," answered the consul. "Wheat has been purposely concealed to raise the price, in connivance with the authorities. Now this profit making has gone too far and has passed the safety line. The bazaars are closed and the bakeries also. We shall hear more about it." The consul looked perfectly calm. The manipulation of wheat prices was a common occurrence in spring before the new harvest was brought in. A lucrative operation for the profiteers, it was very injurious to public welfare.

More news came in the afternoon. The mob had invaded the governor's house. This particular functionary, not being of a warlike temper—he was nicknamed "Pehmbeh Khanum" (cotton wool lady) —fled out of town to one of his estates in the hills. The plaster lions adorning the courtyard of his city residence, which used to provoke our mirth when we called on official occasions, were smashed to pieces, as was the furniture in the reception rooms. The ignominious fate of the lions intensified the ire of Tehran. If one cannot hold power in one's hands, one must at least safeguard its emblems. The palace of the crown prince was not attacked, and the prince remained there, a passive, bewildered spectator.

"What next?" I asked the consul. He took out a silver tobacco case, rolled a thick cigarette, put it into an amber holder, and lighted a match.

"Well," he said, "flour has been brought to the market. The bazaars are open again. The governor will be dismissed and Amin od-Dowleh will probably be appointed in his place. That's all." The consul stopped and resumed his smoking. Above his head the gilded frame of the tsar's portrait shone with the last rays of the setting sun.

As foretold by the consul, Amin od-Dowleh, the grand vizier to be, a staunch conservative and a proud old man of dignified appearance, not very intelligent but brave and strong willed, was appointed governor. The city became quiet again.

A general revolution is much more serious. Its cause is called *zulm,* a theological Arabic expression meaning tyranny beyond the limits imposed on the monarch by the Koran. This implies that the government or the shah himself has ceased to be the father of his subjects and is committing acts of unlawful oppression. If this opinion is shared by the clergy, there is no salvation for the government except immediate retraction.

An outbreak of this kind of revolution had occurred in Tabriz before my arrival. The claim of being the first originator of the trouble may be disputed by the British and Persian governments, and even the Russians were indirectly involved. British politics in Persia became dangerously active in the late eighties with the arrival of the new English minister, Sir Drummond Wolff. In 1890, hastily taking advantage of an oversight of his Russian colleague, Wolff obtained the granting of a tobacco monopoly for an English company—a very risky act to say the least. The Russian legation missed this excellent opportunity to protest on the basis of the commercial clauses of her treaty. The monopoly for the buying and selling of all tobacco produced in Persia was introduced and enacted in 1891.

To understand what this meant, it is necessary to realize that every Persian smokes a *Qalyan* (water pipe), which is as indispensable to him as his food and drink, and that the best *tumbeki* (water-pipe tobacco) is raised and primarily consumed in Persia. The net profit of the operation was calculated at a half million English pounds yearly, to be exacted chiefly from the poorest classes of a population of less than ten million. This concession was signed by the grand vizier and ratified by the shah.

A wave of indignation swept over Persia. The clergy were applied to for help and realized that they had to intervene if they were to remain popular. The chief religious authority in Persia at that time was the *Mudjtehid* (a learned and highly respected priest) Hasan Aga in Tabriz, a decent and serious man. A discreet inquiry at the Russian consulate revealed that there would be no objection from that side.

Then Hasan Aga declared the monopoly tobacco unclean and its smoking a deadly sin, and he publicly broke his water pipe as of no further use. The storm that erupted almost destroyed the authority of the grand vizier Amin os-Soltān and the shah himself. All the towns and villages of Persia followed the lead of Tabriz and brought the country close to anarchy. Finally the grand vizier told the shah that the concession had to be revoked at any cost. The shah agreed. The monopoly was annulled, and a large compensation was promised, to be paid in yearly installments. But the authority of the Persian crown never completely recovered from this shock. The shah was accused of selling his land to foreigners, and the dignity of his long reign was smeared. English prestige in Persia was ruined for a time. After a disagreeable debate in Parliament, Sir Drummond Wolff was replaced by Sir Frank Lascelles, quite a different type of man. The Russian government also recalled their minister and sent in his place E. K. Biutsov, an old diplomat of wide experience, my future chief. In this case, the Russian government sided with the people. Had it continued to do so, things would have been different in Persia and elsewhere.

The downfall of the Persian tobacco monopoly was only one of many conflicts between Russian and English policies. The rivalry of these powers in Asia during a whole century was a continuous menace to the security and peaceful development of that continent. Diplomatic relations in Persia in 1895 represented a struggle between Russian and English influence. The situation eventually improved and then returned to a dangerous level. The chief facts are known; however, the diplomatic obscurity inherent in foreign relations prevents the proper understanding of their connection, and published literature is far from adequate in its elucidation.

It was supposed that Russia was moving from the north through Persia toward the Persian Gulf in order to create a menace for India. On the other hand, it was considered that the duty of England was to raise as many obstacles as she could to prevent Russia's progress and push the Muscovite influence altogether out of the picture. In fact, however, Persia's northern frontier with Russia in the Caucasus was established in 1828, and not an inch of it was moved south by Russia during more than a century of supposedly active policy. And though England exercised pressure on Persia's eastern and western neighbors, not an inch was taken from the territory of Persia proper, and the Persian Gulf remained an open sea. If this can be called a balance of power, it was achieved with mathematical accuracy. Nobody scored in the game.

Russia and England adopted a similar policy in Persia, although their respective positions were entirely different. Both continued the diplomatic strife that centered on Constantinople and the passage to the Black Sea. But Russia did not fear England in Persia. The Anglo-Indian army was not a cause of anxiety for the Russian government. The occupation of southern Persia by English forces would only expose them to Russian attack. All Russia wanted was a Persian government sufficiently strong to remain independent of English control and assure internal security. Her immediate aim was to safeguard Russian merchants and Russian goods from robbers, whether officials or highwaymen—an object, as every Russian consular officer knew from experience, not easily attained. Russia also objected to the presence of English agents in the north of Persia to prevent the stirring of anti-Russian revolutionary movements among Moslems on both sides of the Russo-Persian frontier. In short, England was not a real danger for Russia, but a cause of continual irritation and trouble. Military circles and the conservative press in Russia and England liked to alarm the public with revelations of far-reaching schemes of aggression and imaginary dangers, and ambitious ambassadors often overstepped their instructions. But the cabinets of St. Petersburg and London were primarily interested in the safety of their respective countries and not in the conquest of a famed but poorly developed country with limited natural resources which had been off the gold standard since the time when Alexander the Great took all her bullion and carried it away with Macedonian efficiency.*

Russia was accused of supporting a corrupt and decaying government, but there was nothing else to put in its place. The Persian regime, acknowledged by Russian diplomats to be wretched and hopeless, was better than complete anarchy. And as long as the Persians considered themselves the salt of the earth and other people unclean infidels and inferior beings, no progress was possible. There are things which must be felt to be understood, and the knocks and blows of the foreign powers and their diplomacy made the Persians realize that they had to change if they wanted to survive. Granted, embassies must normally be on friendly terms with the people of the nation to which they are accredited. However, diplomats are not missionaries; they do not come exclusively for the benefit of the land to which they are appointed. They also have duties toward their own country, which has sent them and bears the expenses of diplomatic representation. Diplomats cannot be held solely responsible for the shortcomings of wasteful and incompetent rulers who lack a sense of obligation to their own people and are indifferent to their sufferings.

As long as Persia was surrounded by territories with vaguely delineated frontiers and under even vaguer suzerainty, her rulers could freely indulge their desire for military glory and the kind of immortality achieved through human slaughter. But from the beginning of the nineteenth century England and Russia appeared firmly entrenched in India and the Caucasus, and Persia had her first experience of the acid taste of diplomatic notes. Each time relations between England and Russia became strained, which often happened for no reason other than that of ill temper on the part of statesmen, Parliament, or the press, the Persian question was brought to the fore.

When I came to Persia early in 1895, English and Russian writers had just stopped accusing each other's countries of perfidy, conspiracy, greed, murder, arson, and similar misdeeds. These are forbidden under penal code to private individuals and constitute the monopoly of independent and sovereign states; they are jealously guarded by in-

---

* The Persians remained by sheer necessity involuntary supporters of a silver currency, whatever the opinions of learned European economists, and a hasty move in the nineties by the practical financiers of the English-run Imperial Bank of Persia brought a speedy reward in the form of a net loss of one third the original capital.

ternational law and the intricate net of treaties, conventions, agreements, and exchanges of confidential letters between the heads of governments and their respective chiefs of staff. Persia listened to the acid comments of both camps and believed both, for what good could be expected from infidels deprived of the enlightenment of the Koran?

I found the strain between the Russian and British consulates in Tabriz near the breaking point. The Russian consul general and his British colleague never met socially except on official occasions. But instead of coming to a head, this tension subsided in front of my very eyes and turned into a friendship. I was very glad of the change.

In 1895 the epoch of bickering between England and Russia was drawing to its end. It was the closing phase of the policy of colonial expansion of the Great Powers, which was possible only as long as there were unoccupied lands with a poorly organized native population and a low standard of living. After that the powers met face to face from their adjoining colonial possessions, while the remaining Asian nations grew self-conscious and apprehensive. The first clash came between Japan and Russia and ended in Russian defeat, which signified, in a sense, the defeat of Europe. The aggressive attitude of Germany further weakened and divided Europe so that the diplomatic situation changed entirely. England was among the first to become aware of this fact; she needed to have her hands free of entanglements in Asia, and friendship with Russia assumed paramount importance. The Persian question was the first on the slate.

The ignorance, fanaticism, and backwardness of the Persian people was shocking. I had once complained about this to an officer of the consulate. "You will get accustomed to it," he said encouragingly.

"Never," I answered. "I did not come to the East to get accustomed to its defects but to study them and to fight them."

The consul laughed good-humoredly and shook his head. "I see you are a freshman in our service," he said. "Persia is an independent country. They have the right to live as they like, and they don't know anything better."

But they did. Many Tabrizians had gone to Baku and had seen money flowing from the oil wells. Baku, one of the world's largest producers of petroleum, shone with all the glory of what is called industrial prosperity. Its population was predominantly Moslem, and the Persians were impressed by its wealth. Taghiev, a Russian Moslem of Baku, identical in race and language with the people of Tabriz, was worth thirty million rubles and had an income second only to that of the shah of Persia. What Persia needed were schools, and neither Russia nor England would give them to her.

There are five social classes in Persia. The most numerous are the peasants—illiterate, unorganized, and very oppressed. Hardy and strong on the high plateau and mountains of the northwest where the winter climate is cold and invigorating, they are of gentle and mild character in the warmer regions. I have met honest, kind, hard working people among the peasants.

The merchants in the towns are more clever and well organized. They are selfish, stubborn, poorly educated, and often avaricious, but intelligent and capable of political resistance. Eventually they formed *Anjumans,* or provincial assemblies, and sent deputies to the *Medjelis* (House of Representatives).

The landed aristocracy is not hereditary; it is composed of enriched officials, most of whom are reactionaries. I met many princes of the deposed Qājār dynasty during the days of their glory. Their subsequent downfall was no loss for the country. The semi-independent chiefs of the Kurds and Bakhtiary tribes, still extant, have been greatly curbed of late.

The clergy, very powerful in the late nineties, have been rapidly losing their influence. Some of the old priests I met were excellent people. The Moslem clergy is passing through a critical period.

Functionaries, mirzās, the young intelligentsia, young men educated in American and English schools in Persia, employees of European companies, teachers, and doctors form the fifth class, comprising the most patriotic and educated as well as the most corrupt elements. This group has played an important part in the political struggle both for and against the government.

There are no insuperable barriers between classes. An intelligent Persian of the humblest origin can assimilate the manners of aristocracy with great facility. The grand vizier Amin os-Soltān, also called Atabek Azam, was the son of a water carrier.

I wanted very much to see Persians at home, but our intercourse with them was limited to formal and business calls. Several months passed before I received my first invitation to dine at a Persian house. The dinner was given by the Karguzar Muavin od-Dowleh, a very nice man who was the only one in Tabriz and at the time possibly in all Persia to like European manners and style of life. His imposing house had two large reception rooms overlooking a garden of flower beds with rows of tall trees along the walls.

The guests included the highest functionaries of Tabriz, with the exception of the crown prince and his family, who did not accept private invitations and would attend only public functions. However, there were two princes and an adequate number of dignitaries —servants and dignitaries could be found in any number in Persia at a moment's notice. We sat in strict accordance to rank at a long table set in European fashion. Various pilafs (rice with lamb or chicken) were served, meat roasted on spits, Persian pickles and gravies (*khurish*), no fish—there is little fish in Persia except on the seashore, and Persians do not particularly care for it—and no pork— there are only wild boars to be had, shot by Europeans. Champagne was served in honor of the princes and the foreign representatives, and toasts were proposed to the health of the ladies. Wine is forbidden in the Moslem religion, but Persians are very tolerant in this respect. Prohibition was never popular in Persia; the literature is full of praise for wine, interpreted symbolically as divine love.

"Mamma mia," said an Italian lady in a frightened whisper, "I think there is a man asleep under the table."

"Nonsense," answered another. "It is only a pile of napkins and tablecloths a servant put there to have in readiness." There is so little furniture in Persian houses that things are often placed on the floor. The meal proceeded without further alarm.

Our host, tall, handsome, and gay, spoke a little French but mostly Persian, which was understood by the Europeans present. I heard a Persian praise a strong governor.

"Is he very popular?" I asked.

The Persian looked at me in amazement. "He is dreaded," he answered.

"How do you irrigate the land in St. Petersburg?" one of the guests asked me.

"We do not irrigate it at all," I said. "We have rather too much rain." The Persian looked at me with compassion. Since nothing grows without irrigation in Persia, the unirrigated Russian capital appeared to him to be situated in a dreary desert.

A band was playing outside. As dancing was not accepted in Persian homes, the dinner was protracted, and we left shortly after it.

Such parties were infrequent; Persians rarely entertained foreigners, especially with their ladies.

The only Persians with whom a European was in constant contact were his servants. A European cannot live or travel in Persia without a servant or he will be exposed to embarrassing curiosity, mockery, and occasional ill treatment as an unclean infidel. To be respected a European must be considered a person of rank, a sahib. And though all servants make a certain *madakel* (profit) on the purchases they make for their masters, there are instances of remarkable loyalty, honesty, and delicacy of feeling.

One such instance concerned the Russian consul at Astarābād, L. S. Kokhanovskii, who was expecting the arrival of his children and most of his and his wife's family from Russia. The steamer reached Bendere Gaz on the Caspian Sea, but the consul's family were not on board; they had met a Turkoman boat at sea and changed in order to get to Astarābād more quickly. When the servants who had been sent to meet the steamer returned to Astarābād, a strong wind was already blowing. Men on horseback searched the seashore and came back the next day without having found any trace of the boat. The wind grew in violence, and consternation at the consulate became general. Riders were sent out again and Turkoman tribesmen in the prairies were asked to search the coast. The Turkomans reported that all their boats were in except the one with the consul's family. Mrs. Kokhanovskaia fainted at the news. The consul vainly called the servants for help, but the house looked absolutely deserted. He went downstairs to the kitchen, found the door closed, opened it, and saw the entire retinue of the consulate kneeling on the floor and praying. Kokhanovskii retreated on tiptoe. A few hours later a Turkoman arrived bringing the news that the consul's family was safe in his *aul* (camping place). The wind had come suddenly, and the Turkomans in the boat had set sail and fled before the storm. After much danger and delay, they had succeeded in finding a suitable place to land. It was a lonely spot, and one of the men had to walk a long distance to bring horses from the nearest Turkoman encampment. He was lucky to have found one, as Turkomans are nomads and continuously on the move.

Another case of touching devotion was related to me by my friend N. A. Zarudnyi, the famous Russian ornithologist whose collection birds of eastern Persia was acquired by Lord Rothschild and is now in the New York Museum of Natural History. Mr. Zarudnyi was traveling in the great eastern desert, the worst in Persia, collecting rare specimens of birds, some of which were entirely unknown. It was late in the season, and the scarcity of water forced him to either stay for several months in a small Persian town or attempt a dangerous crossing of the desert. He chose the latter and started off with a servant and a guide, both of whom were very reliable. After a few days there was no more water to be found; the wells they came across were dry. It was too late to go back. They advanced until their horses fell down dead, then walked on foot for some time until they themselves collapsed. They had not had a drink of water for two days. Finally the guide, a sturdy native, said that he knew of a well fifteen miles away and would go alone and bring some water. He warned Zarudnyi and his servant not to move from where they were or he would be unable to locate them on his way back. The following hours were an agony of suffering. They had no idea how much time passed. The servant lay silent, then turned his head toward Zarudnyi and said: "We shall probably die. Don't be afraid. I shall tell God that you are also a Moslem, and He will accept you in His heaven. I am a *Seyid* [descendent of Mohammed]. God cannot refuse the last prayer of a descendent of His prophet." Then they both lost consciousness. When they recovered, the guide was pouring water on their faces. He had walked for thirty miles without stopping, carrying a heavy waterskin on the way back, in order to save their lives.

I mention these incidents because Westerners are prone to underestimate the moral qualities of the Persians. True, Persians are usually unreliable in money matters, inclined to boast, and lie easily. But these are superficial faults and can be attributed to the general decay during the rule of the *Qājār* dynasty. All too often Westerners disparage the Persians while staying with them and miss them after leaving their land.

Madakhel

Nothing was more characteristic of the state of mind I found in Persia than the practice of *madakhel* (literally profit, actually graft), which was the chief factor in business transactions of public and private life. Salaries meant little; the main interest was concentrated in the illegal revenue which the office would bring to its holder. The intelligence of a man was estimated in proportion to the madakhel he succeeded in realizing. Once a sufficient madakhel had been offered and accepted for a certain service, one could be fairly sure that it would be rendered. Practical experience was necessary to calculate the proper amount of madakhel required in each particular case. The importance of the man and of the service to be rendered, and all the attending circumstances, had to be taken into consideration.

The madakhel was flourishing in the seventeenth century, when we begin to have accurate information about Persia from European travelers. Like all the institutions of old Persia, the madakhel failed to adjust itself to modern conditions and became a source of danger for the government and the peace of the land. The shah himself received a madakhel; when a sum was allocated for some governmental purpose, he expected a certain remainder to be returned to his private purse. The grand vizier Amin os-Sultan owed much of his position to the masterly way in which he manipulated the madakhel, but sometimes even he made costly mistakes which hurt both himself and his sovereign.

Every man in Persia paid or received madakhel in some form or other. There were various degrees: the obligatory, the customary, and the exorbitant (the latter prevailed in Tabriz); or, from the point of view of the recipient: liberal, magnificent, or stingy and miserly. The same practice prevailed in trade operations, even in transactions of the simplest character.

I once told my servant to buy a supply of firewood. At the appointed time my little street was filled with a herd of donkeys— small, grayish, long-eared animals, carrying bundles of dry, crooked branches. There are no forests in Persia, except on distant mountains. Old, gnarled fruit trees are used for fuel. The transaction took half a day. It was not only a question of price but of all the concomitant conditions. There were the rebate, the supplement, the premium, according to custom, and the favor, depending on the vendor. Finally an agreement was reached, but at the first move for delivery, the whole storm was raised again.

My servant, Hasan, was an exceptionally honest fellow. I took him straight from a village. The morals there are, as a rule, better than in the cities, where people are more sophisticated. My heating costs being paid by the government, no personal interests were involved, except for Hasan's love of bargaining. The donkeys which had brought the wood stood by with admirable patience, slightly moving their ears and their little legs. At last all was settled and the wood hurled into the cellar. I had long retired to my study, and was busy

with my work, when Hasan appeared to take the payment to the
vendor.

"And the madakhel?" I said jokingly.

"Nothing," he answered, fixing me with his straight eagle eyes of
a hardy mountaineer.

"Impossible," I said.

He stared at me in sheer amazement, then burst into a laugh, ran
out, and returned with a warm muffler. "That's my madakhel," he
said, showing the trophy he had just received.

While Persians were not generally considered very reliable, there
was a whole category of trustworthy people—the caravan men. Without these *charvadars* (drivers), trade and commerce would have come
to a standstill. The time of delivery for goods in Persia is very
vague; nobody can be particular about it, since the journey stretches
through hundreds of miles of mostly waterless desert. But the loads
are delivered according to number, and the wrapping is intact. What
happens to the content of the cases does not concern the driver. If
there are many more pieces of crockery than were originally packed,
that cannot be helped.

My experience with caravans and trade was limited to collecting
data for our commercial reports. The consulate had to be continually on guard to protect the safety of Russian traders, as conditions
were none too good. This necessitated constant correspondence and
personal contact with Persian officials. And last but not least was the
kind of political control which Russia and England exercised over
Persia, often to their mutual disadvantage.

Only one category of people in Persia led a carefree life, immune
from taxation and official interference. They were the *dervishes,*
mendicant Moslem monks considered saints and cheats at the same
time. I was told the following story about them.

The Story of a Dervish

A young man without friends or money started a journey looking
for work. He came to a lonely spot where he saw a small building
with a cupola—the grave of a saint. In a little hut close by sat an old
dervish, who received the young man most hospitably, bade him
stay, and taught him the prayers and the doctrines of the dervishes.
But when the hot season came, caravans ceased to pass by, and they
received no more offerings. The old man said to his pupil: "We shall
starve if we both remain here. I will give you my donkey and some

provisions. Go to some other place where you can meet more people and try your luck."

The old man put the dervish garb on the youth, embraced him, and the newly consecrated dervish, after thanking his benefactor, set forth on his journey. In a few days he totally lost his way and found himself on the border of a waterless desert. He halted at a well to rest his donkey, but the faithful animal lay down and expired from exhaustion. The young man wept bitterly, buried the donkey, threw himself in despair on the ground, and fell into a heavy slumber. He expected nothing but death in this dreary place.

But when he awoke he saw with astonishment a whole caravan around him. The camels were kneeling, and the men sat in a circle, looking with deep reverence on the pale young man wearing a dervish cap, alone by a grave. They said: "We have a dangerous journey to make across this desert, and we have offered prayers at the tomb of your saint. Give us your blessing now that we may travel in peace and reach our destination safely."

The young man in confusion pleaded his unworthiness, but without avail. The travelers made him generous offerings, continued to insist, and he had to comply with their wishes. He held his arms before him, lifted his eyes to heaven, and in a trembling voice intoned the solemn benediction he had learned from his teacher for the preservation of people who are in peril of life. The travelers bowed to the earth, then mounted their camels. The leader raised his hand, and the caravan entered the desert.

Day after day passed, and the young man anxiously waited for news. He lost sleep and prayed at night to the star-covered sky. One night his ear caught the slight tinkling of bells; it grew louder and louder till a whole caravan appeared in the darkness. Men sprang from their mounts and ran to him. They were highly satisfied; their journey had proved a complete success, and they showered gifts and thanks on the young dervish.

More caravans went by, and the young man grew prosperous. Pious hands built a dome over the grave of the donkey. The fame of the young dervish spread far and wide. His old friend heard about it. His curiosity was aroused, and he came to visit his pupil. The latter was overwhelmed with joy at the sight of his master. He kissed his hands and the hem of his robe and begged him to stay and share in his fortune. But the old man refused the offer, and agreed only to remain for one night and to accept some food for the return journey.

They sat down for supper, and the old man asked the young dervish to tell him about himself and his good luck.

The young man related everything and said: "How blessed you are to have a real saint. I feel ashamed to think that I have only an ass in this tomb."

The old man smiled and said: "Don't worry, my son. In the grave of my saint lies the father of your donkey."

Homesickness

Vineyards were still green on the fourth of November 1895, when the first snow covered them with a shower of white flakes. The beautiful vine leaves withered at once and became black, instead of turning red and yellow as usual. The season had closed. I had to face a winter in Tabriz, a Christmas away from home, and God knows how many more, in this distant land. I became homesick.

I sat confined in my solitary house and felt restless in the evenings. Nothing is so depressing in this world as a Persian town at ten o'clock on a winter night. All is silent, asleep, dead, reduced to a state of absolute lethargy, drowned in the darkness of night. Not a single place where a stranded soul could seek a moment of distraction or oblivion. What a contrast with our cities, full at that hour of light and gaiety!

I happened to feel particularly depressed one evening, and in need of some strong physical stimulation. "Saddle the horses," I shouted to my men, who had just settled down for a little chat around an earthen pan of live coals before going to sleep. I ordered two mounted men: my servant and one of my Persian guards. *"Sarkār, kodjā miravim* [Master, where are we going]?" asked Hasan, as if I knew myself. Without an answer I sent them about their business with a movement of my hand.

Through the streets basking in moonlight, the kind of lighting selected by the municipality as cheapest and most effective, we trotted rapidly out of town. The air was frosty but pleasant, and I set the horses at a gallop. We issued from the walled orchards into open fields, a vast expanse of bluish white receding into dimness. We galloped until my horse began to sink in deep snow and nearly fell into a hollow. We made a circuit and reached the western side of the town, where an old mud wall surrounded the city. My companions suggested we go back to the place we had started from.

My excitement had cooled down during the ride but now flared again. "No," I exclaimed. "Never. I won't go back." I became possessed with something of the frenzy of the conquering caliphs who challenged death at the hands of an overwhelming enemy. In my ears rang the Arabian war cry: *"Iftah yā mufattih ul abvāb* [Open the doors of Paradise, oh Highest Door Keeper]!" I rushed my horse to the gate and threw all my weight against it. It opened; it was not locked, only shut. With a whoop I whirled my horse through the entrance and soon was home. I asked my companions: "Where would we have been now, if I had followed your advice?" *"Khudā billir* [God knows]," they answered in chorus.

But I could not go horseback riding every night, and as I stayed in my house reminiscences of years long past appeared in vivid pictures before my eyes.

. . . I am six. I am the little gamekeeper of my father and walk behind him, striving to keep pace with him. We pass the big oaks and tread upon the large meadows surrounded by poplars. Partridges start up with a whir, and some are brought down by the shots, falling lifeless on the grass. A hare falls victim to his own imprudence. My bag is heavy. I drag the unfortunate hare on the ground by its hind legs. Often I have to run to catch up with my father, who is following the excited dog, but I am the happiest and proudest boy in the world.

. . . I am sixteen. I am sitting in a classroom, noisy and animated during the recess. A controversy starts, which threatens to end in a fist fight with a schoolmate, the future governor of a big Russian province, when a dreaded teacher appears, and we all plunge into the intricacies of Latin syntax, which it took Julius Caesar ten years to inflict on the refractory brains of Gauls and Britons.

. . . It is summer 1885. At an open-air tea I sit under a tree outside the fine country house, Iasnaia Poliana and look across the table at the sad, stern face and the deep-set eyes of the great master of Russian literature. People talk around me; Count Tolstoy speaks little. I am awestruck and swallow my tea in silence. We get up. Tolstoy feels the muscles of my arm and with a scornful look turns away. I am annihilated.

. . . It is noon. We are all assembled for lunch in the count's large, square dining room on the second floor. The gathering is fairly numerous. There are Tolstoy's family and that of his sister-in-law, Kuzminskaia, and some other people. The count comes in with my mother and his wife. We take our places at the large horseshoe table.

As we wait for the meal to be served, I look around. The walls are adorned with oil portraits of the count's ancestors, chiefly military men. I recognize the strange uniforms of the eighteenth and early nineteenth centuries. It looks like a picture gallery from *War and Peace*. I notice the showy uniform of General Prince Volkonskii (called Bolkonskii in the novel), the maternal grandfather of the count, a lineal descendent of Rurik, the first sovereign of the first dynasty of Russia. Iasnaia Poliana had belonged to the old general. He had planned and planted the park where I had walked in the morning. The estate itself was part of the feudal principality of the Volkonskie, vassals first of the rulers of Kiev and later of Moscow.

Next was the portrait of Tolstoy's father (Count Rostov of the novel), who took part in the wars with Napoleon. I felt as if the portraits stared silently at us; the other people paid no attention to them but talked and ate. I listened to the conversation and recognized to my surprise the chief characters of *Anna Karenina*. The count was Levin, and his wife Kitty. Only Anna herself was missing. She had committed suicide on the railway close to Iasnaia. It was the sight of her mangled body that had given Tolstoy the idea of writing the novel. It seemed to me that I was living through a scene of *Anna Karenina*. Levin was speaking to my mother, and Kitty smiled, looking at her husband. She was still in love with him. Her sister, Mrs. Kuzminskaia, was the Natasha of *War and Peace*.

After lunch all dispersed, and with them the atmosphere of the novel also. I remained with Tolstoy's sons, about my own age—a new generation not depicted in his great works, which dealt with the period 1805–76. We belonged to a later Russia, disliked by Tolstoy. He felt a stranger toward his own children, although he was a very affectionate father. As he passed before me, I read in his eyes a sad feeling of loneliness.

In the evening the count conducted me to my room. He lit a candle. Under the bed was a hunting dog who growled at me. *"Vona, ona rychit na vas* [Why, he is snarling at you]," said the Count, and he chased the dog out with a stern voice, the voice of a master. For a moment I saw Tolstoy in a new light, not as the romantic Levin deeply in love with his betrothed, not as the moral philosopher, but as the haughty aristocrat who defended the bastions of Sebastopol and fought a bear with his hands after he had missed his shot and thrown away the useless gun.

Tolstoy put the candle on the table and disappeared into the dark corridor. I never met him again. The next morning when we left, he was already out in the solitary woods, a prey to his sad thoughts, which obsessed him with increasing vehemence as he moved toward the end of his days.

. . . I am dining with a very pretty girl, who was later to be the wife of one of my friends. Some fellows at another table look at us out of the corners of their eyes, evidently desiring to be introduced. But I won't do it. We laugh and talk. I feel doubly contented, and we arrange to drive after dinner.

. . . There are troubles at the University of St. Petersburg. Our alma mater is the scene of stormy meetings. The halls resound with angry voices, glass cases are smashed, professors have to suspend their lectures. I happen to meet at that time I. D. Delianov, the minister of public education. I had never spoken with a minister before. He does not look very impressive—a small, sly Armenian with a bald, oval head, a banana-like nose, and a protruding abdomen. He did not come to the university and evidently was glad to have an opportunity to speak with a student.

"Do you suppose you can overthrow the government?" he says, his whole small body expressing defiance. Since nothing in my appearance indicates such intention, he continues in a much calmer, although still ironical tone. "What do you think? Only turkey gobblers think." He waits for an answer from me. As none comes, he looks satisfied with our conversation, in which he was the only one to speak, and nods approvingly with a benevolent smile.

. . . I am going with some friends to the opera, where we have taken a box. "Keep the collar of your fur coat tight," says my mother. "You always leave it open."

"*Sarkār* [Master]," says a Persian voice, "*Agar farmāyeshi na dārid morakhas mishavam* [If you have no more orders, may I retire]?"

I look at my watch. Time to go to bed. One day in Tabriz is over.

Death of Nāser ed-Din Shah

Spring came, a fresh, gay, delightful season, often sung by Persian poets. In my little house with its small court and no garden at all I felt a prisoner and longed for space, open air, trees, flowers, and freedom. I could not stand my confinement any longer and started to explore the orchards surrounding Tabriz.

And there I found the place of my dreams. In a large garden with a a wealth of flowering, fragrant almond trees, a summerhouse stood, fronting a pond with swallows gaily skimming over the surface of the water, and a glorious range of mountains covered with snow in the far distance.

It was fairylike, it was charming, it was all I wanted. I took immediate possession of this lovely spot, brought in a table, chairs, and tea accessories, had my breakfast there each morning before office hours, and received company in the afternoon—a very satisfactory arrangement. I did not know the proprietor, but that did not matter, since he never raised any objections. I felt obliged to him for his discreet hospitality. I enjoyed enormously the brief hour in this garden before the noise and bustle of the consulate and felt perfectly happy in the enchanting place, which looked like a theatrical setting for a scene of Oriental love or tragic death. My impression was not far from truth.

One morning I was quietly sitting in this garden with the cossack whom I was preparing for a noncommissioned officer's examination, when I saw a group of Russian Moslems hastily coming toward us. Clearly something was wrong, very wrong. I rose to meet them.

"Nāser ed-Din Shah was killed yesterday afternoon in Tehran," they said. The death of the shah could easily lead to general confusion. I rushed to the consulate. The acting consul general, my chief, confirmed the news and added that the consuls had been called to the palace by the crown prince, who was the governor general of Tabriz. There was no time to lose; the heir had to be put on the throne at once. We donned dress uniforms, which in this case had the same significance as the oilskins of a seaman in a gale.

A message came from our British colleague, inquiring what we were going to do. I rapidly drew a reply: "The emperor, my august master, having recognized His Majesty Mozaffar ed-Din Shah as sole legitimate sovereign of Persia, I consider it my duty, etc.," and had it signed by my chief. I wanted to make clear to Wood as soon as possible where we stood, since I saw from his letter that he was perplexed. It appeared that, in some unaccountable way, the British consulate in a province ruled by the crown prince had no instructions concerning the succession. Wood rushed to the Anglo-Indian telegraph office, asked for a direct connection with London, and in two hours received a reply.

We drove to the palace. It consisted of isolated buildings and several large courts. On the parade ground was the entire garrison of

Tabriz in nondescript clothes and furnished with old rifles. The streets were thronged with people who for once forgot their leisurely demeanor and hurried in their long, flowing clothes.

We were conducted into a reception room where our French and Turkish colleagues joined us, but the British consul was still absent. We waited, time passed, the fate of Persia was in suspense. Then we heard the clatter of horses' hooves, and the English representative hurriedly entered the room. Downing Street had agreed to accept Mozaffar ed-Din as shah. Persian dignitaries, with evident relief, began to run in and out of the room, and we were soon called into the royal presence.

The king stood alone, according to Persian custom, at one end of a large hall. We were not obliged to prostrate ourselves on the ground and kiss the floor, as the ancient Greeks did, much to their vexation, with subsequent mockeries showered on them after their return home. We just bowed and advanced and bowed again until we had reached the limit of the respectful distance imposed by etiquette.

Mozaffar ed-Din looked at us during this ceremonial performance. He wore a black gown all embroidered with silver, and a diamond plume, emblem of royalty, on his lambskin cap. The new shah was a sickly man about fifty, prematurely aged, with a drooping, grayish moustache and a distressed look in his sheepish eyes. Kindhearted, without will or ambition, utterly harmless and helpless, he was despised by his father and not much feared by his retinue. This was the man who now wielded the limitless power of an autocratic Moslem sovereign.

The monarch listened to our congratulations in the name of our respective governments, followed by a speech by the French consul, Hugonnet, a man of literary distinction. After expressing our sorrow for the death of the late shah, he elegantly swerved by a daring volte-face to the general exultation at the advent of a new king. Mozaffar ed-Din said a few words of thanks in Persian, which were immediately translated and amplified by the interpreter.

The recognition of the new shah by the representatives of Russia, Great Britain, France, and Turkey being now completed, we bowed out, leaving the scene for other actors to play their parts. We were conducted, as simple spectators now, to the upper floor of a pavilion opposite an enormous window in the façade of the palace. The open place before the pavilion was rapidly filled with representatives of the people of Tabriz; the frame of the window was lifted, and the

shah appeared, seated in all his glory. The silence was complete for
a few moments. Then a mullah made a solemn appearance on the
flat roof of the palace and read a prayer mentioning for the first time
the name of the new sovereign. Each time it was pronounced people
bowed in rows, as if heavy waves rolled over this sea of human heads.
This showed that the shah was accepted by the representatives. At
the last words of the prayer, guns boomed the royal salute, announcing the accession to the rest of the city.

The guns stopped, and a poet advanced and read an ode, the first
verse of which was to be engraved on the new seal of state to be
affixed to all decrees of the new shah. That ended the inauguration.
The gates of the palace were thrown open, and a fresh stream of
humanity flowed in. We hastened to retreat through another entrance.

Rejoicing lasted several days. Courtiers were exulting at the prospect of the coveted treasures of Tehran falling an easy prey to them.
Common people were merry with the childish impulsiveness of their
race and sang in the streets:

Shāhe now bāz	A new Shah again
Māhe now baz	A new moon again
Be bāzār āmadeh	Came to the bazaar.
Sharābe molke Rey khorim!	Let us drink the wine of Rey!
Gar hāl nakhorim,	If we don't drink it now,
Pas key bekhorim?	When shall we drink it?

Rey has the best vineyards in the environs of Tehran. But its wine
was to prove sour to the Tabrizians, and the new shah was not to
reign long.

I later heard the details of the death of Nāser ed-Din Shah from the
Russian chargé d'affaires, A. N. Shcheglov, as they were told by the
grand vizier. The monarch had driven with the grand vizier, Amin
os-Soltān, to the shrine of Shah Abdol-Azim, five miles distant from
Tehran. They entered the mosque full of people and stood waiting
for a small prayer rug to be brought for the shah to kneel on and
perform the usual devotions. The grand vizier said that he heard a
short crack and thought a stone had fallen from the vault of the
ceiling. The shah remained motionless for a moment and then sank
to the floor. He had been shot dead by a man who stood close by.
The murderer, a merchant, had sold some goods to the son of the
shah and was flatly refused payment. The merchant had first wanted

to kill the prince but later decided to avenge himself on the sovereign whom he considered responsible for the enforcement of justice in the land. It was more than a private vengeance; it was the first political assassination in modern Persia.*

The grand vizier had the shah transported into the carriage and placed in a sitting position. As they entered the gates of the palace, he lifted the arm of the shah as if the latter were answering the salute of the guards. Amin os-Soltān called Shcheglov and Colonel V. Kosogovskii, commander of the Brigade of Persian Cossacks trained by Russian officers. It was the only reliable armed force in Tehran. Amin os-Soltān sent a telegram to the crown prince in Tabriz and then broke down. Shcheglov and Kosogovskii stayed with him in the palace and helped him take the necessary steps to preserve order in the city. Tehran was stunned but remained quiet. The following day Mozaffar ed-Din ascended the throne at Tabriz and by a telegram reappointed the grand vizier to his office.

Proconsul in Tabriz

My chief left with the British consul general to accompany Mozaffar ed-Din Shah to Tehran, entrusting to me the affairs of the consulate. I sat alone in the praetorium, the mighty proconsul of Russia in Northwestern Persia, a region which, according to the English press, was completely under the sway of Russia, to the detriment of civilization and British interests.

Every morning I received the report of our chief mirzā, a shrewd little man, extremely mischievous and intelligent. He kept us in daily contact with the Persian authorities and the court of the Crown Prince. He knew all that was going on there, all the intrigues, briberies, and extortions of the government of Tabriz, and he shared amply in them. I felt a deep antipathy for him, but I was in his hands and could do nothing without him. He knew it, and his eyes sparkled with malicious joy as he looked at me, the wily devil.

"What is your law on the this matter?" I asked him once, as he was preparing a strong note to the governor about the case of a Russian subject pending for months. The mirzā lifted his head from the paper he was writing on and blinked at me.

"The Koran," he said reverently.

"Do you know it?"

* The assassin was Mirzā Rezā Kermāni, a disciple of Seyyed Jamāl ed-Din Afghāni. F. K.

The mirzā assumed a devout attitude and answered evasively: "The priests know it."

"Can we have their opinion?"

"Certainly," he said. "But the priests cannot call the respective persons by their proper names. They must give a general statement about the case, mentioning the parties concerned by some conventional Arabic names."

"And the case will be settled?"

The mirzā looked perplexed. As was usual with him in such cases, he called for a qalyān. It was brought to him, and for some time I heard nothing but the gurgle of water in the lower recesses of the pipe. The mirzā exhaled an extraordinary amount of bluish smoke, and remained in blissful contemplation of the aromatic cloud settling gradually down.

"Their opinions may differ," he said finally with a sigh.

"And who will decide?"

The patience of the mirzā was at its end. He motioned to the servant to take the pipe away. "Not we, of course," he said sharply and slipped out of the room.

The Shah was nearing Tehran when the Mirza told me that the new crown prince wished to be recognized by Russia. I referred the matter to the legation, received the needed instructions, asked for an audience, and was immediately invited by the crown prince and admitted into the great hall. There he stood, a corpulent young man with small, ugly eyes, looking eagerly at me. He drank in my every word as I announced that the imperial Russian government had recognized him as heir to the throne of Persia. More energetic than his father but cruel and greedy, he wrought havoc to Persia, meantime clinging to Russia much to the embarrassment of our government.

The Journey to Tehran

The staff of the consulate in Tabriz, normally consisting of three officers, was now reduced to one, and the Russian minister at Tehran was uneasy about leaving a young attaché in charge of affairs in the largest province of Persia. This meant that the days of my rule as acting consul general were numbered.

Two senior officers arrived and took over the bulk of the work, relieving me of further responsibility. But the zest of the work went with it, and the consulate lost whatever attraction it had held for me. At the same time Tabriz was deprived of what was called the cream of society, although foam would be a more appropriate term in this case. Mozaffar ed-Din had taken all his favorites with him. a cabinet crisis was sure to come, and Tehran became the center of general attention.

The Russian and British legations were bound to be involved in the resulting muddle. Would they follow the line so genially expressed to me by Wood, or would they seize this opportunity for a good brawl in the usual tradition of Anglo-Russian relations in the East? The diplomatic dispatches of the legations were not communicated to the consulates, and I would have been better informed had I stayed at St. Petersburg, thousands of miles away. As a last blow, I received a promotion to the post of secretary to the consulate at Astarābād, a lonely place on the southeastern shore of the Caspian Sea.

That was more than I could stand, and I asked a friend at the legation in Tehran if he could arrange to have me transferred there. A temporary stay in the capital was all I needed to complete my three years' term in Persia; then I would go on leave and look for something else.

It was a bold but well-timed move. The legation had been taken unaware by the sudden demise of Nāser ed-Din Shah. As often happens in critical occurrences, the minister was on leave and had to return in a hurry. The staff was depleted. The machinery of the central government of Persia was upset by the impact of new courtiers who had descended on Tehran like a swarm of locusts. An officer from Tabriz was just what the Russian legation needed at the time.

As day after day passed, I waited for news with increasing impatience. If everything was settled in Tabriz, my departure for Astarābād would be unavoidable, and I had had more than enough of forsaken places. But things were far from settled in the glorious capital of Persia, and one morning the acting consul general came to the office with a telegram in his hand.

"The minister orders you to come to Tehran at once," he said.

In a flash I forgot all the drudgery of Tabriz.

"Pack my things," I said to Hasan. "I won't stay in Tabriz a minute longer than I can help." Hasan looked sad. He had his family and some land in a village nearby and could not leave.

I hurriedly made my last calls, among them to the American missionaries. They were, I think, the happiest people of all the European

colony. They had arranged a kind of Main Street existence of their
own and, with their teaching and medical service, were an asset to
Persia.

The English consul Wood, rode several miles with me for the last
time. We had become close friends and were sorry to part. Hasan
and the cossack to whom I had given lessons also accompanied me for
a while. Then I remained alone with a qolām and a *chapar shagird*
(postman).

I spurred my horse. Intoxicated with the mountain air and the
sense of liberty, I rode far ahead of my escort. I did not know my
way and did not care, for the iron posts of the Indo-European telegraph stretching from Tabriz to Tehran were my best guides. When
I reached Miāneh, a town I was seeing for the first time, my horse
took me straight to the post house; traveling became extremely
simple.

In the afternoon of the same day I was again riding alone, when
I saw nomads' tents on a plain not far from the road. Nomads were
the only serious consideration for a traveler in Persia. They sometimes robbed travelers, not only for the sake of profits, but also to
assert their independence from the shah's authority. As I passed them,
a commotion started in the encampment; people rushed to me, and
in a moment I was surrounded. They addressed me in such anxious
and suppliant voices that I hesitated to draw my pistol when they
seized the bridle of my horse and turned it from the road. The whole
crowd, with me in the middle, proceeded toward the camp, where I
saw a young man lying on the ground, sick and apparently uncon-
scious. His stomach felt hard and his hands cold, but he swallowed a
laxative and an alcoholic drink I gave him. An old devotee immediately inquired if it was wine. I answered in the negative, quickly
put the bottle in my saddle bag, and intimated that it was time for
me to depart. I left amid the expressions of gratitude of this simple
folk who thought every European was a doctor.

From the town of Qazvin a highway had already been built by a
Russian company, and I enjoyed the long forsaken luxury of a
wheeled carriage. On the seventh day Tehran lay before me on a
slightly rising slope at the foot of the Elburz mountains. The domes
of the mosques dominated the city surrounded by a wall with gates
adorned with enameled tiles. As we entered the gate, I was thrilled
at the aspect of the city, which, after Tabriz, looked quite modern
with its wide, well-planned streets. I was somewhat disappointed to

hear that the legation was at its summer location in the village of Zerghendeh, eight miles away. I was dusty, thirsty, and hungry but had to resume my journey. There was no remedy—*chāreh na dāsht,* as the Persians say. And besides, what did this short ride matter after five hundred miles? I started again over a hot, stony road. Finally I saw green meadows of alfalfa, a shady park, a flagpole, and a fine villa with a flowerbed around a sundial—everything as it ought to be in a legation.

I was conducted to a cottage, with rooms prepared for me. I changed clothes, called on A. N. Stritter, to whom I owed my summons to Tehran, and went with him to the villa. We passed a billiard room and a drawing room with columns, lofty and cool, and came into the library. A small man of about sixty sat there, busy with papers. As he rose I saw a stern face with gray whiskers and a shaven chin, and the cold, rigid, unmistakable aspect of a diplomat. It was E. K. Biutsov (Bützow), the Russian minister. He frowned and said frigidly:

"Have you seen your quarters? We dine at six." He turned without a nod and sat down. Our feet made no sound on the thick carpet as we melted away from his presence.

I returned to my little house surrounded by trees, with the murmur of water running in the irrigation ditches. The rooms were spotlessly clean and well furnished; without a doubt I was in a legation.

At six we assembled: the second secretary, replacing the first, and the attachés, in short all the unmarried people. The minister came in, rubbing his hands and looking slightly more human. He made a rapid movement with his head, which could be considered a salutation, and strode quickly to the dining room. The procession of Persian servants with soup plates started around the table. They were dressed in black livery with silver braid and red lining, the colors of the Russian Foreign Office. Few words were exchanged during the first courses: only when the roast was served did the minister become aware of my presence and looked sharply at me.

"You know these Tabrizians who came with the shah?" he asked with a marked note of displeasure in his voice. The newly arrived greedy favorites were a sore trial for the legations and the people of Tehran. I could say little good about the rapacious horde. The minister nodded. "Yes, yes," he said, "a nice lot. I saw some of them."

After dinner, the minister skillfully played billiards and laughed a short laugh when his partner attempted a difficult shot and missed. Other people sat on the high, stiff benches around the walls and smoked good cigars. It looked decidedly elegant. Stritter dropped in and took me out. I walked through the moonlit avenues of the park as in an enchanted land. There was a restful harmony of subdued shades, forms, and sounds in the silvery, cool night. I thought with joy that there would be no more endless galloping on the parched plains, no more dreary post houses, no more flat cakes baked once a week, no more ten-hour rides which strained me so much that when I dismounted I felt worse.

"Oh, he is all right," said Stritter, referring to the minister, as we walked together. "Come to our house for five o'clock tea tomorrow. You will see him in a much more genial mood."

Biutsov belonged to a German family settled in Russia. For reasons I could never understand, monarchical Russia was largely represented by Germans—nine-tenths of the Russian diplomats were of Russo-German origin. Many of them were capable men indeed. Biutsov was a much better diplomat than the few Russian ministers I knew of who were in Tehran before and after him.

I spent the rest of the evening with the young members of the legation, who made me feel quite at home. Persia seemed far away. I liked my house, the entire legation, and the village of Zerghendeh, our summer place. Other villas were scattered along the gentle slope of the hills, creating a pleasant atmosphere of wealth, space, and leisure. Europeans were more numerous and felt more at ease; they were surrounded by Persians but not oppressed by their presence as in Tabriz.

On the occasion of Mozaffar ed-Din's accession to the throne, the Russian government sent a field battery as a present to the new shah. This was an excellent idea—the shah was as pleased as a child. The Russian legation went in state to the parade grounds to present the guns. We left our carriages and proceeded toward the guns, which stood at the far end of the grounds near a display of various ordnance tools and implements arranged like trophies. We were still walking when we were overtaken by the shah, who stopped his carriage and descended immediately. He wore a black uniform with a double row of turquoises across the breast in lieu of decorations. He was delighted to hear from Biutsov that the guns were ready and literally ran toward them so quickly that we could hardly follow him.

Moshir od-Dowlah, the short, fat, asthmatic minister of foreign affairs, tried in vain to keep pace with the sovereign. I heard his pitiful
complaint—"Je n'en puis plus [I am all in]!"—as he stopped for
breath and was left all alone in the center of the vast grounds. When
the shah reached the guns, he did show a real understanding of artillery and actually pointed the guns himself. It seemed as if he was
ready to start shooting right away without regard to the safety of his
capital, but he postponed the pleasure until the guns could be brought
out of town. It was the only time I saw Mazaffar ed-Din Shah in a
lively mood.

Shortly thereafter, the shah ordered the inspection of the Persian
Cossack Brigade. The review took place a few miles from Tehran.
The shah and his retinue were in a large tent adorned with gorgeous
Resht embroideries—silk on red cloth. The cossacks stood at attention; the chief attraction was the mounted battery, who started at
full gallop, stopped, turned their guns, and opened fire. The Persians
are good horsemen, but they are clumsy with their artillery. The
efficiency of the gun practice of the Persian cossacks amazed the Shah.
Individual cossacks performed various feats such as dismounting at
full speed and jumping into saddle again or hanging under the belly
of a galloping horse.

The Cossack Brigade was Russia's main achievement in Persia,
and it proved momentous. From its ranks rose Rezā Shah, the father
of the present ruler of Iran. The brigade was created in 1882 when,
at the request of Nāser ed-Din Shah, Alexander III commandeered
three Russian officers and a few noncommissioned men to drill about
1500 Persians. Previous attempts at training Persian troops by European instructors had been unsuccessful because of insufficient funds for
the maintenance of the soldiers; now, for the first time, Persian soldiers received good food, good clothes, and full pay. The atmosphere
of the brigade was also congenial to the Persians. They liked the long
cossack uniforms and lambskin caps of Oriental type, the cavalry
service, and the friendly attitude on the part of the officers. Cossack
officers were always democratic in their habits; they were born and
bred in the same villages as their privates, and all cossacks began
service as privates. A Persian cossack could be easily distinguished
from other soldiers by his smart appearance, brisk walk, and quick
answers. He had nothing in common with the slow, dull, underfed
Persian infantrymen.

Life in Tehran

I was sick of consulates and enjoyed my stay at the legation. I had arrived at the end of August; summer was soon over, and we moved to the city. Tehran was a capital endowed with the luster emanating from the presence of the sovereign, his court, high functionaries, the diplomatic body, and the rich people who naturally gravitate to a center of wealth, birth, and power.

One town—Qazvin—tried to imitate Tehran on a smaller scale; others were religious centers and owed their importance to popular shrines which attracted pilgrims. Pilgrimages were still a factor in Moslem lands, as they had been in medieval Europe. The rest of the cities were frankly provincial and proud of it, considering Tehran too Europeanized and of dubious orthodoxy.

Tehran was the creation of the Qajār dynasty and was fading with it. Only the diplomatic body preserved its glory intact, clinging to its comfortable lodgings with the same pertinacity it displayed later in Peking and Constantinople after these cities ceased to be the seats of government. The Russian and English legations owned vast and imposing buildings which were as much a compliment to the Persian capital as to the diplomats themselves, a question of prestige.

I made my calls on the legations and the European colony of Tehran. The chief legation in Persia, next to the Russian, was the English. Its summer home, Gluashek, was not large and scantily irrigated, but its residence in Tehran was grand and shone with the combined splendor of the British and Indian budgets. On reception days the red uniform of the military attaché represented the British army, and turbaned Punjabi *suwars* (cavalrymen) reminded one of India behind the scene. A picturesque native servant circulated with a many-shelved bamboo stand, a superstructure containing all kinds of Reading biscuits, which can last for centuries without losing any of their original excellence. Lady Durand, sad and sweet, presided at these functions. Later, the hostess was Mrs. Hardinge, lady-in-waiting to the princess of Wales, full of the freshness of youth which the climate of India had taken away from Lady Durand.

The ministers attracted my vivid attention. Unlike consuls condemned to a lifelong exile in Persia, they moved freely from one country to another in close surveillance of their policies. Their talk was colorful with plenty of intimate allusions, but very reticent on some matters. A diplomat rarely gives of himself in full.

The British minister, Sir H. Mortimer Durand, belonged to an Anglo-Indian family which had achieved promotion by hard work. He was the ponderous type of successful colonial official and had won distinction in dealing with natives by his talents as administrator, diplomat, and police chief. Coming after the brilliantly destructive activity of a previous English representative in Persia,* he was reserved and on guard with us but later turned to a cautious friendship.

Charles Hardinge, the counselor of the legation—a convenient rank nonexistent in the lists of the Foreign Office, as he said himself —was a different man and struck a different note. He was tall and handsome with dark eyes, dark hair, and a serene forehead, quiet and reserved without being stiff. He belonged to one of the great families of England who went to India as viceroys, as he himself was later to do. In short, he was born with a silver spoon in his mouth and brought up in intimacy with royalty. Of great nobility of character and breadth of view, Hardinge, as undersecretary of the British Foreign Office and as ambassador at St. Petersburg and Paris, was to be prominent in cementing the alliance with France and Russia.

A rather disparate collection of diplomats completed the diplomatic body, consisting mostly of people who could not find or did not merit a better place. It was evident that only Russia and England were interested enough in Persia to send people of real worth. The French had a new building, elegant but strangely constructed. The entrance door led straight into the large reception room where balls were given, so that in bad weather newly arriving guests dripping with rain and melting snow had to make their way among dancing couples. Other legations adorned Tehran with a decreasing degree of luxury and elegance. The American legation, with its barely furnished, unheated rooms, looked cold and desolate. The rest of the European colony tried vainly to keep up appearances with a few rugs and wicker chairs. It was difficult and costly to bring European furniture such a long distance through steep mountain passes, and things often arrived badly damaged and could not be satisfactorily repaired in Tehran. Ladies' dresses and hats sometimes looked like odd curiosities of bygone years or were daring products of local ingenuity. All the same, five o'clock teas and dances followed one

---

* A reference to Sir Henry Drummond Wolff, whose political and business connections in London allowed him to pursue a strong policy aimed at opening Persia to European capital. The Russians, who preferred Persia to remain isolated, considered Sir Henry a Russophobe and his policies destructive. *F. K.*

another, as there were no other distractions. Theatrical and musical artists did not dare approach the forbidding frontier of Persia. But once that first oppressive sensation of exile was overcome, life seemed quite endurable, and young people were gay even in Tehran.

The British took the lead in social activities and arranged a gymkhana—a variety of games on horseback. Some of these just provided plenty of fun for all; others required great skill and involved a certain amount of danger for the participants. The first time I went to see a gymkhana, a great wall made of newspapers was built across the road. The riders arrived at the paper wall at full speed, but the horses, reaching what they considered a solid barrier, reared and refused to assail it. Out of the confused mass of horses and riders, one man succeeded in swerving his mount and, backing it, tore a hole in the paper wall and passed through it. All the riders rushed after him through the opening, and the paper curtain flew high into the air.

A much more exacting game was tent pegging. Wooden pegs were planted in the ground. Horsemen had to pick up the pegs with their lances, at full gallop. If the lance became embedded in the earth, the shoulder of the rider could be dislocated and he himself thrown off his horse. I found that the risk of the game was out of proportion to its pleasure, but it was explained to me that the game served as practice for boar hunting with spears, a really great sport highly esteemed in India.

A popular game accessible to all was the paper chase. A man rode ahead with a paper bag and disappeared in the walled, winding lanes between the orchards, throwing paper clippings to indicate his trail. After a certain time the whole party would start in pursuit, trying to trace him and run him down, in imitation of a fox hunt. But the greatest of all horse games was, of course, polo. I tried it but found it beyond my capacities as a rider.

The English legation encouraged the younger members of the European colony to take part in these games as a remedy against melancholy, drinking, and other uncommendable habits—a highly efficient method, the best invented so far. I was regularly invited but did not take as active a part in these amusements as I would have liked, since the staff of our legation was quite depleted. Several people were away on leave, including the second secretary, who had replaced the first. I was responsible for the whole diplomatic chancellery and part of the consular business.

I became passionately interested in diplomatic work, realizing that relations between Russia and England, which affected the future of Europe, depended on an understanding about Persia which could and ought to be arranged. Sometimes I had to sit up till two o'clock in the morning in the vaulted rooms of the basement, decoding messages which came at the most inappropriate hours and in depressing quantity. My work reminded me of that in our Foreign Office, but the difference was very great. In St. Petersburg my official activities had not gone beyond the narrow range of the Asian Department, whose chief appeared as a mighty, awe-inspiring being topped only by the Olympian heights of the court and the ministers of state. In Tehran I was thrust into the inner circle of the Persian government. I saw Mozaffar ed-Din Shah, who looked just as weak, benevolent, and helpless as he had in Tabriz, his childish eyes now often bewildered. He promised everything, without the slightest idea how his promises could be carried out. He was always short of money but did not care, being less greedy than his father and his son. When he went to Europe, his chief delights were mechanical toys—little puppets who could dance, move, or make some sound seemed to him the highest achievements of European technology and science, and he bought a tremendous quantity of them. And although he could shoot a rifle well and was interested in artillery, a gun was to him only a toy. In 1906, when the revolution started, he granted a constitution and died five days afterward, never aware of its meaning.

I had a taste of Tehran court life. Receptions were few, short, and formal. The large palace, with its beautifully decorated halls and rooms facing gardens with pools of water, was even more useless than the palaces of Constantinople. Because of an absurd etiquette, the "King of Kings," as he called himself, could not sit and eat with other people; he had to sit on his throne in the presence of his subjects. But European representatives objected to standing for a long time. We would enter the hall with the peacock throne, advance, make three bows to the extravagantly bejeweled shah, offer greetings, receive thanks, and back out facing the sovereign. Upon our arrival and departure a band played, flags waved, soldiers presented arms, and street urchins—the only people who enjoyed the sight of uniformed diplomats in their cocked hats—screamed and ran alongside our carriages. These audiences reminded me of the German official receptions, where the kaiser hardly acknowledged the deep curtsies of the ladies, and only the empress was amiable. The English expression "Gracious Majesty" gives an exact definition of the proper attitude of a monarch on such occasions.

I also met the grand visier, Amin os-Soltān, a talented and active man who strove vainly to preserve the treasury from the new party's greed for spoils. His days were numbered; the old regime which he personified could not last much longer.

In 1897 an Armenian servant of the Russian consulate at Tabriz was accused of insulting a Moslem woman who was selling vegetables in the street—a totally false and unwarranted accusation. He fled to the consulate. An infuriated crowd followed him and surrounded the consulate, making it necessary to telegraph the legation at Tehran for help. There was no racial hatred between Persians and Armenians, as later developed in Turkey, and this sudden outburst may be partly attributed to the general tension in a country on the eve of revolution. I received an order to see the grand vizier about the matter. In my presence he communicated by wire with Tabriz. All the conversation was immediately transmitted by the telegraph clerk, as there was no telephone service at that time. I left only after receiving every assurance from the governor of Tabriz that the situation was well under control. This was shortly confirmed by our consul general. Yet two days later came the desperate news that the Russian consulate was in danger and its water supply threatened. This was too much—our legation requested Russian troops be sent, and accordingly they were moved to the frontier with orders to cross it at the first notice. To avoid any intervention, the Armenian was allowed to escape at night in disguise, and everything calmed down. This was, of course, an exceptional occurrence, but normal conditions were extremely unsatisfactory nonetheless.

I had met in Tabriz at the house of the English doctor Adcock, physician to Mozaffar ed-Din, a Persian doctor, Hakim ol-Molk. He looked very humble and obsequious at that time. Upon the accession to the throne of Mozaffar ed-Din, Hakim ol-Molk followed the new shah to Tehran and soon accumulated a hundred thousand dollars in bribes and opposed the grand vizier Amin os-Soltān. I saw Hakim ol-Molk in Tehran, driving in state in a fine carriage and surrounded by mounted servants. Shortly afterward he was exiled and assassinated during his journey. Of this last occurrence the grand vizier was not guilty. Thus closed the spectacular career of an intriguing, unscrupulous Persian.

It often happened that I dined alone with the Russian minister. His frozen attitude disappeared entirely. He proved to be a loving father and often spoke about his family. One of his daughters was a maid of honor to the young empress, and the other had made a rich and happy marriage. He also talked with me about his experiences in his long diplomatic career. "I was the first Russian consul sent to Japan," said Biutsov. "Before leaving I received instructions that my salary would be forwarded from Siberia with a whaler at the first opportunity. The ship never came, and neither did my salary. At the end of the year I wrote to St. Petersburg that the credit of the consulate was exhausted and that there were banking houses at Yokohama. There were also other discouraging factors. There was no heating in the houses, imported stoves were few, and the Japanese did not know how to manage them. I succeeded in finding a room with a stove, in a hotel. In the middle of the night I awoke with a feeling of impending peril. I ran to the door and fell senseless in the hall. The stove had nearly killed me with its carbon monoxide."

The minister had also been in China but did not wear his Chinese decoration. He had received the highest one—a peacock plume—but there was no way of fitting it to our uniform. He laughed heartily while he related to me stories of his past, but if the conversation turned to the present his animation dropped and he lapsed into silence.

On one occasion, moving noiselessly in their socks, the servants had cleared the table and disappeared. We sat alone in deep armchairs at one end of the dining room. I looked at the furrows on the face of the minister and waited. After a while he mentioned some current business in a casual way but gradually became more explicit. He admitted being pessimistic about Persia. He had been in several Eastern lands, but in none had he found such distressing conditions. The acuteness of the situation consisted in the enmity between the Tabriz party and the grand vizier, Amin os-Soltān, the last statesman of prerevolutionary Persia. Tabriz had produced many patriotic men during the great upheaval, but this came much later.

I saw only one alleviating circumstance. Whatever were the relations between the governments in Europe, the Russian and English legations in Tehran were drawing closer together. The reason was that both legations were in the same predicament. They had to deal with the Persian government—a very bad government, but there was no other. It was the sole agent through which the legations could

act in order to protect the personal safety and property of their
respective subjects and their treaty rights. With the coming of a new
and incapable shah, the government began to crumble and became
less and less efficient. This meant that the activity of the legations became less efficient also. That was a matter of prime importance for
both legations and affected directly the position of the English and
Russian ministers. Biutsov and Durand had well-earned reputations
as diplomats and were not disposed to lose them in Persia. They
supported the grand vizier, Amin os-Soltān, who still held this office.

The winter season started, and the grand vizier gave a gala dinner
in his newly finished beautiful palace. It was dark when we drove
into its garden and stopped before the brightly lighted façade of the
house. In the anteroom we were met by the grand vizier, a tall, lean,
handsome man, not much over forty. What struck me most in his
appearance were his luminous eyes and the vivacity of his movements. Persians are usually ceremonious and slow; important people
often look expressionless, if not sleepy. Amin os-Soltān was full of
life and smiles; he walked and moved as smoothly and swiftly as if he
were dancing. He grasped my hand and quickly asked a few questions; then, with an undulating movement of his body in his long
robe of state, he let me pass and was already addressing the next
person. In a few moments all the guests were welcomed and invited
into the dining room, which was hung with Gobelin tapestries, a gift
of the president of France. The silver and the cut glass on the table
seemed to reflect the shining personality of the host, who hardly
touched the food on his plate as he surveyed his guests with rapid,
attentive glances.

Looking at him, I understood the fascination he had held for the
late shah, confined in the dull monotony of a Persian palace with
speechless attendants. The grand vizier spoke and laughed unconcernedly during the whole dinner. Only once his face darkened and
became gloomy. He cast down his eyes as if oppressed by a presenti-
ment of his fate. Then with a jerk he took a cup of champagne, drank
it at one draught, and started to talk with renewed animation. I
wondered at the self-control of the man.

A few days passed. One morning the minister was late for lunch.
He was closeted with Sir Mortimer, who had paid him a sudden visit
at an unusual time. When Biutsov entered the dining room, he
looked older and worried. He did not even rub his hands, but kept
them wide apart, a sign of distress.

"There it is," he said. "The grand vizier is dismissed. Sir Mortimer and I are asking for an immediate audience with the shah. We shall try to save the life of Amin os-Soltān if possible."

Such a step was without precedent in the history of Persia. The joint demand of the British and Russian ministers produced a staggering effect, but it came too late to preserve the position of the grand vizier. They succeeded only in wresting from the shah his consent that Amin os-Soltān should be spared his life and allowed to retire to the sanctuary of the mosque at Qom, where he would be safe.

The next day the magnificent robe of honor of the grand vizier, of priceless cashmere with diamond clasps, was taken from him and returned with the clasps torn from it, a mean and nasty blow aimed at Amin os-Soltān and incidentally hitting the legations, who resented it.

This was the last stroke of the Tabrizians, and it broke their power. The Persian government realized that it could not invite the enmity of Great Britain and Russia for the sake of a gang of greedy courtiers. A wealthy man of Tehran, Amin od-Dowleh, was appointed grand vizier. Dignified and medieval in appearance but of mediocre intelligence, the new grand vizier was one of the most showy representatives of the old regime. For a while he concentrated on internal affairs and neglected foreign relations. Things became quiet again. The British and Russian ministers asked for leaves of absence and left Tehran, Charles Hardinge took charge of the English legation and Andrei Shcheglov of the Russian. With the shah camping far away in the hills and only too glad to escape from the duties of government, Amin od-Dowleh, Shcheglov, and Hardinge were the strongest men in Persia.

During Atābak's long rule he had skillfully managed to be on good terms with both the Russians and the English, taking advantage of their mutual distrust and fostering it when he found it expedient. Would this state of affairs continue under the new grand vizier, or would there be a change? This was the problem in the summer of 1897 in Persia.

The cabinets of London and St. Petersburg considered each other potential enemies and Persia a perpetual apple of discord. Both governments were supported in this opinion by the patriotic public of their countries. But during the last year Biutsov and Durand were in Tehran, the challenge of the Tabrizians brought the two legations together. Under the pressure of existing circumstances, Shcheglov and Hardinge intimated to their consuls to abstain from irritating conflicts. They believed that the Persian question could be settled amicably. Although quite different by temperament, these two men had reached the same conclusion.

That the Persian state was disintegrating was evident to every European living there, but the reason was not clear. The fact that Persia was a despotic monarchy supported by a backward clergy was not enough to explain the situation. Persia had always been ruled by despots. That had not prevented the existence of flourishing trade, industry, and the arts, as well as military strength, a fairly good state of public safety, and a large population, prosperous and contented. What was the matter with the Persia of 1897? Why the continuing decay of the land? I think this depended on a multitude of causes which may be briefly summarized thus: the economy of the rest of the world moved relentlessly forward, and Persia did not keep pace with it. Her exchange of goods was insufficient and her balance of trade adverse. Persia, with her caravan trade and primitive industry, was moving toward bankruptcy in a world of steam power and electric energy. Her currency was continually depreciating in buying power, both at home and abroad.

Another reason for decline was the political support of the Qājār dynasty by the English and Russian governments. Persia had passed through other periods of decay under degenerate and effeminate rulers. Each time an attack from the outside followed by an internal revolution brought a general revival under new men who assumed the guidance of the state. Now the support of the English and Russian legations artificially prolonged the rule of incapable kings, who relied on foreign political and financial aid. This delayed an armed rebellion. At first the revolution adopted a peaceful method peculiar to Persia known as *best*. This meant to take refuge in some inviolable sanctuary like a mosque or the tomb of a saint. A legation may also serve as a kind of diplomatic sanctuary, and a minor offender may occasionally seek shelter in a stable. I found one in my own stable and had to enter into a long argument with the police before the matter could be settled.

The trouble starts with the appearance of an excited crowd in the bazaar. The shops are closed, partly as a demonstration and partly from a well-founded apprehension of looting. As soon as the news of the closing of the bazaar spreads through town—which it does with an extraordinary rapidity—consternation, excitement, and anger become general. If the people do not obtain satisfaction, the second and much more serious phase sets in—the leaders of the extreme elements of the movement settle in a chosen sanctuary. If the mullahs approve of the movement, the third stage—open challenge of the authority of the shah—is reached.

It was clearly outside the competency of the European powers to create a new form of government for the Persians. They had to do it themselves. That was to happen in July 1906, when the people of Tehran clamored for the granting of a constitution, and thousands went into best in mosques and the British legation. The Russian minister refused to give a best in the Russian legation. This was a mistake—you cannot refuse to give a best without deeply offending popular sentiment. In addition, a best does not put any responsibilty upon the host; it merely causes an enormous amount of trouble. But this cannot be evaded; it is part of the job of a diplomat in the East.

In 1906, the grand vizier Amin od-Dowleh was dismissed, a constitution granted, and a *medjlis* (parliament) established. The Russian government bet on the wrong horse by supporting a highly unpopular and incapable shah, whereas, in this instance, the British government's representative adopted a liberal and perfectly justifiable course of action.

A Dinner at the Russian Legation

Shcheglov, my new chief, the Russian chargé d'affaires and gentleman-in-waiting to the tsar, was the son of a self-made man who had introduced his children into the privileged ranks of aristocratic society, where wealthy people were freely accepted. I will not enter into a discussion of the superiority of hereditary nobility; suffice it to say that I do not believe in it. I am convinced that the talents of a race are, like precious metals, deeply embedded in the solid under layer. Whatever good qualities an aristocrat may have were inherited from his humble, toiling ancestors; they are not acquired by the succeeding generations, who lead a life of idleness and self-indulgence if not outright dissipation.

There was a certain amount of successful snobbery in Shcheglov, but he remained essentially a man of Moscow, of the solid common stock which made the old capital the heart of the empire. Shcheglov was short, sturdy, and broad-chested, with clever, gay eyes and a superabundance of health, wits, and energy. He tried to impress me with his peremptory manners, but it did not work.

"Show me our dispensary. You are in charge of it, aren't you?" he said in an imperative tone.

"Yes, sir. I receive the patients and the doctor treats them."

I started to show him around. The dispensary was a small three-room house. "Here is the waiting room, here the consultation room, here the pharmacy. Sit down, sir. We can extract a tooth for you, or perform an appendectomy that won't take long. If you need treatment for your nervous system, that would require more time; but don't be too alarmed. We have handled such cases with very satisfactory results."

"What?" exclaimed Shcheglov.

"Sir, I was just explaining to you, as you told me to, the activities of the dispensary. As for contagious diseases . . ." But Shcheglov had had enough, and I heard him chuckle as he disappeared among the trees of the garden.

He had the uncomfortable habit of working late at night and sending me a bundle of telegrams to be coded immediately. But I had had my training in Tabriz.

"Can you prepare them at once?" he asked me one evening. "Is it too late?" "Oh no, sir. It is only two A.M.," I answered, rapidly vanishing with the telegrams. After that we became friends.

With the coming of summer, the legations migrated to their country houses and for a while enjoyed the coolness of their parks and the beauties of nature. But after some time they became bored with both. Social life was at zero. Except for the Russian and the British, the legations did not own their country estates, and labored under the handicap of a lack of furniture, plumbing, and other civilized conveniences in rented Oriental villas. Our villa, however, was perfectly well supplied.

There was little work to do, as the Persians were quiet after the excitement of the last change of cabinet and the Shah was away from Tehran camping in the hills. Shcheglov, an extremely active and enterprising man, fond of society, was the first to feel the burden of loneliness and inactivity. He arranged a private telegraph station at our country seat and connected it with Tehran, enabling us to receive the news daily from the Russian telegraph agency. But we still had nothing to send by our news wire. Next he planned to erect a monument to the memory of the famous Russian writer and diplomat, A. S. Griboiedov, murdered in Tehran in 1829.* Orders for a bronze statue had been sent to Russia. One afternoon I brought the mail to Shcheglov, who looked with contempt at its meager contents and was soon through with it. We sat silently on the porch of the villa. The trees stood still. In the English legation across the road tennis players could be heard calling the scores, their white figures in constant motion. I think the English continue to play tennis after death in the Elysian Fields. On the high flagpole the British flag, indicating the presence of Hardinge, slowly unfolded, fluttered, then hung limp again as the breeze fell. A slight commotion arose in the English legation, and a cavalcade issued from the gate. Lady Hardinge was going for a horseback ride. Her graceful silhouette matched the tall frame of her husband. Shcheglov looked at them, pondering. "I think I'll give a dinner for them. Yes, that's an idea," said Shcheglov.

Invitations were sent and accepted at once. All went smoothly at first, but a hitch came when the chef was summoned for an economic conference. There was little to discuss: no fish, no game, nothing at this lean season of the year. Shcheglov—a man of the north—did not like lamb, which is not good there. Hunters were sent into the hills and returned empty-handed; the shah was shooting, and all the game was being driven for him. Prospects looked gloomy; we felt worse after each conference, as is often the case. Whatever we tried, our projected dinner lacked what the French call a pièce de résistance—the main roast, which in the Middle Ages was served with a flourish of trumpets. Then luck turned our way. Like genii of the *Arabian Nights* appeared a procession of Persian court servants bearing a wild ram shot by the shah. The situation was saved.

The great day arrived. Mounted English qolāms, preceding the carriage, entered the drive of our park at a gallop, and Lady Hardinge, a vision of English beauty, stepped out of it with her husband. She laughed as she pointed at the violin she had brought with her.

There were H. G. M. Rumbold, P. C. H. Wyndham, and others, even the doctor, Tom F. Olding—the British legation in full, and

* According to *The New York Times* of November 10, 1967, there is presently on display in the Kremlin "a historic diamond, the 88-carat shah, bearing three inscriptions in Persian. It was given to Czar Nicholas I in 1829 by Persia as reparation for a Persian mob's murder of the writer Aleksandr Griboyedov, who was serving as Russian Ambassador to Teheran." *Ed.*

no other guests. The dinner was splendid, with menus printed in gold. Vanilla whipped cream was served with grated chestnut.

"Hardinge, that's really good. We must have it done by our cook," pleaded Rumbold to his chief.

After dinner we moved into the drawing room, and Lady Hardinge played the violin with skill and grace. As Shcheglov had once remarked, all too often women look like grasshoppers about to fly as they lift the violin. Then one of our secretaries played a Slavic song. The Russian and English melodies seemed to enhance the harmony of this meeting. After the music, animated conversation resumed. This was more than a simple social function; there was an atmosphere of cordiality such as I could not recall on previous occasions. Even the English military attaché, Lieutenant Colonel H. P. Picot, a notable Russophobe, assumed an almost amiable countenance. The secretary of the legation, Rumbold, was frankly gay and showed me the trick of throwing his monocle straight to his eye. Hardinge was not as reserved as usual, and he spoke with interest with Shcheglov. It was not the subject of their conversation but the tone that mattered. There was an evident desire to smooth and overcome points of conflict. As the evening drew to its end, for the first time English and Russians were slow to part.

The English, who at first were formal and reserved, gradually grew friendly and genial. They themselves seemed astonished at the ease and confidence they felt in a Russian house and enjoyed this new experience. For generations the English had considered Russia a blot on the face of the earth. They were born and bred anti-Russians. Russia's unrestricted autocracy became more and more repellent to them as Russia moved forward on her path of civilized despotism. The English are by nature extremely independent and intolerant of any authority except their own, accepted by them of their free will. The most die-hard English conservative would seem a red hot radical in the old autocratic Russia, a country without a constitution. The British constitution is not only a matter of law—it is an article of faith, an object of patriotic love, without which an Englishman would lose his self-esteem and his zest for life.

It was the German naval program that forced England to reverse her policy toward Russia. An understanding between the two countries was essential to fight the rise of German seapower, a matter of life and death for England. England's ultra-conservative prime minister, Lord Salisbury, made the first move in January 1897 while I

was working at the Russian legation at Tehran. In a speech in the
House of Lords he surveyed England's policy toward Russia as far
back as the Crimean War (1854–56), in which England had backed
Turkey against the tsar, and said: "Many members of this House
will keenly feel the nature of the mistake that was made when I say
that we put all our money upon the wrong horse." * The noble lords
laughed, but Salisbury meant business. In January 1898 he wrote
to the British ambassador at St. Petersburg that, in Asian politics,
"Russia and England are constantly opposed, neutralizing each other's
efforts much more frequently than the real antagonism of their
interests would justify. . . . It is to remove or lessen this evil that
we thought that an understanding with Russia might benefit both
nations." †

The dinner at the Russian legation took place during the summer
of 1897, midway between the two statements of the British prime
minister. Emperor Nicholas II—or rather his foreign minister,
Count Muraviev—showed little inclination to follow Lord Salisbury's suggestion. It was not until 1907 that an agreement with
England was reached by the Russian Foreign Office under Isvolskii,
although Hardinge was already decidedly in favor of good relations
between England and Russia in Persia by 1897. This was an important fact, as the British representatives in Persia were in effect the
outposts of India, which was surrounded by Afghanistan and Tibet,
where Russia was not represented and had no contact with English
diplomats.

Later, as ambassador to St. Petersburg, Hardinge continued his
work of rapprochment with Russia. From this post he was called
to be undersecretary of the Foreign Office. Sir Arthur Nicolson,
Hardinge's successor, had previously been in Persia and could successfully conduct in St. Petersburg the negotiations about the agreement concerning Persia—the first step toward the future alliance.
From London Hardinge went as viceroy to India, and Nicolson succeeded him in the British Foreign Office—a chain of appointments
too fortunate to be entirely accidental.

In the meantime the Germans continued to increase their navy,
and the apprehension of the English rose accordingly. Sazonov, who

---

* *The Parliamentary Debates* (London, authorized edition, 1897), fourth series, vol.
45, col. 29 (January 19, 1897). *Ed.*
† G. P. Gooch and H. Temperley, eds., *British Documents on the Origin of the War,*
1898–1914 (London, 1927), *1,* 8. The Marquis of Salisbury, January 25, 1898. *Ed.*

succeeded Izvolskii as Russian foreign minister in September 1910, had a talk with the kaiser the following October. The conversation turned to the British and German armaments, and the kaiser said: "That is what provokes the anger of the English against me and my government."

Hardinge, Nicolson, and E. A. Crowe were representative of the trend in the English Foreign Office toward an understanding with France and Russia. Unfortunately the range of the agreements was incomplete. The Balkans remained outside the signed conventions, and through this open door the flames of World War I would suddenly explode. If these conventions, which the Germans called an encirclement, had been complete, World War I might have been prevented.

A Diplomatic Incident

With the coming to power of the new grand vizier, our neighbor, the road in front of his house became encumbered with the carriages, horses, and servants of his visitors, leaving hardly any passage at all. The premier himself behaved in an arrogant way, and complaints about it were heard from members of the European colony. Shcheglov knew it and smiled, but his eyes remained steel cold. He was a fighter and would accept a challenge without flinching. A conflict was close at hand, and I was to be its involuntary cause.

One summer afternoon, as I set out for a horseback ride, I found the road in front of the grand vizier's house totally blocked by carriages and mounted retinues of Persian grandees. I asked for the right of way and met with an impertinent rebuke. I had to turn back, and I made a formal complaint to my chief, the chargé d'affaires, who at once sent the first dragoman of the legation to the grand vizier. The dragoman returned with an unsatisfactory reply— something which had never happened before, as we were on the best of terms with the Persians. Shcheglov's reaction was swift and drastic. (Scheglov was friendly and sociable, but he knew how to defend his interests. He had sharply rebuked the English in Egypt, but that did not prevent him from holding them in high esteem.)

From the house of the grand vizier, the road made a considerable circuit around the extensive property of our legation before joining the main highway. There was a shortcut through our private grounds which we kept open to the public. That presented an important strategic advantage, and Shcheglov fully availed himself of it. He ordered wooden barriers to be placed at both ends of our shortcut, with pickets of Persian soldiers from the guard of the legation. The soldiers were told not to let any Persians pass from the following day on, though Europeans were free to cross. "And the Turks?" asked the Persian sergeant. "Let them pass." The sergeant grinned and saluted. Stakes were planted on both sides of the road with poles placed across them. The Persian soldiers were delighted, expecting a big *tomasha* (show).

Early the next morning came peasants on donkeys from the villages, bringing milk, poultry, and vegetables to the market. They were stopped and turned back; their loud protests remained unheeded. Later, men on horseback and in carriages arrived, entered into heated altercations, and had to retreat. In blatant contrast, a carriage from the Turkish Embassy was let through with military honors to the intense surprise of the Turks, who knew nothing of the happenings.

The climax came shortly before noon with the appearance of the grand vizier driving in state to Tehran. Soldiers in uniform formed a line across the road, barring passage and politely declining all requests. At last the coachman turned the carriage back. The news spread to the capital and became the chief talk of the bazaar.

In the afternoon an ominous silence reigned on our deserted road, while the traffic took the long detour. Even the Europeans preferred not to avail themselves of the shortcut. We sat tight in our legation as if we were besieged. It was like a declaration of hostilities between our castle and the stronghold of our neighbor, a feudal war of the Middle Ages.

This lasted two days. The shah was informed and disapproved of the grand vizier's conduct. Since time immemorial public roads had been under the protection of the Persian monarchs, and no one had the right to obstruct them. On the third day a Persian dignitary came with the message that the person guilty of blocking the way in front of the house of the grand vizier had been apprehended and sentenced to a severe flogging, but the chargé d'affaires answered that he pardoned the offender and asked that his punishment be remitted. The barriers were removed. No complaints were ever heard again about impertinent servants blocking the highway.

A few days later the shah met Shcheglov in the street, stopped his carriage, and had an amiable conversation with the Russian representative. The incident, of course, was not mentioned. All went smoothly after that. The Foreign Office in St. Petersburg was informed of the matter by personal letter.

Glimpses of Persian Life

Persia is renowned for a literature full of rapturous love songs. These are very popular, and every Persian with the least tinge of education is a keen admirer of his native poetry. I wonder where they find the material for these sentimental outpourings, as actual life offers few occasions for them. Marriages are arranged by female relatives, and bridegroom and bride do not see one another before the ceremony itself. After marriage there are no longer grounds to long for a distant meeting, to complain about harsh obstacles in the path of passion, or to suffer from separation—the usual themes of poetry. All obstacles have already been removed, and there is no separation except by divorce—a subject eminently unfit for poetry. I think that most Persian love songs are just flights of imagination, like the long poems in which Goethe, Byron, Lamartine, and Hugo express their heavenly aspirations and speak profusely about Mephistopheles and Lucifer, although none of these writers cared much about religion or met any infernal spirits. Milton and Dante, the only truly religious poets, frankly relied on the text of the Bible as the source of their inspiration.

"Do your women have souls?" I asked a Persian. He looked puzzled and answered: "I do not know. I think they have." As a matter of fact, the Koran is strangely silent about the future life of its female believers. A man is promised quite a number of celestial spouses in Paradise, but what becomes of his earthly ones is not clear. Their destiny is to bear children, for a man must be born into this world in order to gain admittance to the next one. So much is granted, and that is all. The Koran, being essentially a man's book, does not contain provisions regarding women. The tomb of the only daughter of Mohammed is a highly venerated shrine, so there is some hope left for other women, but their status, if any, after death is not explained.

The lot of a woman in Persia was not enviable. She exchanged the harem of her father for that of her husband and spent her life condemned to eternal oblivion by the rest of the world. She had to go veiled and had no right to speak to any men except her nearest relatives. Socially she did not exist; officially she was only a name.

A Russian Moslem woman had a case in the consulate. She came all wrapped up and accompanied by an old man who spoke for her. We had to address him as if she were not present at all—a living mummy. And women constituted the largest part of the population of Persia.

Another case was tried by the Persian court at Tabriz. A wife was accused of poisoning her husband. The charge unfortunately proved true. The woman was condemned to be thrown from the top of the old, tremendously high citadel. She walked without help up the long and steep outer stairs. On her way she confessed calmly and of her own accord that she had poisoned several other people. All Tabriz stood on the flat roofs and witnessed the fall of the unfortunate culprit, wrapped in a black veil. That was the only instance of a woman being executed in Persia during my stay there.

There was a king but no queen in Persia. The word *queen* does not even exist in the Persian language.* The shah's wives had no official position; perhaps there were too many. Their rank depended on the tender feelings of the sovereign. The long-time favorite wife of Nāser ed-Din Shah was Anis od-Dowleh, the only Persian woman whose name was known to every man in Tehran. Her father had owned a watermill in a village not far from the city. As Nāser ed-Din Shah passed by, her veil flew away. The shah saw her and fell in love at once. She was probably the only woman he ever cared for. When Nāser ed-Din Shah went to Europe, Anis od-Dowleh was to accompany him. However, she did not go farther than Russia, for the Persians found European houses lacking in privacy and the accommodations necessary for a harem. Consequently Anis od-Dowleh was sent back to Persia, without being informed of the decision, while the shah proceeded on his journey. A European lady told me that Anis od-Dowleh looked very beautiful leaning on a cushion embroidered with real pearls. This peasant girl was truly devoted to her royal husband and did not survive him for long. Shortly after my arrival at the legation Anis od-Dowleh died.

The only time I saw a Persian household was in Tehran, when I had to seize the furniture of a Russian Moslem. The man was well off, but he obstinately refused to pay an unimportant sum imposed by the consular court. I had to go with the cossacks myself. There were very few things in the outer part of the house. It looked ridiculous, but I was not to be trifled with and declared that I would have to seize the furniture of the harem. The man was mute from aston-

* *Halika,* used in modern Persian for the shah's consort, is of Arabic origin. *Ed.*

ishment at such an unexpected turn of events, but he made no objections and went into the interior rooms. I asked him that the women be transferred to some other place. As I waited, I heard a heated argument in high-pitched, indignant voices and had the uncomfortable sensation that I was getting into a mess. The husband returned—red, panting, and thoroughly discomfited. He made the incongruous proposal that I should accompany him alone, leaving the cossacks outside. Believing that the women had left during all this fuss, I stupidly accepted this offer and followed him through the fateful door.

I found myself in a moderate-sized room with a good carpet, cushions along the walls, two chests, and nothing else. What made the situation decidedly unpleasant was that two veiled women were standing in corners, one sobbing and the other shaking with rage. The husband opened a chest. At that moment the silent woman sprang like a tigress and started to take out garments of velvet, silk, and muslin of various colors and shapes. Each thing was thrown into the husband's face, with appropriate ejaculations. A black servant girl was looking at us from the kitchen door, forgetting in her amazement to veil her face. I fled from this family scene, firmly resolving never again to take inventories in Moslem houses. The next day the sum was paid in full.

My further acquaintance with the local beauties was limited to a single encounter. Once in the environs of Tehran I met a file of closed carriages with galloping bodyguards. One window was open, and passing rapidly on horseback, I had a glimpse of a pale and distinguished-looking girl in a black silk mantle that covered her head and gave a monastic appearance to the Oriental princess.

Astarābād

I knew Persia as well as a young man of twenty-seven could and was quietly waiting for the expiration of my three-year term to go on leave when I was ordered to Astarābād on the eastern shore of the Caspian Sea. To my misfortune, I had been promoted to the rank of secretary of the consulate at Astarābād, and the consul was clamoring for my arrival.

Astarābād was situated on the edge of the prairies inhabited by the Turkomans and had been built as a fort to guard against their inroads. Since the Russians had taken the Transcaspian region, Astarābād, always a very small town, became completely insignificant.

There was no longer any reason under heaven for the existence of this town, and still less for a consulate. But there it was, with no way of escape from the place. I told Shcheglov that I would like to go to St. Petersburg on leave at once. But he insisted that I go to Astarābād first and remain in Persia five more months to complete a three-year stay—like Jacob in the service of Laban. Five more months in the most out of the way consulate that existed at that time! But I was on friendly terms with Shcheglov and needed a good record on my return to St. Petersburg to secure a transfer from Persia.

As a result, my fate and that of Astarābād became linked, and I reached its gates in August 1897. If Tabriz was an abridged and cheaper edition of Tehran, Astarābād could be compared to a leaflet freely distributed on street corners to reluctant passersby. Of course, Astarābād was a province with a capital and a governor, but even from the point of view of a patriotic Persian it was inconspicuous. The governor, Jahānsouz Mirzā, was of royal blood, but that was all that could be said of him; as an individual he was just as insignificant as his city.

The consulate in this sleepy little place, the only decent building for hundreds of miles around, housed a very hospitable consul with a very pleasant family, like a solitary bush with a bird's nest in the prairies. There was also a Russian telegraph station, but otherwise I might as well have been buried at the bottom of the sea. The consul's drawing room on the upper floor looked very well in the evenings when the piano was played. Unfortunately, the jackals that assembled on the city walls would start an accompaniment of their own, whining and howling in a roulade of strange yelps like the weird laugh of a witch in a deserted cemetery.

The Turkomans proved quite a decent sort of people, although they were considered chronic rebels by the Persians and a price was set on the head of any Turkoman brought to the governor. This was never paid during my stay—more likely the Persian would lose his head in any such attempt. The jackals were harmless, the natives peaceful, and a patriarchal slumber enveloped the consulate and all its activities. Still, we managed to send a certain number of letters with our fortnightly mail. The consul complained that answers were slow in reaching us, as if we were completely forgotten by the rest of the world, which undoubtedly was the case.

But there is no tranquillity on this earth; something is bound to happen even in Astarābād, and it did. A rumor spread in St. Petersburg that plague was lurking in some ports of the Indian Ocean, as it always does. Governmental spheres were aroused, and a sanitary commission was sent to the port of Bendere Gaz in our consular district. Shortly thereafter, a fire broke out in Bendere Gaz, destroyed most of the village and, incidentally, the barracks of the commission. St. Petersburg became aware of the existence of a consulate in Astarābād for the first time in the fifty years since its establishment. I was delegated by the legation to Bendere Gaz with special powers to investigate the causes of the fire and to provide the medicinal personnel with whatever assistance was needed.

I found the doctors and nurses quite cheerful in the new quarters to which they had migrated with all their pharmacopoeia, which they had rescued from the fire. Since I had not been instructed to rebuild the whole village, there was nothing for me to do. However, I had enough practical experience to realize that my immediate return would not meet with approval in high quarters. I stayed as long as—in my estimation—St. Petersburg expected of my zeal for the good of the service, the urgency of the situation, and the seriousness of the case. Time passed pleasantly enough, and eventually I received a telegram from my consul calling me back. There were many things to be prepared, including our yearly commercial report and the Christmas celebration. After that I was free to leave Astarābād in January 1898. Snow was lying on the thick green leaves of the orange trees as I mounted a Persian horse for the last time, and the consul and his family waved to me from the balcony.

My stay in Persia had been a disconcerting experience. The East was a failure—it may have been great in the past, but now it was like a ruined medieval castle which is picturesque from afar but at close range reveals crumbling walls, cracked vaults, and empty halls, often roofless and in any case unfit for habitation. I was fortunate only in the people I had met. The Russians and other Westerners were very pleasant—possibly their sense of isolation in a foreign land stimulated friendly ties among them. And some of the Persians were likable—the race certainly has a future. As in old Russia, it was not the people but their mode of life and particularly their governmental system that were obsolete and decaying.

But my main concern was not with Persia. The relations of Russia and England were of much wider importance for the East and all Europe as well. Petty quarrels about Persia endangered the balance of power.

The chief mistake of European diplomacy during the nineteenth century and up to the eve of World War I was that statesmen concentrated their attention and started wars on questions of secondary importance while neglecting the vital issues. France opposed Russia at the Berlin Congress (1878) and expressed anti-British sympathies in common with Germany during the Boer War (1899–1902), while the French frontier remained exposed to a German attack. English diplomacy was concerned with Russia's advance to Constantinople and problematic menace to India, while Germany was building a navy threatening the very existence of England.

A whole complex of diplomatic alliances had to be created along new lines if peace in Europe was to be preserved and the integrity of the territories and sanctity of the treaties successfully defended in case of war. The immediate need in 1897 was that people who knew Persia should make their voices heard in St. Petersburg and London. It took ten years till this actually happened during the stay of Sir Arthur Nicolson as British ambassador in Russia.

A steamer took me from Bendere Gaz to Petrovsk, where I boarded the Moscow express and entered the rapid stream of European life after three years of stagnation in Persia. I saw my mother and my friends in St. Petersburg—I was wild with joy. How smoothly and easily life moved along the familiar, well-laid, civilized lines. What a relief to hear and speak one's own language without worrying over the meaning of uncanny words and stupefying guttural sounds. What a pleasure to be home!

My friends welcomed me warmly but with some curiosity as a man resurrected from the dead. "Is it possible that you have really been in Persia? What is it like?" I was asked a hundred times, particularly by the ladies. I had to relate all my experiences in a land which seemed so far away that it lost its reality even for me. I was glad to be back and sad that three years seemed to have slipped out of my existence altogether.

"You don't seem eager to return to Persia," said my dear chief, N. G. Hartwig, who was now vice-director of the Asian Department. "Well, let us see. Something may turn up. You are not in a hurry to go away?"

"No, sir," I answered, with such sincerity that he smiled at me and nodded.

"Come and see me later; we may arrange something for you."

St. Petersburg looked glorious and mighty. The tsar was fortifying his new Far Eastern possessions and planning a conference on general disarmament to be held at The Hague. The Dutch, who had a large colonial dominion in the East Indies with a population of over forty million and no defenses worth speaking of, approved of the idea. The conference conformed entirely to the way of thinking of Nicholas II, who never saw the practical side of things. He was born to succeed to a throne and lived in an atmosphere of mystical grandeur. Was he not the anointed of God and was not his own orthodox faith the only true one, leading to assured success in this world and salvation in the next? This reasoning seemed perfectly logical to the tsar and was not open to question.

During the early years of his reign natural shyness had prevented the Tsar from assuming personal guidance of affairs. Nicholas II first came into view as a very polite and unassuming young man. In order to keep on his epaulets the initials of his father, "A III," he continued to wear the uniform of a colonel. St. Petersburg observed with mild amusement the shy and hesitating manner of the new sovereign.

"Well, how is our colonel?" was often heard in society circles. "Still paying court to his bride?" In fact, the death of Alexander III occurred after the bethrothal of Nicholas II, but prior to his marriage, which had to be celebrated in a hasty and unostentatious fashion. At the ball given for the occasion, the ladies, sparkling with diamonds, danced in black dresses—quite an uncommon sight.

At the council of ministers, in the chair recently occupied by the impressive bulk of the late tsar, who seemed to be cut out of a solid block of granite, now appeared the slender figure of his successor, making a rather poor show amid dissenting statesmen.

A friend of mine, the son of a high dignitary, said to me with a grin: "The minister of finance, Witte, is getting impossible. Imagine what he said to a colleague: 'How can you fail to see the point? Even the tsar understood it.' " The emperor, of course, was not present at this encounter of his advisers.

By sheer force of inertia, the Russian monarchy moved on along the lines of policy laid down by Alexander III. The young tsar was merely a successor without a personality of his own, a puppet in the hands of the old ministers.

It was the new foreign minister, Count M. N. Muraviev (1897–1900), a born courtier and flatterer, who by his adulations prompted the tsar to step forward as a world leader and to convoke The Hague Conference on General Disarmament. The next move, in complete disagreement with the conference but in conformity with the tsar's growing spirit of megalomania, was the creation of the office of viceroy of the Russian Far East and the increase of naval and military armaments on a huge scale.

One of the ways in which Count Muraviev catered to the awakened ambition of the tsar was by opening new legations in distant lands where Russia had no interest whatever, such as Abyssinia and Morocco. However, it was at the tsar's own initiative that the Foreign Office was ordered to establish a legation in Bangkok; the tsar had promised it to the king of Siam during the latter's visit to St. Petersburg. A suitable person for the post of minister was soon found, but the appointment of a secretary met with difficulties. Several young men were recommended by influential persons, and Count Muraviev, in order not to offend them, declared that he already had the right man in view and charged Hartwig to find one without delay.

I was leading a happy and carefree existence when I noticed with dismay that my leave was running out. I was afraid to go too often to the Foreign Office lest I be confronted with an order to go back to Persia. Yet I felt that something had to be done. I delicately broached the question of my transfer to Turkey, and received a very satisfactory reply with the promise of a promotion. Now I could freely visit the Asian Department, awaiting my appointment. A post in Turkey would be very satisfactory, as that country was within easy reach of Russia, and my mother could visit me there. But fate willed otherwise.

4 Siam

Spring 1898. I was walking through the narrow, dark stupendously
high-ceilinged corridor of the Russian Foreign Office in St. Petersburg when I met Hartwig, vice-director of the Asian Department,
who stopped me and asked briskly: "Would you like to go to
Bangkok?"

"Yes," I answered with the recklessness of youth. A single word,
but it sent me to the other end of the world on my first diplomatic
errand.

I came home and told the news to my mother. She did not look
happy at all; she sighed and clasped her hands together. During the
next days my head whirled. I felt that I must make some inquiries
about Siam.

The first man I came across was a young secretary of the Foreign
Office. "Siam," he exclaimed opening wide his eyes. "Oh, yes. There
are decorations there. That's important. Two of them: the Cross of
the White Elephant and the Crown of Siam." And he left me in a
hurry.

I called on the assistant chief of the Far Eastern Section. He received me rather coldly. "But it is you who are supposed to know
everything about Siam. That's why you are going to be appointed
there," he added sarcastically. "Serpent," thought I, hastily retreating.

I went straight to the office of the head of the section. He was
much more friendly and outspoken. "We know nothing about this

place," he said. "There are no files. This is the first time a legation is being sent there. We are preparing the secret instructions. There is not much in them." He shrugged his shoulders. "You have to read them, though."

I did; they were very vague. In this extremity, I entered the office of a friend.

"You ought to learn something practical about your new duties," he said. "Well, the foreign service is about the same everywhere. It is nearly twelve now. Go downstairs; there you are sure to meet some secretaries of embassy on leave. They will tell you all about it."

I rushed downstairs and entered a room where elegant young men were smoking cigarettes, some standing, some sitting unconcernedly at their desks. My appearance left them absolutely indifferent. I inquired from one of them what would be my duties in a general way in the Land of the White Elephant. That produced a slight sensation. I felt that people were listening to me without so much as turning their heads. The secretary I was addressing had just come from London.

"You will know that only on the spot, when you arrive there," he said.

"Try not to catch cholera at the same time as your chief, if you can help it," observed another. "Beware of tropical diseases."

"What are these diseases?" I asked.

A silence fell. But diplomats are not browbeaten so easily.

"Elephantiasis," said one looking triumphantly at me. "White elephantiasis," quickly retorted another. An uproar followed, and I beat a hasty retreat.

I got a book about Siam, but it dealt chiefly with the Buddhist religion; that did not seem so urgent. I felt nervous. No one in the Foreign Office showed any interest in Siam after the appointments had been settled. I had yet to meet two important persons concerned with my future activity. One of them was to be my chief in Bangkok.

I called on A. E. Olarovskii, the newly appointed minister to Siam. He had been consul general in New York and had just arrived from there. His wife was an American. He did not say much about Siam, since he was chiefly concerned with his presentation to the tsar.

The next time I saw my chief he had already been presented and was in high spirits. The tsar as Heir Apparent had visited Siam on his trip to Asia and was on very friendly terms with King Chulalongkorn.

"Dreadfully hot there," the emperor had said to Olarovskii. "Order a white uniform."

"That would be against the regulations, Your Majesty."

"Who will care about regulations down there?" said Nicholas II.

My chief left for Siam, but my appointment stuck in the bureaucratic channels, and I still sat at my desk, although everybody seemed to urge my departure. "What, you haven't left yet?" I was asked by almost everyone I happened to meet, as if my departure depended on me.

One afternoon I was sitting gloomily at my desk when an usher entered and informed me in a particularly deferential and subdued voice that the minister of foreign affairs wanted to see me immediately. We passed through large offices with shining mahogany desks, everything bright and lustrous but still looking like offices, and entered the minister's private apartment. The floors were carpeted in red, the furniture upholstered in silk—even the air I breathed seemed different.

I was ushered into a vast drawing room. A door opened and Count Muraviev walked in. He wore a black uniform with silver buttons. Uniforms were the rage at that time. The count, a middle-sized, middle-aged man with a gray moustache viewed me ironically but not in an unfriendly way. He sat down, motioned me to a seat, and started to speak. His talk was short and to the point. France, our ally, was having difficulties with Siam. It was necessary to help her settle them without endangering the independence of the Siamese kingdom or provoking the armed intervention of England. He meant: Make things better if possible but not worse on any account. In a few minutes I learned more from the minister about foreign policy than from all the libraries of the world.

"Your chief," he said, terminating his audience, "may become sick and have to leave. In that case you will be alone there. Whatever happens, you will be held responsible."

I bowed. He shook hands with me with a parting smile. I was never to see him again. He died suddenly during the Boxer uprising while I was in Siam.

En Route to Siam

My mother went with me to Sebastopol on the Black Sea, where I had to embark. It was the last I was to see of her and Russia for three long years. Parting on board a steamer is particularly distressing, much worse than at a railway station where the train moves off at once. The ship was slow to leave the quay. My mother could see me very distinctly on the deck, since there were few passengers besides myself. And I looked at her standing alone on the pier, without a single friend in the city. Our eyes remained fixed on each other till they grew dim with the distance as the ship pushed away into the foaming sea.

I was sitting sad and dejected, when I heard a friendly voice. It was Academician N. P. Kondakov, professor of the history of art at the University of St. Petersburg, on his way to Constantinople. Whatever may have been the defects of old Russia, her academicians were first-rate, and Kondakov shone among them. A man of overwhelming knowledge, he talked not only to, but with, his students. He listened to them untiringly, guiding their minds with his remarks, which were touched with a slight irony that would turn sharp as a razor blade when a student was obdurate. He used to start his lectures hesitatingly, as if undecided which point to explain first. He said he never prepared his lectures beforehand.

"Frankly, I wonder how students have the patience to listen to me," he once said laughingly. However, when launched on his subject, he was as brilliant as a rising sun, illuminating vaster and vaster horizons.

I talked to him about central Asian mosques with enormous portals and large interior courtyards, where believers assembled in the open with the sky as a dome over their heads. "A pretty image," he said, "but it won't do in a scholarly treatise." All my eloquence fell flat.

At Constantinople we visited the museum with the sarcophagus of Alexander the Great. "You see this border of vine leaves. Here art has reached the utmost limits of elegance. A step more and it would lapse into decadence and affectation."

We entered the Mosque of St. Sophia. "Look at that," he said. "Una cosa da divino [It is divine]," he added in old Italian. "There is nothing to criticize." His specialty was art in Europe, but he was conversant in all branches of his field.

"Bring some Malay krises [knives] inlaid with gold for our museum, if you happen to see some in Siam. They are of remarkable workmanship," he said.

From Constantinople I continued my voyage alone, but in Piraeus a nice Russian couple came on board.

"I like the colors of our regiment, pink and dark green, like those of a moss rose," said the lady, whose husband was a Grodno Hussar —a fine regiment of the Guards, who did not lead as fast a life as the Tsar's own Red Hussars. "All the foreigners I meet," she continued, "are pressing me with questions about the new empress. I cannot tell them she is not liked, and what else can I say?"

In Egypt I changed for a big ocean liner bound for Singapore and met a French naval captain.

"Do you know Pierre Loti?" I asked. The novelist, whose books were selling by the hundreds of thousands, was a naval officer.

"Julien Viaud, you mean?" he answered, calling the writer by his real name and not by his pseudonym. "Yes, of course. He will be put on the reserve list. It is time for him to be promoted to admiral, and this can't be done."

"Why?" I said.

"Why?" repeated the captain with astonishment. "Because it is utterly impossible. *Comment voulez-vous qu'on confie une escadre à une personne qui écrit des romans* [How can you entrust a battle squadron to a man who writes fiction]?"

I did not know what to answer. Certainly Columbus and the great admirals I had heard about had not displayed marked literary activity. But was it an insuperable obstacle to naval distinction? Caesar's books were famous and popular—not among schoolboys, of course—and yet he did command fleets. But that was so long ago. I remained silent.

After the arid sands of Suez, Ceylon brought us our first impressions of the tropics: the caress of the heavily scented air and the luxuriant expanse of flowering trees covered with pink and purple blossoms. There were too many of them, too much of everything—of color, perfumes, and strange shapes. Nature in the tropics does not give you the frank, friendly welcome of our fields and woods. It attracts, ensnares, and enslaves you, body and soul, powerfully but without violence, pleasantly but irresistibly. I enjoyed in full the charm of Ceylon. My stay was too short to affect my strength. I walked and drove, regardless of heat and sun; like all newcomers, I hardly felt them. Their poison works slowly, and its first attack is almost painless. I even took the train to Kandy, the old capital in the hills, with the Peradenia Botanical Gardens, where there are no hothouses and rare exotic plants form lofty avenues—the climax of Ceylon.

I was back in time for the steamer. Bronzed children in small boats clamored for coins and plunged after them into the transparent emerald water. One boy had a mutilated arm. I was told that it had been bitten off by a shark. Nevertheless he dived with the same gusto as the others. The tropical sea is not to be trusted in its treacherous appeal. Sharks are everywhere, and in the Indian Ocean there are poisonous sea snakes as well.

We left the calm harbor, entered a choppy sea, and doubly regretted leaving Ceylon.

Our next stop was Singapore. A Malay coachman took possession of me and all my belongings and drove rapidly away from the ocean liner, my last link with Europe. I was swallowed by the East.

The driver took me to the Raffles Hotel, the best at that time. It is not named for its owner but for the founder of Singapore, who turned a small, swampy island into a beautiful city and the tenth port of the world. Singapore is the gateway to the Far East, and a very attractive one. The city is clean, civilized, colorful, and hospitable. There is no red tape and never was. Raffles did not tolerate it, which accounted for the success of his colony and created a precedent for the other English settlements in the Far East. All are free to live and trade. There is, or at least there was, no "protection" —an odious term that designates prohibitive customs duties. Gratitude to Raffles is expressed in all sorts of ways—even a creeper, a parasite that grows on the Malaya vine and has ill-smelling flowers and no leaves, is called "Rafflesia" in his honor. Surely the great governor deserved a better plant.

I took a suite in the hotel. As a matter of fact I was already home, since I had reached the tropics and Bangkok was close by. But what a new and strange home it was!

In front of the porch of the hotel stood Ravenala palms, each with all its leaves spread fanwise on its top. It seemed absurd that a tree should look like that. I felt inclined to turn my back on it and say "There ain't no such thing," like the farmer who saw a giraffe in the zoo for the first time. But finally I became reconciled to this very decorative though unusual shape.

"Queer, isn't it?" I thought. "Well, let it be as it is. Don't pretend to impress me, stupid thing. I can be just as tropical as you are." To prove the point I dressed all in white, shoes and sun helmet included, and walked bravely into the blazing street.

"Don't overdo it," said the consul, who had an apartment in the same hotel. "Keep in the shade, or you'll regret it later."

In the shade! As if there was any shade, with the sun staying at the zenith! And besides, I had so many things to see and to do. I had to buy rattan chairs and sofas for my house in Bangkok—upholstered furniture was much too warm—and order a number of white suits, since they look smart and clean for a very short time only. The chief inconvenience in the tropics is a kind of double perspiration—one is your own and the other comes from outside, from the moist air.

"You'll get sunburned if you expose your wet skin," said the consul, as if I had a single dry spot on me.

I went to the bazaar and saw people of all colors, dressed in all sorts of clothes except European ones. In a narrow street there were cages with parrots, called *loris,* delightful little pets with feathers of wonderful hues. These birds were much too delicate to be brought to our cold climate. I entered a small passage, and a long muscular arm covered with red hair threateningly stretched toward me from a cage. I saw a big female orang, her eyes blazing with fury and despair. With her other arm she pressed to her breast a small, innocent-looking baby orang. She drew back her arm and looked at me with misery and anguish. She certainly seemed more human than the girl on the steamer who had screamed at a little seasick boy: "Get out of my way, you dirty little thing!"

I was in rapture with Singapore. "What a beautiful gulf," I said to the consul, "with all these islands looking like baskets of fresh verdure."

"Don't go there," the consul warned me. "They are batteries masked with creepers. Singapore is a fortress."

I was sorry to leave, but a cable had already been sent to Bangkok, and, moreover, I was burning with the desire to see Siam, now so close.

Bangkok

I left Singapore on a small steamer with a single passenger beside myself, and a very silent one at that. My sense of loneliness was increased by a deserted sea. We were outside the main ocean traffic. Siam's isolation was the principal reason for its survival. Concealed in the interior of the gulf that bears its name, the country long kept its independence intact.

England and France, pressing on both sides from British Burma and French Indo-China, finally joined their frontiers in the north, completely enclosing Siam on land. The sea remained its only outlet. I knew that the country was defenseless and that its collapse could produce a violent collision between its two neighbors. Interference by Germany was also possible, and she had already outdistanced us in sending a legation to Bangkok. Are we too late in coming, I asked myself, and shall we be hopelessly entangled in an impending disintegration? Our relations with England were bad enough. Shall we embitter our relations with a friendly France and have to make an ignominious retreat, leaving Siam in the throes of a foreign invasion and the interior disorders inevitable in the collapse of a state? I looked at the sea, baffled, but it gave no answer.

The ship seemed to make no progress at all; her old engine throbbing, she remained in the center of a vast expanse of water which always looked the same. The elusive country appeared to recede before us. I began to doubt the very existence of Siam as day after day passed and no land came into view.

But there it was at last, all around us. We were steaming up a large, muddy river—the Menam—both its shores covered with dense vegetation. Palms were waving their feathery leaves. Long spikes appeared above the trees. Pagan temples with high roofs and gables curved like horns stood in the clearings. Brown men in light canoes swayed in the swell left in the wake of our ship. Then came rice mills and piles of teak, the standard exports of Siam. Shores were crowded with floating houses, the favorite dwellings of the Siamese. At last big stone buildings came into view—banks, stores, hotels—indicating the presence of a large city. I heard the bell of an electric tram running up the main street. Our ship was moored; my chief stood on the landing waving his sun helmet. I was in Bangkok.

Olarovskii welcomed me heartily. We drove through the European quarter, clean and neat, with houses surrounded by gardens, then along a crowded street leading through the Chinese town full of offensive smells, until we passed a gate in a low, thick wall, the entrance to the Siamese or Royal City. We turned to the left and stopped before the porch of a white, two-storied building with a lawn descending to the river and a tall flagpole flying the Russian flag. It was the legation.

Two long bungalows flanked the lawn, one on each side: the office and the secretary's house, which was to be my home. Olarovskii conducted me there. It was quite bare. Lizards, unavoidable roommates in Siam, ran up the walls and looked at us. The windows were without panes, which are useless in the tropics, but had shutters for protection against rain and sun. The inspection finished, my chief took

me to the veranda of the legation and said: "We shall make the
necessary visits tomorrow. Now let's have a talk."

He stated the situation. The colonial expansion of the European
powers in Asia was reaching its limits. England and France were unable to come to terms on how to divide Siam. A peaceful settlement
was in the interest of both countries, but excited national sentiment
was against it.

My chief stopped. On the river passed a procession of long canoes
with high prows shaped like snake heads. Siamese walked in the
street, men and women alike wearing *panungs* (which may be called
skirts for lack of a better word). I felt hot and very uncomfortable;
my shirt became sticky, my collar was melting, a moist spot appeared
on my jacket between my shoulder blades, and Olarovskii resumed
his talk.

The present frontiers of France and England with Siam were
politically safe and economically sound, but that did not seem
enough to the colonial powers. In this conflict of the mighty the
voice of the intended victim was yet to be heard. There were still a
king and a government in Siam, which meant a mind, a will, and a
responsibility. What was their line of conduct? What kind of men
were ruling the country? Were they capable of making a decision at
a crucial moment?

My chief looked at me, waiting for an answer, but I could give
him none. I sat bewildered by what I had heard and by all that was
going on around me. Here we were alone in the middle of Bangkok,
a strange, exotic place. Opposite us a Buddhist temple loomed high
above unknown trees. Back of us stretched a crenellated wall with an
old round tower, which probably had seen combats with arrows flying and spears and swords clashing on helmets and shields. Farther
down could be seen masts with foreign flags and white gunboats with
cannon and sailors. What could I say?

Since no reply came from me, Olarovskii wiped his forehead,
looked around, and said in his usual calm voice: "Boy, bring us
cocktails."

That was the end of the conference. The affairs of state were bad,
my house lacked everything, and only the official visits could be
made at once. But Olarovskii looked cheerful and practical, and I
felt that I had to be the same.

Making Calls in Bangkok

We started our visits the next morning. The Foreign Office was located inside the palace enclosure. Large green lawns stretched to its white wall, crowned with the oval merlons of Siamese fortifications. Above them rose the horned roofs of green and orange tiles and the fantastic spires and cones of the palace buildings and temples. The royal residence looked like a fairy castle, something like the Moscow Kremlin but more ornate, lighter, and more aerial.

I was distracted by all this oriental magnificence, and wondered how we could discuss serious matters among such theatrical surroundings. But the Foreign Office proved to be a European building, and it was with a sense of relief that I entered a large room with solid and severe English furniture.

We were greeted by a small man with a full face, a high forehead, and intelligent eyes. It was the foreign minister, Prince Devawongse. Olarovskii presented me and immediately broached the question of the pending commercial treaty. Our task was simple. We had to negotiate a trade convention, the first treaty between Russia and Siam, on the basis of the most-favored-nation clause. This meant that any new privilege granted by Siam to another state would be automatically extended to Russia and reciprocally by Russia to Siam. The most-favored-nation clause was universally accepted at that time. It was abandoned after World War I and became equally universally abhorred.

The prince exchanged phrases with Olarovskii without saying anything definite, then developed a sudden interest in me. As I was to learn later, Devawongse was a past master at turning from a serious subject to some trifling matter, and he never gave an answer at once. His policy was to gain time. He knew how to talk and write much and say little. His attitude was always defensive, and he failed to take the initiative at the opportune moment. In short he was temporizing, and the ground was slipping from under his feet.

He seemed to be enchanted to see me and fired the usual volley of questions—whether I had had a good voyage, whether I liked Bangkok, and so forth—each question to be answered in the affirmative. My answers seemed to meet the approval of the Siamese minister, who swayed in his chair and laughed louder and louder till I was stunned with this outbreak of hilarity. Then he suddenly became serious, assumed a countenance of respectful reserve, and informed my chief that the king was to attend in person the coming religious festivity in the big *vat* (temple) on the other side of the river and that I could be presented to His Majesty there. Having delivered this statement, the prince rolled in his chair in a new fit of merriment, intimating that he had nothing more to say.

I met the other ministers. They were all of royal blood at that time. With a single exception they had all visited Europe and spoke English fluently. The exception was the minister of the navy, Prince Prap Parapak, a delightful old Siamese and a mighty elephant hunter, about whom more will be said later. But in the last resort everything depended on the king, and I had not seen him yet.

We called on the French and English ministers, who were career diplomats, firmly set on an established line. The American minister, Hamilton King, had been a college president and enjoyed his new experience in the diplomatic field.

The German minister, Herr von Saldern, was a Prussian Junker of the old stock. He had been consul general in Stockholm, where he was slighted by his legation, as is often the case with consuls. This he would not tolerate. In his study he had an engraving representing his great grandfather seated paralyzed in an armchair, with Frederick the Great standing before him, holding his weak, loyal hand. A Saldern could not be snubbed. He complained to Prince von Bülow. The memory of Frederick II still worked after a hundred years, and Herr von Saldern was sent as minister to Bangkok.

At the first reception in Siam he appeared in the uniform of a Prussian lieutenant of uhlans. The uniform was tight and the heat stupefying. At the next reception Herr von Saldern wore an ample, open, embroidered diplomatic coat and beamed with relief.

When I dined with him, soup was served in ancient pewter plates, a substitute for silver, which was not common among the Prussian gentry living on lands chiefly productive of sand and pine trees.

The minister and his colony were active. A German shipping line was established between Singapore, Siam, and Hong Kong in China. The British paper in Bangkok tried to put a good face on this ominous venture. The Germans talked about the Netherlands Indies. "What rich lands," they said, "which could be still richer, if . . ." The rest remained unsaid.

In the meantime I provided myself with all the necessities, comforts, amenities, superfluities, and vanities of European life in tropical Asia: electric lights, *punkahs* (fans), mosquito netting, and so on. A cook, a coolie, a boy, and a coachman formed my household, all speaking different languages and belonging to different races. Everything was fine, but what heat! The air I inhaled seemed to be composed of vapor alone.

"Hot, isn't it?" said Olarovskii. "Have a cocktail." That was his usual manner of meeting any untoward occurrence. "That's better," he would say.

I would feel better indeed. And besides, had I not given my word to Hartwig that I would stick to Bangkok, whatever it was like?

"This heat is awful," said Mrs. Olarovskaia.

"My dear," answered her husband, "I cannot change the climate of Siam. Have you seen your dressmaker?"

"Well, no. I must speak to her at once." And out she went.

"That's the way," said my chief. "Have another?"

"No thanks." I had not had his experience of New York clubs in the early nineties when people made great fortunes and led hardy lives.

Olarovskii had spent half his life in the United States as consul general in San Francisco and New York, had married an American, spoke English at home with the members of his family, was thoroughly Americanized in his habits of life, and yet at the same time retained a purely Russian character. Short, powerfully built, jovial, expansive, and hospitable, he was fond of hard work, poker, company, and good food. He took charge of the culinary matters of his household, and every day he gave his cook the most detailed instructions. He liked and knew horses and drove his break himself. He was embarrassingly frank, openly anti-English, but notwithstanding was popular in the English colony. Altogether he was an extremely likeable man and a very sensible diplomat, active and resourceful.

I remember hearing that during the Boer War Olarovskii met an English friend at his club. The Englishman had exclaimed excitedly, "Fatal news! General Butler had a reverse and lost some of his guns."

"Why fatal?" came the reply. "Excellent, on the contrary. It depends on the point of view." The Englishman was aghast, but it was impossible to be cross with Olarovskii for any length of time.

The American minister, Hamilton King, a very strict man, offered his first dinner without wine. Olarovskii objected jokingly. Drinks were brought and placed on a separate table behind a screen, to which the men disappeared. But then the ladies protested, and

Olarovskii supported them. Finally wines were brought to the dinner table, to the satisfaction of all.

Olarovskii had a habit of appearing on the lawn of our garden hatless, his bald head shining in the full midday sun—a very dangerous practice in the tropics. His wife, his daughter, and I would run after him with sun helmets, but he would escape into the house and wave to us from an upper story window. There was a special Providence for him.

King Chulalongkorn was enormously amused by Olarovskii, appreciated his solid qualities, and treated him as a trusted friend. Olarovskii clearly stated to him that his government must stop having difficulties with France, even at a price. The king agreed. In 1893 French gunboats had come to Bangkok and threatened the city. English opinion was excited against France. A clash about Siam could bring a crisis in Europe. France had recalled her gunboats, but left a garrison in the town of Chantaboon on the eastern coast of the Gulf of Siam.

Some of the Siamese statesmen were in favor of accepting an English protectorate. But another party raised the objection that this would not be a solution, as France would claim a large portion of Siamese territory, and the partition of Siam would bring not only a loss of independence but also the total disintegration of the country.

Soon after his arrival, Olarovskii proposed the cession to France of a piece of territory in the extreme northeast of Siam as a compensation for the evacuation of Chantaboon. The offer was actually made by the Siamese government in 1898 but was rejected by the French legation.

King Chulalongkorn

I was anxious to see the king. It was he who had brought us to Siam by asking the tsar to send a legation to Bangkok. I knew that the king was in earnest when he made this request. He had already toured all the capitals of Europe, and several new legations had recently been opened in Bangkok. They had greatly enhanced the international prestige of Siam but were not enough to assure the safety of the country. Being mere observation posts, they took no part in the march of events, giving a free hand to French and English rivalry.

The British legation was quiet but stood firmly entrenched, gradually introducing English advisers to the Siamese ministers. The head of the police force in Bangkok was a British officer. The French legation resented the rise of English influence, as France was far from friendly with England at that time and was cool to the Siamese authorities. The German legation was not much of an aid to peace. A conflict between France and England would suit the kaiser, and King Chulalongkorn soon realized this.

But what did he expect from us? We were the allies of France and had not come to oppose her interests. At that very time the French were increasing their demands, and the king was resisting them. A mass of inflammable material was accumulating at the Siamese Foreign Office and at the French legation. The king knew that a spark might be enough to consume him and his kingdom. Where was he heading?

On the morning of the day appointed for the festivity at which I was to be presented to the king, a Siamese steamer took us to the landing of the temple. No other passengers were on board, and no invitations had been issued to the diplomatic body, the ceremony being strictly religious. But the news that the Russian minister was to be present leaked out. I presume it was Olarovskii, who, with his usual loquacity, was the cause of it. Be that as it may, the British and French ministers also came in their steam launches, along with quite a number of French naval officers. My presentation, so well conceived by Prince Devawongse, became much more complicated than was intended.

We were informed that we would have to wait until the function inside the temple was over. The interior of Siamese temples is always very small, and there was no room for so many foreigners. To increase the confusion, it began to drizzle, and there were several short but violent downpours. We could not be presented during a torrential rain and had to wait again. On the other hand, it was necessary to complete the ceremony in order to release the Buddhist priests, as they could not eat after twelve o'clock and would have to stay hungry till the next day. It was already past eleven.

In an interval between the showers we were hastily summoned. We proceeded up an avenue of magnificent trees, unfortunately dripping water on our heads, and reached the entrance of the sacred enclosure. On each side of the gate stood an enormous enameled statue of a guardian demon; they certainly could not be called angels, with their distorted features, bloodthirsty eyes, and open mouths with protruding fangs. We looked with amazement at the monsters standing before the abode of the calm, divinely merciful Buddha.

We entered a paved courtyard. The doors of the temple were still closed; from inside came a slow and melodious chanting. The crowd of people in the courtyard made way for us, and we were conducted to reserved seats. Shortly the sky darkened, thunder rumbled, and rain poured down on us. We relinquished our places of honor and sought refuge under the porch of the temple.

The Siamese did not seem to mind the rain. The bearer of the royal umbrella, a glorious thing of gold and red brocade, proudly stood defying the elements and holding straight his emblem indicating the presence of the monarch. We waited, wet and depressed. Even Olarovskii, the most talkative man I ever met, remained silent.

Then the sun came out again, drops of water glistened, the heavy doors slowly opened, and the whole pageant of Siam presented itself to our eyes. The interior of the temple was visible, with its lights, the little spirals of smoke from the burning sticks of scented wood, the clean-shaven Buddhist clergy in their yellow robes, the mass of uniforms of the Siamese officials. A general in white colonial drill strode toward us, a very handsome man of about forty, with a straightforward look in his black eyes. He was not tall, but he was well shaped and wore his military uniform of European pattern extremely well. It was Chulalongkorn.

For all his composure, the king was visibly annoyed when he saw our drenched state, and he shortened his talk with us. He asked me about the health of the tsar and when I had left St. Petersburg. As I answered him, I felt that I looked as if I had swum the entire distance from Russia to Bangkok. The king departed, and we rushed after him to the steamer, home, and dry clothes.

An Evening Reception at the Palace

I was not at all pleased with our presentation and with the whole proceeding. I had the impression that it was a failure, and partly by our fault. Certainly if we had come alone, some place in the temple would have been found for us, and we would have seen more of the ceremony and the sovereign. Mrs. Olarovskaia was of the same opinion.

"There will be another reception at the palace next week," said Olarovskii, who never lost his countenance for long. "Let us finish our mail. Mother, shall we have fish for dinner today?"

By contrast, at the next audience everything went without a hitch. There were showers during the day, but they stopped before the reception, which was to take place in the evening. The steps were already dry when we mounted the royal staircase leading from the court of honor to the first floor of the palace. Like all noble stones, marble may be wet but is never damp—water cannot penetrate its polished surface.

The reception was the largest of its kind I ever saw in Siam. Malay rajas and representatives of other vassal states were summoned and stood along the left wall of the throne room. Opposite them and aligned on the right side were the diplomats and the members of the European colony. Down the center was an open aisle leading to the throne at the far end. The great white hall was ablaze with electric light. We took our designated places and waited. The hall was full and silent like a church.

A chamberlain struck the pavement with his ebony staff; a closed door was thrown wide open, and the king entered and bowed. The men returned his bow, and the ladies curtsied; the reception had begun.

The king approached the diplomats first, stopped before each of them, extended his hand, and said a few words. He was sparing with his words but never short of them. His manner was simple but regal; he was every inch a sovereign. The king moved calmly, looked directly at the person with whom he was speaking, and listened attentively. Sometimes a slight smile seemed to flash in his eyes rather than on his lips. All was still in the large hall, and only one voice was heard at a time.

My chief became nervous with heat, expectation, and forced immobility. His neck reddened above the silver-embroidered collar of his uniform. The king saw this and, it seemed to me, purposely lengthened his conversation with the person next to us. Then, as if nothing had happened, he turned to my minister with a cordial welcome: "How are you, sir? Glad to see you, Mr. Olarovskii." The king pronounced the difficult syllables of the Russian names very carefully and never made mistakes. The sovereign spoke at length, calmly and amiably, with the Russian minister and his wife. Fortunately His Majesty used English, as Mrs. Olarovskaia's attempts to speak French were far from successful. The king pressed my hand and moved on.

It took a long time for the sovereign to make the tour of the hall.

He did not look tired, but I wondered how he felt after conversing
with nearly a hundred people. Presently we were invited to another
room for refreshments. The king had vanished. We were glad to
move and speak freely. After a while I saw the king again. He was
sitting in an armchair, resting, in a remote drawing room, talking
with a young prince who stood before him.

The queen made her appearance later. She was dressed in the
Siamese fashion, which is very much alike for men and women. She
wore a white jacket and a silk panung, like all the ladies of the upper class in Siam, but with a wealth of lace and diamonds. The big
sapphire presented to her by the tsar shone among her jewels. She
was in the happy period between unripe youth and mature age. Her
black hair was cut short the Siamese way, she had beautiful eyes,
and her manners were easy and dignified. She stopped to talk with
Mrs. Hamilton King, the wife of the American minister, and with
other ladies, offered her hand to be kissed by the men, and moved
on.

People felt extremely hot as they strolled through the rooms seek-
ing a breath of air. Olarovskii and Hamilton King stood at the entrance of the hall, talking. The king laughed as he passed them.
"You chose the coolest place. There is a draft here," he said. Again
the bang of the chamberlain's staff. The reception was over.

As we recovered our freedom and hastened into the open air, I
thought about this man who had kept us so long and who evidently
was glad himself that the ceremony was over. This stately, well-
shaped, intelligent Siamese, who wore the insignia of the commander in chief of an army that was practically nonexistent in the
European military sense and held unlimited power over a totally
defenseless nation, had to withstand the impact of the two greatest
colonial powers. The diplomatic body, who on state occasions assembled before his throne in the brilliantly lighted palace, was all
that stood between him and impending destruction.

Two powerful statesmen—Lord Curzon, viceroy of India, and
Paul Doumer, governor-general of French Indo-China, the future
president of France—were facing each other and moving toward a
collision. What would become of Siam, caught between them, and
what would be the effect on the great powers themselves as they
crashed together? The Siamese foreign minister, Prince Devawongse,
was content to let things drift, as they did, but the king thought
differently. A much stronger man, he clung to his independence,

although he saw the increasing menace of the situation. In a moment of despondency he said to Olarovskii: "There is no way out. I hope that the tsar will give me a refuge in his dominions so that I can finish my last days there." Even my chief, who at fifty was as cheerful as an American boy of fifteen, came from the audience depressed. He discussed the situation with me.

"There is nothing we can do. . . . Have a cocktail, or rather, let us have a bottle of mineral water." A bad sign. We took the Vichy in silence. Then his ingenious mind started to work again.

"Prince Devawongse . . . No, nothing to hope for in Siamese diplomacy. The French legation . . . No, too deeply set on old lines. I have had my experience with diplomats. Let us try something else. . . . After all, this is purely a question of colonial policy. That's it. What do you think are the ideas of the governor of the French colonies in Indo-China?"

I made a gesture of complete ignorance.

"But he must have an opinion. In fact, it is he who would become immediately involved if something happened here."

"I suppose so, but . . . " I stopped short.

"All right, I see. The only thing to do is to have a Siamese goodwill embassy sent to Doumer to invite him to come here and have a talk with the king. Yes . . . It will be hard . . . But we cannot sit here doing nothing till Bangkok goes ablaze."

The last argument was decisive, and my chief started to work.

Paul Doumer, Governor-General of French Indo-China

The sending of a Siamese embassy to Saigon was approved by the king, but there was still the question of how this embassy would be received by Doumer. If he declined to come to Bangkok, the situation would be made worse. We could not incur such a risk without being informed of the attitude of Saigon. We lacked this information and could not get it in Bangkok. We ran into an impasse.

A solution came by mere chance. The health of Mrs. Olarovskaia was poor, and the doctor said that a change was necessary—a sea trip to Java or Saigon would do her good.

"Saigon?" said Olarovskii. "All right."

"But I do not speak French," exclaimed his wife.

"Never mind," replied my chief and remained thoughtful. Then he turned to me and added: "That would be an occasion for you to go also."

Olarovskii was a man of ideas. To see Doumer before the arrival of the Siamese embassy was just what we needed.

I felt that it was my duty to go to Saigon, according to Olarovskii's suggestion, although this placed a great responsibility on me. I knew that if I remained in Bangkok, the embassy would almost certainly fail. Doumer would welcome it with the usual French politeness, would telegraph to Paris for instructions, and would probably be told to wait for the return of the French minister to Bangkok, who was on leave and not expected back for months. Doumer would consequently give a noncommittal reply to the Siamese, and the whole thing would fall through. And Doumer would not have been able to act differently.

It was necessary that he telegraph to Paris at once his firm resolution to accept the invitation. For that he needed a definite assurance that the Siamese were ready to be friendly and meant business. He also had to be sure that the reception would be thoroughly satisfactory to him. And he lacked certainty on both these points.

My presence in Saigon would change the situation. The arrival of a member of the Russian legation in Siam, coinciding with the sudden appearance of a Siamese embassy, could hardly be considered fortuitous and in any case would offer a serious guarantee, not to be rejected without careful consideration by a daring and resolute man.

Our party, consisting of Mrs. Olarovskaia, her daughter, a governess, and myself, sailed on a small steamer and in a few days arrived at Saigon, which had been advised of our departure by the French legation. Two aides met us and accompanied us to Government House. We entered the hall. Paul Doumer stood before us, an extremely good-looking man of about forty, with a commanding expression in his black eyes, crisp hair, and impressive manners. I never saw a more handsome and efficient Frenchman. His later photographs do not convey the impression of extreme vitality which was so striking when I saw him in his prime. He did not speak fast, as most Frenchmen do, but very distinctly, enunciating every word clearly and precisely, using his beautiful voice to full advantage. His movements, on the contrary, were quick, although elegant and dignified. A man without haste, but with no time to lose. He invited us to stay in his palace. A moment, and he was gone.

As I learned later, he habitually left town at about four and went to Cape St. Jacques, where his family lived in a villa high up in the hills. He was very regular in his habits, and when he saw that he might be obliged to dine with Mrs. Olarovskaia and miss spending the evening with his family, he quickly closed his office and escaped on a steam launch.

We stayed a day or two in the empty magnificence of his palace and then also moved to Cape St. Jacques, where there was a very comfortable hotel. Mrs. Olarovskaia started her cure of fresh air and sea bathing, both excellent in this resort. I went with her to call on Mme Doumer, a kind lady devoted to her home, who did not speak English, and again I saw her husband, a fascinating personality of a type entirely new to me. Whether it is common in France or not I cannot say, but, as far as I know, it has never been portrayed in French novels.

An ordinary Frenchman likes to sit in cafés, to take aperitifs, mostly absinthe, to discuss actresses and other females in a rather joking way; in a word, to treat everything outside of his work in an unconcerned, light-minded manner. French families are usually small; boys are emancipated early and left free to sow their wild oats. Parents are concerned chiefly with paying their offspring's debts. I am speaking, of course, of France at the turn of the century.

Doumer was different. He himself supervised the education of his boys, four of whom were killed during World War I. Starting in very modest circumstances, he had moved forward rapidly. His fields were politics and finance. Still young, he became minister of finance and entered the small circle of men who held in turn the portfolio of finance, passing it to one another with the change of cabinets. They were all controlled by the Bank of France, which was then in the hands of an equally restricted, even hereditary, oligarchy. The bank was considered by most a bulwark of strength, but by some a cause of stagnation and an impediment to progress, a matter of much disputed opinion. Doumer was a radical, belonging to a party now staunchly conservative, but which was considered leftist in the nineties. A cabinet fell, and Doumer was offered the post of governor-general in Indochina, as some people said, to keep him out of Paris.

I could not be the first to speak of the Siamese embassy and had to wait until the news of its departure for Saigon produced the expected effect. Time passed. I knew that Prince Prap, minister of the navy, was keeping a gunboat under steam and that Prince Damrong, minister of the interior, had offered his assistant as ambassador; yet the embassy did not leave Bangkok. To distract myself, I walked in the palm forests and plunged into the glorious surf of the Pacific.

Then one morning I saw a Siamese man-of-war in front of our hotel. The envoy, vice-minister of the interior, was on board. There was not a single diplomat for hundreds of miles around, except myself, who kept quiet in the hotel. That day I was called to see Doumer. I entered his study. Doumer looked at me. "A Siamese embassy is coming," he said. "What does it mean? Do you know?"

"The Siamese are good neighbors," I answered, "and they want to be friendly with France."

Doumer asked me a few more questions, then fell silent. "I'll have to telegraph the minister of colonies," he said slowly. A pause. "But he won't refuse," he added with a flash in his eyes.

That ended the conversation. I still felt my heart throbbing, but there was no longer any reason for it.

In the afternoon I had a telephone call from Doumer's office. "What kind of reception would be given to us in Bangkog?"

"The same as for Prince Henry, the brother of the German emperor."

Down went the receiver. The invitation was accepted.

Mrs. Olarovskaia finished her cure, and we all left for Bangkok. As a memento of her stay in Indo-China she received a decoration from the emperor of Annam (now South Vietnam), a vassal state of France. The accompanying scroll said in translation that she was rewarded for her piety to the souls of her departed ancestors, her perfect obedience to her husband, and her exceptional skill at weaving silk tissues.

"My goodness, if I ever . . . " said Mrs. Olarovskaia, and she remained pensive. Was my chief's American-born wife thinking of the spinning wheels of colonial times? Many American families treasure ancestral relics, and memories of old traditions haunt the few remaining houses of colonial times.

High Visitors

I was back in Siam with the family of my minister. The die was cast. There was nothing to do except wait and see. No news from Paris and London—the best news possible. The date of Doumer's arrival was announced officially. Still all remained quiet in the political spheres.

The French squadron anchored before the estuary of the Menam, too shallow for big ships. Bangkok assumed a festive appearance, with French and Siamese flags decorating the streets. A yacht brought the governor-general to the landing, and he drove in state escorted by the royal bodyguard. I called on him. He smiled as he saw my Russian diplomatic uniform. I was no longer a globetrotter, visiting Saigon. Doumer told me that he was impressed by the large diplomatic body in Siam, especially by the presence of the Russian and American ministers.

Diplomats are lacking in European colonies, where native princes are controlled by the colonial governor, and where Western civilization is imposed and not voluntarily accepted. King Chulalongkorn decided to establish direct contact with the heads of the European nations, visited the capitals of Europe, and opened Siamese legations in politically important centers. As a result, the establishment of Japanese, German, Russian, and Italian legations followed in quick succession. The American, British, and French legations were already in Bangkok.

The "Marseillaise" was sounded as Doumer ascended the steps of the palace. The meeting with King Chulalongkorn was very cordial. In the evening a dinner was given at the Foreign Office. All the diplomats were present when Doumer rose and proposed the health of the king and queen of Siam. Devawongse answered the toast. The basis of an accord was laid. The rest was to be settled in Paris and Bangkok through diplomatic channels, a complicated but chiefly routine task.

It was my happiest day in Siam when the French statesman entered our legation the next morning and shook hands with Olarovskii. What more could Count Muraviev have asked from us? The Siamese were amazed. How little is needed to make peace, though even less to start war. A brilliant reception took place in the palace halls. Doumer sat next to the king, while Siamese dancers in gorgeous brocade, with pointed golden tiaras on their heads, performed the sacred ballet, thousands of years old, which heavenly beings dance before the gods on the sculptures of the great temple of Angkor. Musicians, seated on the floor, played on strange instruments like those represented on Buddhist bas-reliefs dating from before

Christ. In a symbolic dance at the end of the performance, French and Siamese flags were waved and united by a garland of flowers. It seemed as if Buddha himself had granted a new lease of life to his faithful people.

After the departure of Doumer, the reaction of England was expressed by the sending of her Far Eastern squadron under Admiral Sir Beauchamp Seymour, a display of her naval strength without any political pressure. A dinner in his honor was given on board the cruiser *Mahachacri,* the largest ship in the Siamese navy.

I noticed that the British naval officers wore beards like the Admiral himself or were clean-shaven like his flag-captain, Sir David Beatty, who later fought the Battle of Jutland. The German kaiser, when he put on his uniform of honorary English admiral, thought that he looked every inch a British seaman, although with his prominent moustache and shaven chin he was breaking a cherished tradition of the British navy. A sailor must be clean-shaven like King George VI or have both beard and moustache like his late father.

It was cool on board ship, but the city was growing hotter every day. When Tsar Nicholas II came to Siam as Heir Apparent, he suffered so much from the heat in his tight military uniform that one of his first questions to the king was "Haven't you a cooler place in Siam than Bangkok?" They went to Ayuthia, and the tsar spent most of the time there in his shirtsleeves, as the king told us once, laughing. Ayuthia, the old capital up the Menam, served as a summer residence and a meeting place for the elephant hunt.

I saw the gardens there during a night entertainment arranged for the count of Turin, a cousin of the king of Italy. It was already dark when our special train arrived at Ayuthia. The road to the palace and gardens was illuminated. Music was playing everywhere. Choirs were singing among the flowering bushes. We were conducted to a brightly lighted shooting gallery. The Italian prince took careful aim and fired. A Siamese girl ran to the stand and back and presented him with a garland of flowers and a silver bowl of Siamese work as a prize for his markmanship.

We moved further on. On an open place a tree was lighted and adorned like a Christmas tree. We were invited to take souvenirs from it. I plucked something, as the king was passing by. "What did you get?" asked His Majesty. "Show it to me." It was only a cracker. "Take something else," said the king and walked on. But I was too embarrassed to try my luck again.

Diplomats were talking under a jasmine tree about a Central American republic which had flourished for thirty years under the same president. A diplomat compared it to other states and said: "Nothing like a strong hand to keep a democracy going."

"You call it a democracy?" someone asked. A polite silence.

"What have you there on your shoulder?" It was a beautiful cicada with iridescent wings of red and green, which looked like a jewel.

"Oh, it is nothing. The other day a cobra was found in our living room."

"Not a daily occurrence?" asked a newcomer.

"No, it is rather rare."

Fireworks blazed on the velvety sky. Hundreds of lights were reflected on the surface of the large pond in front of the palace. A marble pavilion shone white above dark waters. We were offered wreaths of scented flowers. They looked pretty on the black evening clothes. Finally the band played the Siamese anthem, which meant it was time to leave.

We felt tired as we sat in the railway car, full of the heavy aroma of the flower wreaths. The train raced without stopping through the tropical night till we reached the station in Bangkok. Policemen ran to wake our sleepy coachmen, and we drove home through streets which seemed strangely silent after the enchanted vision of Ayuthia.

The next morning I was again in my office resuming my daily work, but its monotony was interrupted by the strange life around me. One morning in a suburb peopled by Hindus I saw boys, smeared with black, celebrating a holiday in honor of God Krishna, the Dark. The boys were from Madras, and as I had no idea of south Indian dialects the following verses must be accepted as poetical fiction without any relation to reality but one of chance:

> The girl singing:
>   Take the calf and bring the cow.
>   Give us milk; we need it now.
> The boy prancing:
>   "Take the broom and sweep the house,
>   Bring the cat and catch the mouse,
>   Wash your hands and bring some water,"
>   Said the mother to the daughter.

Prince Prap Parapak and the Elephant Hunt

One morning I had started to write a commercial report suggesting the development of Russian trade with Siam, nonexistent as yet, and had run short of facts and ideas. I continued to sit in the office in the state of prostration recommended by Buddhist teaching but without the required concentration of thought.

The office was located in a lofty bungalow without a ceiling. It was almost dark under the roof, but the sun glared through the open door to the veranda and was painful to the eyes. I had just closed them when I heard a slight, dull sound and saw a thin green coil wriggling on the floor not far from my feet. It was a house snake, a harmless creature which had fallen from the roof beam and broken its spine. A servant carried it outside, where it had to wait for a new avatar (reincarnation), since the Buddhist religion grants immortality to all living beings without discrimination. I made sure that there were no crossbeams above my head and resumed my immobility.

But my slumber was gone. My senses became acutely awake. After a while I seemed to perceive a shuffling of bare feet. The sound was approaching, became distinct, and a shadow fell before my door. I lifted my head; a young Buddhist priest was standing at the entrance.

He looked like a nobleman. All priests try to look dignified in their own way; it is part of their profession. But the Buddhist priests are particularly striking. The young man before me had his head and eyebrows shaven; only his eyelashes were spared. He was clad in a yellow garment of antique style. With a graceful move of his hand he invited me to give him an offering—a highly meritorious act, according to Buddhist tenets. I gave him a silver coin, a *tical*. With a rapid motion he threw a flap of his mantle over his extended right palm, and the coin disappeared into its folds. A priest cannot receive money in his naked hand. A nod of acknowledgment, and he walked away with the dignity of a Roman senator.

I was filled with admiration for his poise, which I could never equal. We always look stiff and pompous in our tight official clothes. Dignity requires a certain expansion of the wearing apparel. That is why priests, university professors, and judges wear wide ceremonial gowns. And besides, priests have a certain impressive way of doing things. They always make you feel you are their inferior.

"Hello," said Olarovskii, appearing in the office. "The king has ordered an elephant hunt. Let's go and see Prince Prap, who will be in charge of it." The aged but sturdy Prince Prap Parapak personified for me the old Siam. He was our oldest and staunchest friend, but he was not very easily approached. The first thing he did when we met him was to expectorate all the betal he was chewing. Even then he was not ready for a talk. This required the presence of a trusted interpreter, as the old man spoke no language but his own and did not mince words.

Pending the arrival of the interpreter, delicate yellow tea was served in Chinese cups. Prince Prap was very simple in his tastes, but if he cared for anything he knew how to get the best. He lived in a small house on the shore of the Menam, next to the palace and opposite the naval arsenal on the other side of the river, which was his stronghold as secretary of the navy.

Like all Siamese, Prince Prap disliked the sea intensely and had never been on the ocean, but he took his office very seriously. Every morning he went over to the arsenal and stayed there all day surveying the operations. His hoarse commands and fierce swearing could be heard miles away. He kept the little Siamese fleet in very good condition, the ships ready to sail at short notice, and his devoted marine corps was the best armed force of the kingdom.

The loyalty of Prince Prap to the king was limitless; he spoke his mind openly to him, and the much younger sovereign showed him an almost filial affection. Prince Prap did not mix in court intrigues, but everybody was afraid of him and kept at a respectful distance.

When Olarovskii took a house for the legation, many things had to be arranged, and the work moved slowly. Then Prince Prap came to the rescue, and the legation was invaded by sailors who worked like a swarm of ants. With extraordinary rapidity everything was painted, fixed, and put in order. A tall flagpole was erected on a concrete base. In their zeal to please their chief the sailors planted a large palm tree in the middle of the lawn. The tree had to be removed later, for it did not take root, but it looked grand at the opening of the legation.

But the favorite occupation of the old prince was the elephant hunt. It had nothing to do with the navy, but it was the national sport of Siam, and Prap Parapak, Siamese to the bone, delighted in it. And who but he could manage it on a large scale, requiring as it did utmost skill, arduous work, and what may be called strategic talent?

Elephants were the pride, the love, and the glory of Siam; they were not killed, only caught. An elephant hunt did not imply a wholesale butchery, but, taking into consideration the size, power, intelligence, and, in the final moments, fury of the animals, it was fraught with danger for the hunters. It was a contest of wits, and man was not always the winner. I doubt that the Roman circus or a Spanish bullfight could easily equal the excitement of a royal elephant hunt in Siam.

Except for nine or ten thousand tame animals, elephants are wild in Siam and live in small herds in the forests. How they arrange their family affairs I do not know, but the members of a herd live in perfect harmony. They are entirely inoffensive if not interfered with. Only lone males are dangerous and become a nuisance to their own kin and to all mankind, as is often the case with old bachelors. The tame elephants I saw were wonderfully intelligent, patient, and altogether lovable creatures.

Once in several years a royal hunt is arranged to trap elephants. Only young animals are kept for training; the others are eventually set free, since they cannot be tamed and do not multiply in captivity. The hunt is a big affair and is considered a national festival. Hunters are sent weeks ahead to locate and assemble the separate herds. When several herds are united, a single bull takes the lead. In 1899, two hundred elephants were driven under the leadership of an enormous bull fully ten feet high at the shoulders. Hunters drew the tremendous herd from the jungle down to the outskirts of the city of Ayuthia to the stone enclosure for trapping elephants, called a *kraal* by the Europeans.

Inside, leaving a passage along the stone wall, was a second enclosure—a stockade of huge wooden pillars, each one separated from the other by a space large enough for a man to pass through but too narrow for an elephant. The space between the stone wall and the stockade served as a refuge for the hunters. On the wall was a pavilion for the king; the rest of the wall was reserved for privileged spectators.

We arrived from Bangkok on a steam yacht and spent the night on board. On the following morning we were invited to take our places on the wall, for the elephants were quite close to Ayuthia.

From the top of the wall I could see thousands of people in back of the kraal. In front of us the plain descended to a small river, and further beyond in the blue mist stood the great forest of Siam, covering practically the whole country except the clearings with rice fields. People talked excitedly, pointing at the forest where the elephants were supposed to be, but nothing could be seen. A hush came as the king took his place. His presence was made known by the appearance of a tall fan made of brocade and osprey feathers, which an attendant kept in continuous motion above the head of the sovereign.

At the king's order a signal was given. For some time everybody waited in tense expectation. Then a cloud of dust, moving and tossing, was seen at the edge of the forest. It was the great herd rolling toward us. The king nodded approvingly to Prince Prap, whose wrinkled face beamed with contentment. The appearance of a huge herd of wild elephants at a designated place and time was a great moment in his life.

Soon the animals could be better distinguished, a dark gray mass, with uplifted trunks emitting a queer discordant trumpeting. The a wide shifting front. The big bull walked proudly ahead. Close to elephants crossed the small river, which became black with their glistening bodies, and came nearer. On the plain the herd formed him followed tame elephants whose long tusks flashed white in the sun. The herd marched behind, with the mothers taking care of their offspring.

The leader approached the kraal and stopped. All the herd stopped with him. He seemed highly disturbed and looked suspiciously at the kraal—the critical moment. The tame animals moved still closer to him. There was a kind of discussion among them, by gesticulation and grunts, unless these sounds expressed a language unknown to us. The big bull objected. Then the tame ones surrounded him and started to push him with their bodies—an undignified situation for a leader. The tame elephants acted at the instigation of the hunters. Each elephant had a man, his *mahout,* sitting on his neck. A man riding a tame elephant can enter a herd of wild ones, and they will not attack him or pay any more attention to him than if he were a bird. The tame elephants insisted. It was loyalty to man and treachery to their wild brethren.

Finally the leader agreed. With a sharp cry and uplifted tail and trunk he rushed into the entrance. The whole herd pushed in after him. The gate had seemed large. It proved small for the onset. With piercing squeals the elephants tumultuously jammed in. A shout of acclaim rose from the Siamese to greet the success of the hunters. Oil was thrown on the elephants to make them more slippery as they passed through the gate. The babies protected by their mothers entered unharmed, but a half-grown elephant was squeezed to death. The gate was closed behind the last animal.

From our elevated position on the wall we looked in bewilderment on a wild sea of elephants in a state of extreme confusion, amazement, and indignation. The males became angered and dangerous. The leading bull, mad with rage, attacked the wooden pillars with his mighty tusks and shoulders. His impact was tremendous. It seemed as if the whole herd was going to support him. The hunters behind the stockade tried to repulse the elephants by pricking them with lances. This only made them more furious.

At that moment Prince Prap appeared on the wall. The terrible expression on his face reminded me of that of a war god idol come to life. He roared an order that could be heard through the bellowing of the elephants. Naked hunters glided between the pillars and threw themselves among the infuriated beasts. With masterful agility they put a heavy rope noose around the hind leg of the giant bull and fastened him to a pillar. One hunter narrowly escaped being trampled to a pulp under the ponderous feet; another got stuck between two pillars as a charging elephant passed by with viciously upcurled trunk and projected tusks. Prap, with his blazing eyes and extended arm, defied the tumult, and the elephants, with their leader out of the fight, calmed somewhat.

Prap ordered the hunters out and sat down. After spending a whole day under the tropical sun, with the loud shrieks and dreadful smell of the infuriated beasts, we were happy to retire as evening came. The elephants were left alone for the night. Some of the males were bleeding, but the females and the young were unhurt. I wondered whether a human crowd under similar circumstances would have shown the same consideration to women and children as these panic-stricken animals.

The next day the elephants were set free, since they could not be kept long without water. They were released one by one and ran in every direction. Spectators on the plain also took to their heels. One man in his fright was running in front of an elephant. In a few strides the enormous beast overtook him and with a movement of his trunk sent him rolling for several yards. An old woman sitting on the grass, paralyzed with fear, received a slight slap from a passing elephant.

A young animal was caught by a rope around one of his hind legs

as he walked out of the gate on his way to liberty. He was quickly
tied to a post and would probably be kept for training. At first he
emitted heart-rending shrieks for help, but seeing that it was of
no avail, he resolutely knelt on his forelegs, put his forehead to the
ground as though to turn a somersault, and brought all the weight
of his body against the rope. It burst with a bang, and the liberated
animal took to the forest amid general applause.

The young elephant that had been crushed at the gate was sold
to the Chinese and eaten at once. The big bull, the monarch of the
forest, had become so enraged that he created havoc and had to be
shot. The hunt was over. We sailed on the steam yacht back to
Bangkok.

The wild excitement of the Siamese facing raging elephants, tropical monsters issuing from the jungle, was in striking contrast to
the usual calm of these people and their reverential behavior in
the peace and quiet of a Buddhist temple. Which was stronger, the
jungle or the god?

The Siam of Buddha

Two factors made Siam what it was—the tropics and Buddha.
The tropics are still there, and their influence is supreme. During
eight months of the year a merciless sun strikes the land of Siam,
the plants, the animals, and the men. A few months more of it, and
all would be dead or forced to flee.

Then the rainy season sets in, and all revives. The impulse, the
power, the rapidity of the growth of tropical vegetation are incredible. Every plant, insatiably thirsty, greedily drinks the falling drops.
Everything grows on the ground or above, with orchids and creepers
suspended in the air. Any habitation left by man is covered with
growth and occupied by snakes which have escaped from their inun-
dated burrows. A Buddhist temple deserted by its monks is invaded
by venomous reptiles, like the tenets of pure Buddhist faith by
savage superstitions.

Men obey, adapt, and circumvent tropical nature by means of
canals, irrigation, and houses built on piles or floating rafts. One
man, Buddha, defied nature.

Buddha had walked through the jungle of Indian life with absolute contempt for its dangers and attractions. He considered the
gods of his time quite inferior beings, afflicted with the passions of
mankind and forming part of the material world. Buddha went a

step farther than Einstein and, renouncing every form of existence, moved out of space and time into the realm of the absolute.

I admired Buddha but could not adore him. He had created a unique philosophical conception of the living world which still holds good, unproved yet not refuted. The principle of life remains unknown. His moral code embraces the whole of nature. He reached the limits of the human mind and then stopped, on the threshold of immortality. Our science has not advanced much since. He was only a man and did not pretend to be a god. His teachings are not a religion, and he left a void to be filled after him.

A Christian tradition, traced to the eighth century, reproduces his story under the names of Barlaam and Josaphat, splitting his personality in two. Josaphat is the king's son and Barlaam the teacher. The real Buddha was both.

The Siamese treat Buddha in the same way that they treat nature. They respect, obey, and evade his teachings. The clergy has accommodated the exigency of the religion to the shapes and moods of every sort of person, in conformity with the clemency of the Great Enlightened.

Buddha is supreme above the common weaknesses of human flesh, but he is full of mercy for struggling mankind. Everything is pardoned but nothing conceded. The law of perfection is there, immutable as ever. It is very exacting, or not at all demanding, depending on whether a man belongs to the clergy or to the lay community. The clergy can have no wives; the laity, as many as they like. Every man is free to choose his own path of life, except for a short time spent in a monastery that is obligatory even for a king's sons. About one percent of the population remains in monasteries for life, and there is more than one temple for every thousand inhabitants. Women are exempted from monastic life. Whether their religious standing is too high or too low I could not determine, but certainly Buddha had a mother.

Religious discipline is lax for the laity, strict for the clergy, and does not concern the chosen ones who have no will and no wishes of their own and are immersed in contemplation before entering into *Nirvana* (nothingness). Exactly what this means is known only to those who have attained it. A man who has kept something of his individuality is dragged by it into a new existence and is reborn in a new form of life, which may be a lower or a higher one according to his previous merits or demerits. To be reborn as a white elephant is considered a very respectable, almost divine state, although Buddha did not mention it at all.

The laity occupy a markedly inferior religious position. They pray on their knees, while the monks are seated. And only monks can be priests.

Buddha did not speak of punishments in an inferno. He probably considered that continuous life in India under the various forms of existence was a kind of retribution in itself. To escape the rotation of rebirths was the greatest bliss. But in the temple of Kandy, the most famous Buddhist shrine of Ceylon, I saw a picture of hell very expressive in its details. An old woman was fervently praying before it. Did she have some misgivings about her own future fate, or was she concerned with the present condition of her late relatives? I did not ask.

The true road to salvation is to become a monk for life. The monks live in *wats* (monasteries), unless they prefer to be solitary hermits. Each wat forms a *sanka* (congregation). When the monks pray, they keep a line of long threads in their hands to express the perfect union of their spirits. In the morning they go out to collect alms, for they are forbidden to engage in any profit-making or productive trade. The offerings they receive are chiefly food, which must be consumed before noon and may not exceed the needs of a day. They cannot kill animals but may eat their meat if the sin of killing has been committed by someone else.

There are no parishes and no cathedral temples, for temples can be built only in monasteries. Buddha did not build temples or worship in them, and he recognized no idols. But his grave has become a center of adoration, and consequently each wat must have a *stupa* (mound) in which the remains of a saintly person are buried. Inasmuch as believers needed something more tangible to venerate, temples were built with a statue of Buddha, often of a large size out of proportion to the dimensions of the building. A temple is strictly the shrine of the god, not a place of congregation.

Monasteries must be built in a wilderness. But as this is not practical—both for the monks, who depend on alms, and for the laity, who desire to visit the temples—these are constructed close to the towns, and the wilderness is reduced to the limits of the sacred enclosure. The city gradually moves to the temple, which is surrounded by houses, and finally becomes part of the town.

The priests are often called to pray in the houses. They start with the words in Pali, an ancient dialect akin to Sanskrit: "*Namo tao Buddhao Bhagavatao Arahatao* [Glory to Buddha, the Lord, the Great Enlightened]."

Such was Siam, the abode of Buddha, as I saw it in the late nineties.

The Franco-Siamese Agreement

Doumer had left Bangkok, fully satisfied with his visit. The large number of Frenchmen who came with him were also pleased and were impressed at the sight of the French tricolor flying in the streets of the city. But after their departure, life resumed its previous course. Undoubtedly Doumer had sent a very favorable report to Paris, which must have produced a certain impression there. But that was all. Detailed negotiations were necessary for the drafting of a treaty, and these were not within the competence of a governor-general. A French diplomat was needed for that. A new French chargé d'affaires, Hector de Panafieu, was immediately dispatched to Bangkok when the news of Doumer's visit was reported in Paris newspapers. But the cautious diplomat, naturally enough, showed no disposition to produce a second stir and quietly waited for the return of the French minister.

Things dragged on. Doumer left for France, and the Siamese grew restless. Early in 1900, Olarovskii went on leave, after a final audience at which he presented me to the king as the Russian chargé d'affaires. I was alone at the legation, and a heavy responsibility fell on me. A mere expression of sympathy toward France was not enough on the part of Siam. Something concrete had to be proposed at once. That could not be expected from Prince Devawongse, who was only too glad of the temporary truce in his relations with France and would not move. I also saw that no lasting settlement could be arranged without removing the cause of the friction between the two nations and placating their feelings.

For several years the French had kept a small armed force in Chantaboon, on the shore of the Gulf of Siam. The town was unimportant, but its occupation angered the Siamese and affected the prestige of the king. Evacuation of the troops from Chantaboon was the first point to be considered. The second was its exchange for some other Siamese territory that would be suitable for the French without upsetting the economic balance of Siam.

I studied the Franco-Siamese frontier and came to the conclusion

that the region of Battambang in the southeastern corner of Siam—
containing the famous ruins of Angkor, the ancient capital of Cambodia—would suit the interests of French Indochina exactly, without prejudice to Siam. Communications between Bangkok and Battambang were very difficult, and the kingdom of Cambodia was
already a French protectorate. All this looked very well in theory,
but there was a practical side to be reckoned with. The land in
question was totally unknown to me. I decided to see Prince Damrong, the minister of the interior. No one knew the country better
than he and his chief assistant.

Damrong listened to me attentively. He approached the large
map of Siam on the wall, indicated an area on it with his pencil,
holding it in the air without touching the map, and said: "Is this
what you mean?" I nodded.

"It might be done. There are fisheries there belonging to the
queen. That can be arranged. But don't forget I am not the master
here. I'll have to speak with the king and give you an answer afterward." A few days later I was informed that the king had given his
consent to the proposition.

The second step remained—the approach to the French. After a
five o'clock tea at the Japanese legation, I walked out with the
French chargé d'affaires and told him about the offer of Battambang. "There never was a question about Battambang," he said. "I
cannot raise it."

That blocked the regular channel of communications with
France, by means of her representative in Bangkok. There was, of
course, the Siamese legation in Paris, but it could be of little use in
this case. The Great Powers transact all their serious business with
smaller countries through their ministers there.

Nothing could be accomplished even after the return of Olarovskii. Since I was leaving Siam, I could go to Paris and have a talk
with Doumer at the very seat of the French government. It was my
duty to let him know the latest developments in Siam. Whether he
wanted to press toward an agreement or beat an honorable retreat,
my information would help him.

Here I interrupt the course of my narrative and pass directly to
my arrival in Paris. I went to the Colonial Office, located in a wing
of the Louvre. Doumer was sitting there looking as regal as ever.
I was apprehensive lest he had forgotten about Siam, but on the
contrary he showed keen interest. He seemed to be in no great haste

to return to Indochina, and the settlement of the Siamese question would be the crowning achievement of a splendid administrative career in the East.

The proposition was entirely new to Doumer. He listened with increasing attention as I explained to him the location of the territory offered in exchange for Chantaboon and the advantages of the region. I stressed the point that the exchange would not increase the burden of the colonial budget, since it would simply extend the existing protectorate over Cambodia and not involve any political complications with the local population, who were ethnically identical on both sides of the frontier. Strategically the position would be the same, or indeed improved.

Doumer grasped the point at once and asked only whether I was sure of the consent of the king and whether Olarovskii shared my opinion.

"Completely," I answered.

Doumer looked pleased. I did not know that Théophile Delcassé, the foreign minister, had entirely changed the orientation of French policy and was striving for an entente with England and for the rapid elimination of all France's colonial entanglements. England disliked the French occupation of Chantaboon, and its evacuation would please her.

"My friend [Antony] Klobukovski will go to Siam as minister," said Doumer. "He will be in Paris in a month. Let us have lunch with him."

In a month I had promised Hartwig to be at my new post in Ashkhabad, central Asia. I told Doumer that I had to leave Paris, that I had already said everything, and that Klobukovski would find no difficulty in making a treaty.

That was the last time I saw Doumer and my last contact with Siam. I may add that a treaty was signed between Siam and France along the stated lines and has worked satisfactorily ever since. Siam made some concessions to England and lived in complete harmony with her neighbors.

Three intelligent men are enough to save a nation. In Siam they were King Chulalongkorn, Prince Prap Parapak, and Prince Damrong. I am glad to offer this tribute to their memory.

The Return from Siam
December 1900

At the end of November 1900, my chief came back from Russia. It was my turn to go home on leave. I made parting calls on my Siamese and European friends, had an audience with King Chulalongkorn, and bid farewell to Olarovskii and his hospitable family.

I had my last breakfast in Siam with my blue-eyed cat and my small dog. As I talked to them, a servant brought me a letter from Prince Damrong and two spears with ringlets of gold, a farewell gift to a departing friend, to protect me on my journey from snakes, wild beasts, and robbers. I met none, and the spears proved a bit cumbersome in the steamer's cabin and railway cars. But I liked them and faithfully brought them to St. Petersburg.

I was glad to be going back to Russia, for my health was failing after three years in tropical marshlands, but at the same time I felt sorry to leave Siam. As the boat moved downstream, the palms and temples of Bangkok glided before my eyes. I looked at the beautiful shrines dedicated to Buddha, the only man of his time who recognized no idols and no gods yet was adored after his death by millions of devoted worshippers. What fate was to be theirs?

The country held promise for the future but was going through a critical stage, full of uncertainty. Would it remain independent or be absorbed into the colonial possessions of its neighbors? Was it better for an Oriental state to work out its own salvation or to be brought under European control and trained in the ways of civilization by a competent foreign administration? There was a party in Siam in favor of the latter solution, but the king was against it, and Russia supported him.

Japan was an independent Far Eastern state, but she owed her freedom to her insular position and to the poverty of her land and its lack of mineral wealth. The Great Powers maintained a kind of equilibrium in China which they called "The Open Door Policy." But Siam occupied a precarious position. One factor was in her favor: England and France were near the limit of colonial saturation. Germany was advancing her claims. A repartition in Asia could lead to a war in Europe. The Siamese question was receding into a safe backwater.

The course of my meditations was interrupted by the tossing of the steamer on a rough sea until we reached Singapore. I spent a pleasant day there, making calls and buying seashells. The eyeless mollusks are skillful artists, whose dwellings are inlaid on the inside with mother-of-pearl and on the outside with enamel. How they could produce such color effects was beyond my comprehension.

I changed steamers and on the big liner met General V. V. Sakharov, who was returning from the Far East after the Boxer disturbances. There had been some fighting at Taku in June, and the Japanese sailors had rushed barefooted up the sloping escarpments of the Chinese fort. This had been constructed according to European specifications and did not provide for such a contingency.

"Have you been in Japan?" I asked General Sakharov.

"Yes, on my way from Vladivostok," he answered.

"What is your impression of the Japanese army?"

"Excellent, as far as I could see it." I wonder whether he was the only man in the Russian army who held such a view at that time. But then Sakharov had a mind of his own. A sprightly, active man, he was capable of initiative but never had the occasion to develop it. The minister of war, A. N. Kuropatkin, who took Sakharov as his chief of staff during the Russo-Japanese war, did not pay much attention to his opinions. During World War I Sakharov commanded the army on the Rumanian front—the last army to accept the tsar's abdication.

According to the advice of my doctor, I stayed in Egypt for a while. It would have been too risky to go to Russia in December straight from the tropics. The climate of Egypt is excellent for invalids but has its drawbacks. I missed the worst of them—the *hamsin,* a hot wind blowing sand. This sand is extremely fine and penetrates everywhere—you drink and eat it with your meals; you breathe and inhale it even in a closely shut room. There is no escape from it, and it is dangerous for the lungs.

Thoroughly recovered, I took the steamer to Russia. We docked at Odessa on December 24. I rushed to the post office, where I found a letter from my mother with keys and receipts; then to the railway station, where a trunk was waiting for me; then back to the hotel. It was very cold, and I shivered in my light overcoat. Sitting in my room I read and reread my mother's letter, a recent one, unlike the month-old letters I used to receive in Siam. In the trunk were all the things I needed—a fur coat and cap, gloves, woolens. How neatly they were folded and packed by my mother's hands. I could almost hear her anxious voice inquiring about my health.

But at the railroad station I had heard dismal news: the line was blocked by snowdrifts, and trains were not running that day. A Russian railway station was always a source of confusion, but I had not expected it to be as bad as it was. True, I had been told by railway officials whom I had seen that morning that service would be resumed tomorrow, but what did "tomorrow" mean in Russia?

The counselor of the embassy, who had traveled with me from Constantinople and was staying at the same hotel, went to see the commander in chief, who told him: "You won't be able to travel by railway for several days. I am sending sledges to bring passengers marooned in trains on the way, and I have ordered soldiers to clear the line of snow."

The next day was Christmas, and a small tree was lighted in one of the cars at the station to cheer the waiting children.

Another companion from the steamer, a naval officer, suggested that we go by sea to Sebastopol in the Crimea. The tsar was there, and the line would certainly be kept open.

We took the first boat sailing from Odessa. It was small, the cabins had a strong smell of rats, and a young first mate was in command. Fog set in toward evening, to complete the unfortunate combination of circumstances. In the morning, as I awoke, the ship was strangely still. My naval friend looked into my cabin.

"We are aground on a shoal," he said.

"Are we sinking?"

"No, we cannot. The bottom of the ship is resting on a sand bank, and the sea is calm."

I dressed and went on deck. All around us was a dense fog, with strange noises close by, like the rumble of a carriage on a paved street. The mist cleared. We were inside the port of Eupatoria. Sailing boats were anchored close to us. The captain reversed the engine and got the ship afloat. We set out again, as the ship was not supposed to call at Eupatoria. In the afternoon the fog settled down for the second time. We were going full steam ahead.

The naval officer said to me: "Now we may sink or sink somebody else. The captain is a fool, but this is the only way to reach Sebastopol in time, if nothing happens." Nothing happened. We moored at the pier at Sebastopol and found the train ready at the station. I noticed that all the people there were looking in the direction of a short, broad-shouldered general who walked up and down the platform, talking with an officer. It was Kuropatkin, who was returning from Livadia after a personal report to the tsar, and who, later on, was to lose the Russo-Japanese war.

I had only a glimpse of Kuropatkin at the Sebastopol railroad station. However, the following summer I had to accompany him on his trip through Bokhara and saw much of him at close quarters. He was a slow-thinking man, incurably convinced of the superiority of the Russian army over all others, about which he had only the slightest knowledge which he regrettably never felt the necessity of supplementing. I must add that he was a brave, honest, and kind man in his own clumsy and tactless way.

The train started. Three more days, and I saw St. Petersburg, my mother, and my home.

5 Russia Again

I arrived on December 31, 1900, just in time to greet the New Year with my mother. She looked a bit older but still svelte, cheerful, and full of spirit.

My next call was to the Foreign Office. I was instructed to report to the minister, Count V. N. Lamsdorf, whom I had met before as chief of the chancellery. He was short, with a very high forehead and a soft, affable manner. There was nothing bureaucratic or imposing about this leisurely, well-bred man of good society. This, however, was only his manner—he was clever and hard working but did not like to give that impression or to appear exacting toward his immediate subordinates, who were devoted to him and very efficient. A certain attitude of assumed nonchalance was typical of the entire department. To show excessive zeal was considered to be in bad taste.

Lamsdorf, who succeeded Muraviev as minister of foreign affairs in June 1900, had never held a post abroad. He belonged body and soul to the Russian Foreign Office and to St. Petersburg. He liked its climate, its rainy, gloomy autumn, and its dark protracted winter with short sunless days. Perhaps he liked them because they gave him a pretext to sit without stirring in his comfortable study.

He asked me about the climate of Siam. I explained that it was rather trying. He listened with interest, evidently feeling happy to be in St. Petersburg and not in the tropics.

"Well," he said with an apologetic smile, "there is no ideal climate."

"Pardon, count," I answered, "there is one."

"Which is it?"

"The climate of the country where one was born and bred."

Lamsdorf looked thoughtful. "You may be right, after all," he said. "As far as I am concerned, I like our climate here."

Our conversation continued, revolving on trifles. Lamsdorf was not interested in Siam, nor in the fate of our legation there, nor in anybody outside the restricted circle of his collaborators. The rest of the world he treated with polite indifference. He was not married. Although he belonged by birth to the high society of St. Petersburg, he did not care for it. All his interest was centered on his desk and his work. He was the chosen pupil and intimate friend of the old minister, N. K. Giers. Sheltered by the latter, he made a perfect secretary, transacting the entire correspondence with Europe. He delighted in writing official papers, safely entrenched in the privacy of his office and sure of the approval of his beloved chief.

But when he became head of the ministry of foreign affairs, Lamsdorf found himself in a different and very exposed situation. He was obliged to deal directly with the tsar and with the other ministers. When he happened to dislike their opinions, he disliked even more to express his disapproval and became perplexed.

As long as the colonial expansion of Russia was directed by the minister of finance, S. Iu. Witte, Lamsdorf relied on him. Good relations with the Ministry of Finance were one of the traditions of the Russian Foreign Office, just as distrust of the War Ministry was another. We considered the military a kind of Don Quixotes, aggressive and inefficient. Lamsdorf shared this opinion, but in 1903, after Witte's dismissal, he fell back before a joint attack of admirals, courtiers, and generals. Lamsdorf did not lack intelligence, but he lacked nerve and a fighting disposition. He felt he was getting into a quagmire but could not resign the conduct of foreign affairs, a sacred trust confided to him by the dying Giers.

When I saw Lamsdorf, there was still a possibility of an agreement with Japan, but Lamsdorf was not thinking of Asia. All his attention was absorbed by the kaiser, an extremely restless military man whose threats and offers of friendship were equally embarrassing and endangered the Franco-Russian alliance, the pivot of the Russian foreign policy established by Alexander III, Giers, and Lamsdorf.

The return from Siam was a landmark in my life. The East had lost a good deal of its attraction for me: Siam had been too much of a good thing. Its climate, nature, and people were so different from ours that I had become sick of exoticism. What I needed was Europe, and especially Russia. As chargé d'affaires in Bangkok I had held an independent and responsible position; after that, bureaucratic, subordinate work in the Asian Department had no appeal for me. Where could I go?

During my stay in Siam, the consulate in Astarābād had become vacant, and I was appointed to it. But the idea of returning to Persia was so unpleasant that I grew disgusted with my career at the Foreign Office, where success was working against me. At the same time I developed a strong affection for my country and an interest in its life, from which I had been separated during the years of my absence. To stay in Russia became my chief desire; it amounted to an obsession, and my career seemed an obstacle to this.

The problem was difficult; it required much thinking and very delicate handling. Officially I was consul at Astarābād, the youngest consul in the Russian service. Advantage had to be taken of this situation, and further consular service in Persia eliminated at once. After careful study of the Foreign Office list, I came to the conclusion that the post of commissioner for frontier relations at Ashkhabad, Transcaspia, in Russian Central Asia would suit me to a "T." Ashkhabad was a Russian town connected by railway to St. Petersburg and quite close to the Persian border, so that my previous experience would not be lost. I went to see Hartwig, head of the Asian Department, and mentioned casually during the conversation that I would prefer not to return to Persia.

"Well," said my chief in a rather stern voice. "What is it you want?"

I explained in a meek voice that I would like to exchange my consulate for the post of commissioner at Ashkhabad. I would be closer to the Foreign Office and directly under Hartwig's orders. This last consideration mollified my chief.

"All right," he answered. "I shall telegraph to the commissioner and inquire whether he is agreeable to this exchange." The answer was affirmative, and I was transferred to Ashkhabad. The salary was smaller, but life there was extremely cheap and much more comfortable than in a Persian town. Besides, I received an extension of my leave. I could stay a few more weeks in St. Petersburg and study the life of my country.

Tsar Nicholas II had already been on the throne seven years and
had brought no change in the government of Russia. Autocratic
rule extended over the whole empire like a sheet of ice paralyzing
every green sprout of political activity. But under the frozen surface
life was throbbing and would soon burst through.

Until 1905 the reign of Nicholas II had been a mere continuation
of the reactionary regime of his father. The ministers of Alexander III still ruled over Russia. The individuality of the tsar disappeared behind them, and he was therefore only incidentally included in the blame they incurred. It was the regime that was hated
by the opposition, not the person of the young emperor, who was
considered insignificant and remained safe by virtue of it.

In the meantime the Russian intelligentsia came to the fore. This
comprised all the educated people who took an interest in politics
without playing any role, as there were no house of representatives,
no votes, and no elections. The intelligentsia criticized the government, was rebuked by it, and finally succeeded in making it very
unpopular. Russia became revolutionary minded before the coming of the revolution. No political activity was allowed by the government, and the interest of the public was diverted to literature.
That was an attractive field, easy to explore, and it would give me
some insight into the general trend of public opinion and its reaction to the existing regime.

I noticed a change in Russia, slight but rather disquieting, as if
on a radiant summer morning you suddenly feel a certain uneasi-
ness. The air seems oppressive, the sunlight dimmed; clouds begin
to gather from nowhere. A puff of wind comes, makes the leaves
rustle; a few heavy drops of rain fall; then for a while all seems
quiet. A puff of wind again, a gust, a blast, a peal of thunder, and
the whole sky turns into an Armageddon. Rain comes in torrents,
and woe to the wanderer who does not find a shelter betimes. And
this is only a passing spell of bad weather. A social cataclysm is much
worse, yet it can be prevented if people heed the ominous signs.

Russia, as I knew her under Alexander III and in the early days
of the reign of Nicholas II, was both oppressed and depressed. Except for a few terroristic attempts and isolated agrarian disturbances,
people showed no fight and desired none. The great writers—the
only spokesmen for the nation—had often exposed the abuses of
autocracy, the inertia of society, and the backwardness of the masses.
But they had all died of old age at the end of the nineteenth century

Tashkent, 1906. *Far left, seated,* is A. D. Kalmykow; *second from left,* N. P. Ostroumov; *third from left,* Lieutenant General D. I. Subotich, governor general of Turkestan; *far left, standing,* A. A. Semionov.

A. M. Kalmykova, mother of the author. Prominent in the promotion of elementary education for children and adults and in teacher training.

Senator D. A. Kalmykow (1835–89), father of the author.

Aleksandra Akimovna Ryndovskaia, by first marriage Chernova, née Kovalevskaia (1830–1905), maternal grandmother of the author, for forty-five years head of the Girls' Gymnasium at Ekaterinoslav. This school, founded in 1860, was considered the best of its kind in Russia.

Major General F. V. Neiolov, 1903, stepfather of the author's wife.

M. Ia. Neiolova, by first marriage Shilovskaia, née Sobko (1852–1928), author's mother-in-law.

Vladimir Sergeievich Shilovskii (1843–97), author's father-in-law. Collaborated with S. Iu. Witte in railway construction and was director of the Moscow-Vitebsk line. He belonged to the twenty-fourth generation of one of Russia's oldest families; the genealogical tree of the Shilovskie goes back to the beginning of the thirteenth century.

Left: A. D. Kalmykow as a gymnasium student with his paternal grandfather, Aleksandr Nikolaievich Kalmykow (1812–89). *Right:* Lieutenant General Aleksandr Aleksandrovich Michelson (1863–1919) and his wife, Aleksandra Vladimirovna, née Shilovskaia (1877–1969), the author's sister-in-law, dressed for German court functions. Aleksandra Vladimirovna is wearing an ancient-style Russian costume by special request of Kaiser Wilhelm II. General Michelson was military attaché in Berlin and a member of the Russian delegation to the Second Peace Conference at The Hague, 1907. He later commanded the Moskovskii Regiment of the Second Division of the Imperial Guards. In 1916 he was knighted by George V of Great Britain and made Commander of the Legion of Honor by the French government.

Vera Vladimirovna Kalmykova, née Shilov-skaia (1884–1919), the author's wife. The portrait was taken of her as a young bride during her honeymoon in Italy in 1903.

A. D. Kalmykow and his family in Crete, 1913. The two children *seated in front* are, *left,* the oldest son Vladimir, and *right,* the daughter Aleksandra. *Behind them,* held by Vera Vladimirovna, is the second son, Andrei.

Uskub, 1912. A. D. Kalmykow is *seated; standing,* four war correspondents, two to each side of Mr. Bukovich, who became mayor of Uskub after its occupation by the Serbs.

Bokharan dignitaries and Russian officials in Tashkent, taken between 1906 and 1910. A. D. Kalmykow is *seated third from the right.*

except Tolstoy, who alone was fully alive and had started a spiritual revolution of his own—religious, moral, and social, a kind of ethereal bolshevism without recourse to force. With Tolstoy the criticism of individual defects became universal and attained its culmination. It was a condemnation of Russian life as a whole. He attacked with his pen, and from a purely ethical point of view, the church, the state, married life, and all the activities of society—public, private, industrial, and cultural. Under the broadsides of his denunciations people were taken aback, stultified, confused, and they finally ceased to pay any attention to him at all. His influence waned even before his death.

Tolstoy recognized only the principle of love and nonresistance to violence. But can one love injustice? Can a man tolerate it when the victims are the beings he cherishes most? Tolstoy relied on God, although, like Dostoevskii, he never was quite sure of God's existence.

The symptoms of the coming disturbance appeared in the writings of the younger generation. Two tendencies could be observed: one spirited and protesting, the other gloomy and despairing. Gorkii was the daring stormy petrel. Andreiev, his opposite, was a poet in prose, with a sense of impending doom like that of Edgar Allan Poe and Maeterlinck, but more realistic, closer to actual life, expressing not only the individual fears of a distressed, defenseless being amid fantastic surroundings but the agony of the more sophisticated section of Russian intelligentsia, oppressed by the feeling of its helplessness in the face of approaching disaster.

It was my own fault that I failed to make the acquaintance of Andreiev. I went to see a friend who had a villa not far from St. Petersburg, across the Finnish border. We walked along a very pretty forest path running high above the sea and ending in an open, bare, and rather desolate plateau. I saw a high stockade with a kind of blockhouse inside. The house must have had a fine view of the gulf, but that was all. With no trees, it was a sad, lonely place.

"Here lives Andreiev," said my friend. "He has a motorboat and often cruises in the gulf. Sorry, I am not acquainted with him and cannot introduce you." It appeared that Andreiev had spent a lot of money arranging his place. The house was built of huge logs and furnished in the primitive, ornate, and barbaric style of the old Norse sea kings, fitting well into the rude Scandinavian landscape and in harmony with the melancholy mood of the owner.

I could easily have gotten a letter of introduction from my
mother, who knew Andreiev, but I hesitated to call on him. I
doubted that we could understand each other. I was a born optimist,
forward looking and full of expectations. Andreiev was desperate;
life seemed to him like Dante's Inferno, where there is no hope
whatever. He once tried to commit suicide, but the bullet narrowly
missed his heart. He seemed to owe much of the tender beauty of
his early writings to the influence of his wife, who died prematurely. His style became bitter after this loss.

I was more fortunate in meeting another star of our literature,
even more reticent and difficult to approach.

"Who is the most popular writer in Russia?" I asked my cousin.

"Gorkii," he answered, "is the idol of our younger generation.
He writes about tramps, people who have failed in life and belong
to the dregs of society. They are very interesting."

I met Gorkii at my mother's. He had no permanent home of his
own and was constantly on the move, collecting and accumulating
impressions. He was tall, with a large sunken chest, long limbs, an
awkward gait, and a thoughtful, slightly disdainful expression. As
he entered, he seemed to fill all the available space in the little
study. He fixed his gaze on me, with the professional indelicacy of
a writer, and sat down sullen and silent. I apparently belonged to
the set of people he could only attack or ignore. Out of regard for
my mother he could not do the former, so he chose the latter.
My mother made most of the conversation. She told him that he
would never be a writer of fame unless he published his short stories
and novels in book form instead of scattering them in various
magazines. He listened with a peculiar mixture of indifference and
attention and agreed. Two years later his name was widely known
throughout Europe.

Many authors attempt to describe poverty, and some have experienced it themselves. Yet there is always something lacking in
their perception. They have never belonged to the poorest class and
do not have its complexes. They are only keen and sympathetic ob-
servers—deep divers, yes, but not born inhabitants of the depths.
A scientist can make an excellent study of ants and bees, but he has
never been an ant himself, and the psychology of an insect is
foreign to him.

Gorkii had been one of the human insects he describes so well. He had been a tramp and remained a tramp even when he earned considerable money. He felt at home at the bottom of society. In his writings there is no condescending pity, no forced amiability, no virtuous indignation—just comradeship toward wretched beings. There is no attempt to dramatize the situation by depicting a social hell or by making its inhabitants look helpless and utterly despondent. On the contrary, they display a remarkable vitality and power of resistance. They continue to live, to feel, to fight over their love affairs.

What is more, there is a buoyancy in them, in some of them at least. They endeavor to work out their salvation with their own hands against all odds. They feel oppressed but not crushed. That distinguishes them from all the previous characters in Russian literature. Gorkii is the first revolutionary writer of Russia. Yet he was not a revolutionary himself—he was too impractical, too sensitive to be a man of action. He had a simple mind, thoroughly incapable of systematic thinking. He was not a theoretician, only a dreamer and a great artist.

He saw clearly people moving in the dim light of a cellar and painted them vividly. He knew the society of the small bourgeois and hated them, their habits, and their conceptions. A pure proletarian, he disliked the well-to-do, the government, and the monarchy. He could not understand the complicated organization of modern society. When communism came, he disliked it also and opposed it. Later he became converted to it and was received into the intimacy of the new rulers of Russia. But he saw all in a kind of mist. That is why he could never describe the revolution in being. The greatest revolutionary writer of Russia never portrayed a single revolutionary leader. Like a deep-sea fish brought to the surface, he gasped and remained blinded and powerless.

I decided to stay with my mother until the last day of my leave. That was due her. Then I called on Hartwig and asked him in a very innocent way what itinerary I was to follow to reach my destination. My chief answered good humoredly: "That we leave entirely to you." This was just the answer I was waiting for, and I threw the bomb I had kept ready. "Then I would like to travel via Paris and London."

A disquieting silence followed while the heavy caterpillars that were the eyebrows of my chief moved ominously. Then he looked at me and smiled. "Do as you like," he said, "provided you are in Ashkhabad on the 20th of May." I may add that I kept my word.

I went around the capitals of Europe. My trip was splendid. The European cities vied with one another in an amazing display of reckless luxury. The twentieth century was ushered in as an era of progress, peace, and prosperity. Europe was guided by farsighted statesmen of conservative tendencies; socialists were branded as impractical dreamers and unpatriotic pacifists. Preparedness for war was supposed to be the best guarantee of peace.

But the champagne youth I saw in Paris and London were doomed to die on the fields of battle, torn to pieces by explosives, riddled by machine gun bullets, asphyxiated by poisonous gases. So much for peace and progress. It did not mean that the governments of Europe were worse than their predecessors; I personally thought they were better in many respects. But they proved unable to foresee, provide against, or circumscribe the coming conflagration. On the whole, western Europe looked quiet and peaceful. Democracy seemed firmly established, and I saw no signs of the acute discontent so keenly felt in my own country. Only when I returned to Russia, on the way to Transcaspia, did I perceive symptoms of the approaching trouble.

Some of the young men whom I had known as schoolboys were rapidly advancing on the road to wealth and honors. They were doomed to disappear with the advent of the Revolution, and none had time to become cabinet ministers except P. L. Bark, who was to be the last minister of the imperial regime. He had always been prominent, even in school. A calm, solid, good-natured fellow, very efficient but not at all of the pushing type, he was receiving the highest salary in Russia—100,000 rubles a year—as president of the North Bank at St. Petersburg, when he accepted, without haste, the portfolio of the Ministry of Finance.

I stopped at Kharkov to see an old schoolmate of mine, a young and successful lawyer with radical tendencies. As we passed a policeman at his post on the street, my friend said distinctly: "Down with autocracy." The policeman winced but did not move. "See how we have trained them," my friend said with a boyish laugh. "All the young people here are either Social Democrats or Social Revolutionaries."

The Social Democrats, or SDs, as they were called, had a platform based on the support of factory workers, practically along the lines of German socialists of that time. But the SDs had no factories of their own and were not working men themselves. Some engaged in propaganda in the mills, but the majority had a purely academic attachment to their program. They talked about it and discussed it among themselves with great zest. But that was all, as the government had forbidden public meetings, speeches, and printed pamphlets.

The Social Revolutionaries, or SRs, wanted the partition of land among the peasants and were confronted with the same difficulty. They had no lands to give away, were not peasants themselves, and knew nothing about agriculture.

Both parties were motivated by a sense of social justice, and both proposed economic reforms. They asked for a more equal repartition of incomes and taxes, a better standard of living, and protection of the working classes from economic exploitation. My young friends of Kharkov did not need these reforms personally. Most of them were lawyers, were their own bosses, and were economically independent; some even owned property.

To put their program in practice they needed political rights, a legislative chamber, and control of the budget and of the entire activity of the administration. They did not wish to destroy the government of the tsar; rather, they wanted to share in its powers, to act through the legal channels of the governmental machinery. Here they ran into an impasse—the government refused to grant a parliamentary regime. Russia was to remain under an autocratic tsar.

These opposition parties were not restricted to Kharkov; they existed throughout Russia. The young men protested but could do nothing. They had no force at their disposal and were out of contact with the masses. Some hotheads tried propaganda and failed; the masses did not stir. The influence of the young people did not extend beyond the limited circles of the intelligentsia. They were leaders without followers, officers without an army—and purely theoretical officers at that. However, their lack of success did not disappoint them; they enjoyed their liberal activities in full. "The future is ours," they would say. Notwithstanding their revolutionary appellations, neither party was revolutionary at all, and they could wait. The extremists formed separate terroristic organizations.

I shared the views of the reformers but not their optimism and did not join the ranks of any party. I saw that the intelligentsia was unable to influence the government. Would it be able to win the confidence of the masses and lead them? No leader was in view. Lenin, at thirty-one, was totally unknown outside a narrow circle of quarreling Socialists and found little response even among them.

In 1901 Russia was not ripe for a revolution. Economic forces were working changes in what is called a normal way. Such a course, however, could only proceed slowly and provided there was no external interference. The tsar was everything in Russia but not in the outside world. A war with disastrous results would shatter his authority in the eyes of his people. It was necessary to keep away from wars, and the tsar did not. Here the Ministry of Foreign Affairs and the Ministry of War enter the picture.

The Russian Foreign Office was a strictly conservative, monarchical, reactionary, and bureaucratic institution, with plenty of obsolete traditions imposed on it and a good amount of pretence, snobbery, and conceit. But we had one important advantage: we were the only Russian institution that was in constant contact with foreign lands and governments, inflicted rebukes on them, and received hard knocks in return. In short, we were trained fighters and had a practical knowledge of the outside world.

The Foreign Office was an efficient organization. That does not mean, of course, that we were always successful—nobody is. We formed a separate, restricted, independent institution and defended our independence against any encroachments. Our chief adversary was the War Office. The conflict was perpetual, incurable, and on the whole beneficial. It constituted a balance of power. There were only two instances when the diplomats gave way to the military: the first, in the last days of Lamsdorf's ministry, before the Russo-Japanese war; the second, during the few months preceding World War I, when Sazonov accepted the point of view of the minister of war, V. A. Sukhomlinov. In both instances the result was a crushing defeat for Russia.

The War Office was just as reactionary and monarchical as the Foreign Office, but there were other considerations of much wider import. The Russian military lacked practice in wars of large scale. World wars are, or at least were, of such rare occurrence that the generals had no practical experience in conducting them. They had to rely on books, maneuvers, and peacetime routine, with a few colonial expeditions against untrained and poorly armed natives in undeveloped territories. These protracted expeditions were often costly in men and money and, although in the long run successful and proclaimed as such, were with few exceptions quite unimpressive performances. In a word, the commanders who had to lead the fighting forces were not fighting men trained in actual warfare, and whatever they had seen of war was of little importance for the conduct of operations on the scale of a world war. Such a war implied the mobilization of the country's entire male population and resources and imposed a strain of unprecedented proportion. It was a problem far exceeding the conceptions of the military men who were to assume responsibilities in World War I.

Ashkhabad and all of Russian Central Asia were under military administration, and I was to have ample opportunity to see it at work. I do not mean to imply that this administration was bad but only that military men had a simplified idea of the infinite complexity of civilian work and life.

Ashkhabad*

I was told that Transcaspia was a kind of Russian Arabia consisting chiefly of a waterless desert with oases, camels, and the like, the difference being that winters were cool. This was true. As I crossed the Caspian Sea and approached the land, I saw a range of barren reddish rock. At its foot a cluster of small houses stood in the sand that covered the streets. Only Arabs were lacking to complete the picture. This was Krasnovodsk—"Red Water Town"—the port of Transcaspia. The rocks were red all right, but no water of any color was to be seen among them. There was the sea, of course, but for drinking purposes people had to be content with a few shallow wells. According to local standards, this was enough. You cannot be demanding about the water supply in central Asia.

There was not much to be seen in Krasnovodsk, and I went straight to the railway station, by far the best building in town. I wondered why Russia had taken this land, which lacked even a solid surface to tread on and where, at the time of the conquest, our soldiers had to plough their way through deep sand carrying heavy kits and rifles. The railway gave me the answer. It provided the best land access to central Asia, eastern Persia, Afghanistan, and India and was the sole reason for the existence of Transcaspia. Re-

* After the revolution the town was renamed Poltoratsk. A few years later, as Ashkhabad, it resumed its original name in its Turkoman form. *F. K.*

move the railway, and Transcaspia would vanish into nothingness. Most of the people in Transcaspia—except the nomads, of course—had something to do with the railway, and the rest were there because of it. I myself belonged to the latter category. Before the construction of the railway, which immediately followed the Russian occupation, frontier relations with Persia existed only in the form of sweeping inroads of Turkoman raiders into the interior of Persia. Prisoners brought from there were sold as slaves in the markets of Merv and Bokhara, a highly profitable and honorable business, according to local conceptions.

After the Russians had taken the land, the Turkomans ceased to cross into Persia. It was now the Persians who flocked to Transcaspia, selling the Russians eggs, poultry, fruit, vegetables, and charcoal. Persian villages and Russian settlements became interdependent and interrelated. The intercourse was very lively, almost daily. The office of commissioner for frontier relations was created to safeguard it, as its interruption would have sorely affected the supply of our settlements. All went very smoothly to mutual advantage.

As our train left Krasnovodsk and bravely entered the desert, the passengers gathered in the dining car. It was amply supplied with provisions, fortunately for us, for there was nothing else to eat or drink for hundreds of miles around. A well-furnished table was very attractive in the midst of a desert, and I fully appreciated the advantages of railway communications.

In the morning the country looked a bit better. The blue mountains of Persia on our right drew closer, and rare little streams flowing down their slopes created a narrow belt of scantily irrigated land along the Russo-Persian frontier. I looked at the stations where we stopped: there was the obligatory garden with a dozen parched trees around a small artificial pond, where a diminutive fountain—fed from the railway cistern—splashed during the five-minute stop of a passenger train.

Building the railroad was a real achievement, accomplished surprisingly well by a handful of soldiers, with a ridiculously small outlay of money, in a short space of time. It seems that the dry, pure, exhilarating air of the desert had transformed the slow, sluggish, lubberly ways of the Russian infantrymen. One cannot be slow in a desert, so one learns to be quick. Tracks were laid across waterless sands considered impassable; wells were drilled, irrigation canals dug, trees planted. The conquest was made by the impetuous General M. D. Skobelev and the settlements by his chief of staff, A. N. Kuropatkin, an incompetent strategist but a good farmer.

The train reached Ashkhabad. I took a carriage, which left a cloud of dust behind us. All was dusty—the houses, the streets, the thirsty trees bordering the sidewalks—with little irrigation ditches pitifully dry. The hotel offered a refuge from heat and dust. Calls were made after five. Till then I had to share in the torpor of the city.

The sunset brought a resurrection. Bands started to play in the garden of the Military Club, reserved for the aristocracy, and in the public park, open to all. The society of Ashkhabad was small but very active. Was it the great distance separating them from Russia that made people cling together? Was it the dryness of the climate that made men breezy, like the Americans from the western states? I could not tell. In any case, Ashkhabad was not a sleepy provincial town of Russia, and people were different here. Ashkhabad was full of societies. Every man of some standing had to be president or vice-president of some society and a member of most of the others. No, Ashkhabad was not a dull town, and I was drawn into the swirl.

I had to join the Military Club, the Horse Racing Society, the Shooting Club, and the Society for the Relief of the Poor, beside the Oriental Society and the Museum Committee. Only a yacht club was lacking in Ashkhabad, for the largest water surface was provided by a bathtub. I was saddled with the duties of secretary for the Committee for the Construction of a Cathedral, and we did build one. I also took part in the founding of the first mosque of the Persian sect of the Babi.

This harmless, progressive, liberal sect was founded by the Bab, who was shot in Tabriz in 1850, close to the wall of the citadel at a place which I tried in vain to locate. The Babis were persecuted in Persia in my time and had to conceal their faith; I had never met them there. They came to Russia and even spread to America, where they were called Baha'i.

The Babis in Ashkhabad formed a closely knit community of honest, law-abiding people, somewhat reminiscent of the early Christian churches in the first century after Christ. The great event in the life of the Babi colony was the arrival of Hadji Mirza M. Taghi, a Babi chief, and nephew of Bab, from Yezd, Persia in 1902. A rich, wise, kind old man of Biblical appearance and dressed in floating

Oriental garments, he looked like one of the Magi who came to
Bethlehem to adore the birth of Christ. Hadji Mirza M. Taghi had
been consular agent for Russia, England, and France in his native
town for many years. Although widely respected, he was finally
forced to leave by persecution which continuously increased in violence. I had been informed beforehand about his arrival, and he was
warmly recommended to me by my friend and future brother-in-
law, Dr. D. M. Vinogradov, who had visited him in Yezd.

After being welcomed with due reverence by all the Babi community of Ashkhabad and meeting with a hospitable reception on
the part of the Russian authorities, Hadji Mirza M. Taghi decided
to settle in Ashkhabad and, as the crowning act of his long religious
life, to build there a beautiful Babi temple, the first on the continent
of Asia. He lived in a very simple manner but spared no money for
the completion of the temple or the cause of his religion.

I presented Hadji Mirza M. Taghi to the military governor of
Transcaspia, General D. I Subotich, who agreed to lay the corner-
stone of the Babi temple. It was an impressive ceremony, this Russian recognition of Babism as an established religion at a moment
when hundreds of Babis were being slaughtered in Persia. The Babi
community presented General Subotich with a picture by the famous calligrapher, Meshkin Kalam, representing a bird on a tree.
The picture was formed with the letters composing the verse, "On
the Tree of Eternity sits the Bird of Truth repeating: 'He (God) is
one, is one, is one.' "

Although the Babis in Ashkhabad kept the outward appearance
of old-fashioned Moslems, their conceptions were entirely different.
Babi women visited European families and enjoyed a freedom unknown at that time in Moslem countries. The Babis had a small
book called *Kitabi Siossieh* (*The Book of Behavior*). They considered that each man had a divine spark which must be kept pure during his lifetime in order to ascend to heaven. The Babis in
Ashkhabad presented various stages of evolution, ranging from a
purely Oriental to a European way of life. However, they retained
their Persian attire, whereas in European Russia they wore western
clothes.

I was glad to hear that after the revolution the persecution of
Babis ceased in Persia, and I have no doubt that they will prove to
be excellent Persian citizens. They are certainly good examples of

what may become of a Persian liberated from the suffocating atmosphere of an old decaying past.

One of Russia's successes in Ashkhabad was the People's House, which provided good food for a few cents. The value of nutrition is keenly appreciated in a desert country where nothing grows. There was no labor problem, since Ashkhabad had only one factory, but that did not simplify the situation. There were many workmen in the railway workshops and in the railway battalions, recruited from among factory men. All these people were open to revolutionary propaganda. In case of a strike, the whole province could be paralyzed at a moment's notice, as did happen in 1905.

But all was quiet as yet. On holidays, military parades were held on the plaza, attracting a mass of spectators. Troops were reviewed. The railway school took part in the performance, and its boys cheered with their young radical voices the corps commander who greeted them. The year 1901 was probably the last year when reforms could have been introduced by the government with perfect safety.

A picture of old Transcaspia would not be complete without including Tarnovskii. He personified the restless spirit of a new land. No man was safe from him, not only in Russian Central Asia but in the whole empire. As a young officer he had been appointed commander of a lonely post on the Afghan frontier. Tarnovskii found the opportunity good, crossed the border, and occupied the first Afghan village on his way. Then he telegraphed directly to the tsar, presenting him with his conquest. A thunderous telegram from Alexander III to the commander in chief relieved Tarnovskii of his post and put an end to his military career. Tarnovskii consoled himself with the thought that he, a mere captain, had received a personal reprimand from the emperor—a rare occurrence in the annals of the Russian army. He reappeared as manager of the Russian State Bank in Bokhara. Tarnovskii was an enterprising man and never lacked adventures. A tiger came close to the railway—a thing never heard of before. Tarnovskii organized a party of hunters. They met the tiger, opened fire, and the tiger charged. Here the details become somewhat confused—what is certain is that Tarnovskii escaped unharmed, the tiger was killed, and a soldier was mauled to death.

I had hardly entered into my manifold duties in Ashkhabad when a telegram from St. Petersburg ordered me to take charge of the

political agency in Bokhara at once. No explanation was given. I
boarded the next train to New Bokhara, the seat of our political
agency, a few miles away from the capital of the native state of
Bokhara, a protectorate of Russia. I was met by a cossack guard and
a member of the agency who reported to me what had happened.
Of course, Tarnovskii was again the cause of the trouble. He had
assaulted the acting political agent and was shot by him in the chest.
I found Tarnovskii none the worse for his wound, sitting in an armchair with the proud mien of a Roman emperor. The likeness was
complete, as Tarnovskii was scantily draped. He welcomed me and
started to talk volubly and without sense. He was suffering from fits
of temporary insanity. I put him on a train and sent him away.
But before he reached Krasnovodsk, he interfered in a quarrel, beat
the wrong man, and presented his excuses in his most chivalrous
manner. That was the end of Tarnovskii in central Asia, which
seemed dull indeed after his departure.

Tarnovskii was the last troublemaker. The mixed population of
Ashkhabad lived in perfect harmony. The freedom of the surrounding desert seemed to permeate our little city. I liked Ashkhabad.
Life there was so normal, pleasant, and easy. There were no expensive restaurants, no luxury shops, no display of wealth. In this sense
it was quite a provincial town, but without the priggishness often
found in one.

As summer advanced, Ashkhabad got hotter and dustier every
day. Fortunately I could move to a resort in the hills. General
Kuropatkin, when he was governor of Transcaspia, had settled this
point. The Russian possessions extend along the mountain range
which forms the frontier of Persia. After prolonged negotiations
Kuropatkin succeeded in obtaining the little valley of Firuza, cool
and shady, with a clear swift brook. Every summer the administration of Ashkhabad moved there. It was a perfect arrangement, a little
paradise for unpretenious people.

Whatever the defects of Russian administration, it shone in contrast to the neighboring states of Persia and Bokhara. The railway,
unique in the Middle East, produced an enormous impression on
the minds of the natives. The tremendous bridge over the Oxus
hung high in the air, a fairylike construction. Civilization appeared
at its best in the desolation of the desert. Ashkhabad was the only
place where I felt proud of Russia.

In 1902 came the first tremor. I was talking with a railway stationmaster, a Ukrainian, who cautiously asked me if I knew what was going on in the province of Poltava. I answered that there was nothing wrong there, since the papers had not mentioned anything. The stationmaster looked at me dubiously. I was mistaken. The peasants were attacking and robbing the estates in Poltava. The papers were censored, but the news spread through the railways. The railwaymen were well organized and informed. They proved it during the general strike over the empire.

In the autumn the chief of the railway gendarmes, old General Malykhin, president of our Shooting Club, called on me to speak about a pheasant drive. Malykhin looked gloomy, which was contrary to his habit. He was usually a merry man, a good sportsman, and an even better storyteller. He knew a great many anecdotes and could not make even the shortest visit without relating one of them, with his usual dry humor, which would provoke an explosion of laughter. This time he was exceptionally silent.

I was unpacking a bronze empire writing set, arranging the sphinxes and winged victories on my desk. Malykhin gazed thoughtfully at the gilded statuettes. Probably they reminded him of the palace furnishings he saw when he accompanied the tsar on his hunting trips as head of the secret service men. The sight of the gay and noble figurines seemed to increase his dark mood.

"Do you know what is going on in Russia?" he asked abruptly.

I looked at him in mute surprise.

"Yes," he continued with a grim intonation, shaking his white head. "Not we, but our children for certain will see things beyond the wildest flights of our imagination."

He took leave of me without any further explanation, as if he had said too much. I remained perplexed. Malykhin was in touch with the Police Department in St. Petersburg and was fully informed of the progress of revolutionary sentiment.

"Well, well!" I thought. "Where is our government leading the country?" I did not think much about it, however, as I had other things of absorbing personal interest in mind.

I had arranged in my little house the Jacob-style furniture sent by my mother, added some Bokhara carpets, and had put my collection of books in order. The English works were about politics and travel in Asia; the French ones concerned the art of the Dutch and Italian Renaissance. I felt perfectly happy and soon was to be happier still. With the coming of winter Ashkhabad became delightfully clean and cool. Snowflakes floated in the air before my eyes, forming a haze, spotlessly white and transparent like a nuptial veil.

Old Customs

I received an invitation to dinner from the new chief of staff. It was summer, and we were all staying at Firuza, a village in the hills. The table was set under a large walnut tree. The hostess placed me next to her daughter, seventeen, with a delicate face and hair the color of ripe wheat. Pâtés were served on green plates with a swallow painted in the center.

"Are you not afraid that the swallow will carry away your pâté?" I asked my neighbor.

She looked at me, opening wide her eyes, and burst into a laugh that rang in my ears. A few months later we were betrothed.

In the beginning of our acquaintance, I could see her only two or three times a week, including church. We were both shy. I paid visits to her mother, who used to call her to join in the conversation. Later she came of her own accord.

But when we moved back to Ashkhabad, I began dropping in almost every evening. According to the Russian custom, tea was served in the dining room in a close family circle at about nine o'clock, the most pleasant moment of the day. The general, a stern, hardworking man, looked companionable then, having finished his daily tasks. The mother talked about Moscow life, spiritualism, and vegetarian diet. I was ready to swallow anything as long as I could look at the slender girl at the other side of the table. We spoke little together, our eyes rarely met, but I felt a new sense of peace and well-being when we were in the same room. If she left it even for a moment, I felt disturbed and ill at ease.

There seemed to be a kind of special atmosphere that surrounded us both and isolated us from the rest of the world. Her presence became indispensable to me, like the air I breathed. I asked for her hand, and it was given to me. From that moment I was allowed to pay regular court. We could sit alone and talk together. Time seemed to fly past us. My betrothed became eighteen, and the date of our wedding was set soon after.

Our marriage was to take place in the evening. In the morning I sent my bride a bouquet of orange blossoms and white violets by my best man. Later he went to inform her that I was going to the church, where I was the first to arrive. There were no printed invitations to attend the ceremony, but all Ashkhabad filled the church, which was all lit up and animated by the murmur and movement of the people.

I did not wait long. She entered the church on the arm of the general, and they walked to the middle of the nave, where I met them. We advanced alone to the priest and stepped onto a piece of silk laid before the lectern. People were eagerly watching us, for there was a belief that the one who trod on the silk first would have the upper hand in the household. Since bride and bridegroom walk together, there is usually quite an argument among the public about who was first.

She appeared as frail and ethereal as the long veil which decended from the orange blossoms on her head. She was altogether something new and unreal. Only her voice was the same as she answered "Yes." We exchanged our rings three times to form a chain and walked thrice around the little lectern with the Holy Gospel. We held lighted candles in our hands, the priest preceded us, the attendants held crowns above our heads, and the choir sang.

"Kiss your wife and you your husband," said the priest. Our lips lightly touched each other's cheek, and my bride lowered her eyelids as she drank wine from the same cup as I. That was the end. We were united for the rest of our lives.

We drove to her home, which was hers no more. A military band struck up a march as we entered the house and knelt before her mother, who gave us her blessing. We stayed during the reception, receiving congratulations, then drove to my house, which was ours now.

The rapid succession of happy days, weeks, and months which we spent there till we left for a trip abroad can be better described in verse than in heavy prose.

> It seem'd as if
> The march of time
> Had turned back
> Its flying course.
>
> We heard the harps
> Of angels singing
> And lived alone
> In Paradise.

> You are my Eve
> And I your Adam.
> Give me your hand
> And walk with me.

I received a formal leave and took my wife to Florence to present her to my mother, who was staying there. My mother was delighted with my choice and cherished my wife with all her love—she had always wanted to have a daughter. From Florence, the three of us went to Rome. There is a charm in Italy, where ancient art looks young and beautiful in its natural surroundings, defying time. I think it is due to the effect of the sun. Its rays glide with a caress over the marble fountains of Rome, whose gay, unceasing flow of sparkling water is the source of Italy's life and youth.

I called on the Russian legation at the Vatican for a letter of recommendation to see the Pope, and I met the Russian minister, K. A. Gubastov. He later became assistant foreign minister and was very friendly with me. I also saw the secretary of the legation, who looked pale and of delicate health. He complained that he had to finish the mail for the departure of the diplomatic courier but finally agreed to prepare a letter for me at once. This secretary was S. D. Sazanov, who became foreign minister of Russia six years later, and had to face the ordeal of World War I.

The Russo-Japanese War and the First Revolution

Early in 1904 Japan declared war on us. The news was received in Ashkhabad, as everywhere in Russia, with amazement. The tsar had said publicly on the eve of the New Year that there would be no war. However, there it was. The public, totally misinformed about the strength of Japan, remained unconcerned over the outcome of hostilities. Only the ignorant common soldiers understood what war would mean. They realized instinctively that, since Russia was strong, the country that attacked her must also be strong. But Russia called on them, and they went unflinchingly to her defense.

We were summoned to the public square to hear the ukase of the tsar about the declaration of war. I was deeply moved, looking on the gray mass of soldiers standing at attention. A general speaking with me called them "holy cattle." "Holy," yes, I thought, but why "cattle"?

A reason for the war had to be given, and a very unsatisfactory explanation was offered. It was stated that Japan had objected to a Russian concession in Korea. But why should Russia seek this concession at the risk of war? The whole transaction was very unpalatable. People of rank were financially interested in it; that was widely known but could not be stated officially. Therefore, Japan was accused of greed, ambition, and high-handedness in beginning hostilities before declaring war and of violating the neutrality of Korea.

The invectives against Japan did not produce the desired effect, and public opinion blamed the inefficiency of the Russian authorities. When the telegraph announced that two of our best ironclads had been damaged at Port Arthur, a general observed: "Our admirals there are the same kind of fools as everywhere." I have mitigated somewhat the blunt expressions of the old warrior. Even taking into consideration a certain mutual antipathy which existed between the navy and the army, the trend of censure was unmistakable. I sent a servant to a store to buy some Japanese toothpicks, and he grinned: "Yes, the Japs know how to polish the teeth." No offense to me was meant. It was a kind of self-criticism peculiar to the Russians, which now often tries the patience of the Soviet rulers.

On the whole the reaction in Ashkhabad was mild. We added a Red Cross section to our numerous societies and donated a complete equipment for a field hospital. Some officers volunteered for the war and did not return. Their widows went to church in black. There was no mobilization in central Asia, and we had no troops to spare. I was glad that the vast mass of Moslems inside and outside our dominions remained perfectly quiet.

In Russia the situation was different. The mobilization was unexpectedly large and the expenditures enormous. Besides, the war promised no profits. But it was not a mere question of losses. The mentality of Russia was affected. The conservatives had relied on the bureaucratic regime and felt that it had blundered badly. The liberals, always quarreling among themselves about abstract points of various theories, united in a common condemnation of absolutism and bureaucracy. Labor was indignant, burdened by heavy sacrifices imposed for the sake of Manchuria and Korea, which meant nothing to them. The government was confronted with foreign war and a potential civil disturbance. But the tsar shrank from an open disavowal of his ministers and a speedy peace with Japan. Nicholas II first wanted a victory—General Kuropatkin had promised it to him.

War is chiefly a matter of ways and means. Kuropatkin could not win. He chose the southernmost part of Manchuria as a theater of war. The Russian headquarters and the army were thirty days away from Moscow, connected to it by a single-track railway. The Japanese were twenty-seven hours from Yokohama and had command of the sea. They played with Kuropatkin like a cat with a mouse.

The tsar was sorely afflicted by the reverses, but he tried not to think about them. In wartime, during the report of a minister, he said: "Do you know that I shot six fine cock pheasants this morning?" The minister was aghast.

In the spring of 1904 I went to St. Petersburg. The personnel in the Asian Department looked ghastly, and the rest of the Foreign Office was not much better. I called on V. N. Lamsdorf, the foreign minister. Our talk was meaningless, as it had always been. The count knew nothing about Asian affairs and did not care about them. It was his appearance which struck me. He used to have a smiling, affable countenance and delicate, velvety manners; his talk had been smooth, almost oily. He liked to produce a pleasant impression on his callers, and he would forget them as soon as they went out. He was full of ecclesiastical unction, like a prelate desirous of being popular.

All that was gone. He now sat shrunken in his armchair, his full face nervous and twitching. He seemed to avoid looking at me, as if apprehensive that I should read in his eyes the agony that convulsed him. He knew that all Russia put the blame for the war on him, and he felt guilty. And guilty he was for not stopping the absurd Korean concession and for letting the direction of Far Eastern affairs slip into the hands of A. M. Bezobrazov, E. I. Alekseev, and A. M. Abaza, who promoted the concession. Of course the military command was responsible for the mismanagement of the war, but it was the duty of the foreign minister to offer his resignation if there was no other way of preventing a disastrous conflict.

I left St. Petersburg with a heavy heart. My chiefs in the Foreign Office were crushed, and a good deal of Russia's power as well, unless an improbable victory redeemed the situation. Ashkhabad was in a mess. Cholera broke out in Transcaspia and spread to the garrison of Merv. My father-in-law, who was acting as temporary governor and corps Commander, rushed there and stamped out the epidemic, but he looked visibly shaken on his return. Notwithstanding his severe and gruff manners, he considered his soldiers part of his family.

In the fall of 1905, pending a formal appointment, I was called to Tashkent, the capital of Russian Central Asia, as acting political secretary for frontier relations to the governor-general. The Russo-Japanese war had just petered out, not on the bloody fields of Manchuria or at a solemn conference in a great capital, but in a small city in New Hampshire—Portsmouth, of all places. It was the right time for the belligerent parties to talk business, for both were short of money. As the story ran, the Russian delegate, Count S. Iu. Witte, former minister of finance, met J. P. Morgan in New York. Witte could not speak English, and Morgan did not speak French. Yet they got on very well together. A business proposition, worked out by Witte, was accepted by the Japanese, and an excellent treaty was signed. But a wave of discontent swept over Russia and reached Tashkent, where the railwaymen were the first to organize a protest.

I was still in Tashkent and had no exact information on what was happening in Russia. Telegrams in the local papers were short. The mail was slow in reaching central Asia, and events moved quickly and in an unprecedented way. I had to depend more on what I saw than what I read. Judging by Tashkent, the situation was serious enough.

The worst of it for me was that I had to return to Ashkhabad and was dependent on the railway service, which might be discontinued at any moment. I was with my wife and my little daughter, who needed fresh milk every day. If my departure was delayed we could be caught by the declaration of the strike at some station in the desert, without any food at all. There was no time to lose.

As soon as the political secretary returned, I went to the governor's palace. All was quiet there. N. N. Teviashev, the old governor-general, looked as comfortable as ever. I received his authorization to leave and drove straight to the railway station. I wanted to reserve a private car, one of the privileges of colonial service.

The station was black with people, and a meeting was going full swing, resounding with shouts of "Down with the government!"

A martial-looking gendarme with fierce whiskers was observing the scene from a safe distance.

"What does this mean?" I asked.

"It is like this every day," he answered calmly.

It did not impress him. The people assembled at the meeting were hard-working men who had no quarrel with the local authorities. They were protesting against the government of St. Petersburg and clamoring for a constitution. That was too complicated for the

brains of the guardian of peace in Tashkent and left him apparently
indifferent. The stationmaster assured me that the train would leave
in the evening for Samarkand, according to schedule, and that a
special car would be attached for me. That was all he could say.
During a revolution no one knows for sure what will happen the
next day or what will become of him. I had to take the risk, and I
left the same evening.

The critical moment came when we crossed the Oxus River and
entered into the desert that separated it from the Merv oasis. At
every station the train crew could receive the order of the declaration of the strike. A reddish sun set behind the hillocks of sand. My
wife was giving milk to the baby from a bottle. Both were gay, and
I had to appear to be. I lay down, listening to the sound of the
wheels which were still turning, the only thing that mattered.

In the morning we came to Ashkhabad, and the first news I heard
in the office was that a general strike had been declared over the
whole empire and that trains, mail, and telegraph services were to
stop from that day on. In Russian Central Asia this meant that trains
were detained in the desert at stations with a limited water supply
in tanks. But the orders of the central executive committee were in-
exorable and counted more than the will of the tsar.

As I sat in the government building, a revolutionary procession
passed before the windows, celebrating the declaration of the strike.
Workmen were carrying red and black flags (they were not sure
which would be the right color) with large inscriptions. Soldiers
from various regiments were conspicuous, much to the despair of
my father-in-law. Only the cossacks were absent. They did not share
in the movement.

On the same day two governments were established in Ashkhabad
—the official one, which continued to function within the limits of
the city, and the revolutionary one, which controlled the strike in
the entire province by means of the telegraph. There was a truce
between them. The military governor commanding the province
and the army corps, General E. E. Usakovskii, a Pole, showed much
good sense on this occasion. He was a lazy, pretentious man, but he
had humane qualities and refused to have recourse to military force
—only partly reliable, as it would lead to bloodshed and civil war.
The generals were against the governor but hesitated to provoke
an open revolt of their troops.

The only place that opposed the strike was the fortress of Kushk on the frontier of Afghanistan, a dreary place full of malaria. The strategic railway branch that connected Kushk with the rest of Transcaspia was left without rolling stock, but that did not stop the commander of the fortress. He assembled his men and wanted to move on foot to the rescue of Ashkhabad, on the way hanging from telegraph poles all the railwaymen, civilians, Jews (there were none there), rebel Russian peasants (also nonexistent in that region), university students, and the like. Russia was to be a land of soldiers commanded by the tsar. All the rest were useless, pernicious, and un-Russian. The general was stopped by a telegraphic order from Usakovskii, the only telegram that was allowed to pass during the strike.

On October 17 (old style) 1905, the tsar granted a constitution. The strike was called off, and the first revolution demobilized, considering itself victorious. But it was not.

The revolutionaries thought that a parliamentary system implied, as in Great Britain and France, a parliamentary cabinet responsible to the Duma (house of representatives) and nominated by its majority. The tsar considered that the choice and dismissal of the ministers rested solely with him, as it did with the president of the United States. But in America the ministers, or secretaries as they are called, do not take part in the sittings of the House. In Russia they did. The right to interpellate the ministers had never been denied to the Duma in Russia. Thus an impossible situation was created. The appearance of the ministers in the Duma after they had been voted down provoked storms of protest.

During the sessions of the first two Dumas, the tsar, not content with executive power, controlled, or rather paralyzed, through the conservative upper chamber, the entire legislative activity of the Duma. The fundamental law on elections was altered by a decree of the tsar, and therefore, the new (third) Duma, subservient to the government, did not have the confidence of the nation.

By an excessive use of his powers, the tsar undermined his authority. Public opinion swerved toward a second revolution; some parties became converted to the idea of a republic. But the masses, who had resumed their everyday work, were disinclined to fight again. They had fulfilled the program of their leaders, whose fault it was that the struggle had proved abortive.

The tsar, who was satisfied with the old laws, cared chiefly for his executive power and had kept it. The political parties, which

needed new laws and strove for legislative supremacy, were unable
to legislate under the new constitution. The vanquished tsar
emerged from the strife as the chief winner.

There was an essential misunderstanding that was eventually
bound to destroy everything. Many people believed that the monarchy existed and would exist forever in Russia because it was ordained by God, imposed by law, and indissolubly linked with the
idea of Russia as a state and nation. Hereditary tsars, Orthodox de-
nomination, and Russian nationalism, according to this opinion,
formed a single entity. One conception could not be dissociated
from the others else all would collapse and there would be no more
Russia. Their slogan was orthodoxy, autocracy, and nationality.
The fact that other nations had parliaments and were limited mon-
archies or republics with no monarchs at all, did not impress the
conservatives. The liberals contended that Russia had to follow
the same evolution that other nations did, that unlimited tsarism
had outlived itself, and that any obstacles put in the path of liberty
would only accelerate the downfall of the tsar.

Ashkhabad, after a brief spell of excitement, became sullen. Revolutionary elements turned to underground work. Several people
were threatened, among them my father-in-law, who fortunately was
soon transferred to another post in Russia. Personally I had nothing
to fear, but I felt oppressed. I had put all my hopes on a constitutional regime and saw now that it would not work.

Early in 1906 I went to Kushk, accompanying the new governor-
general of Russian Central Asia, General D. I. Subotich, on his inspection tour of the frontier. Subotich, a Serb by origin, was a brilliant man with liberal views and a keen mind. He was soon
dismissed. We found the brave general commanding the fortress—
the only man who never had malaria—gay and hospitable, the soldiers sick and loyal, and everything as usual in Kushk. But the place
was not to be treated lightly. There was something undauntable in
its atmosphere.

The governor-general, who was also commander in chief, with a
sudden impulse common to military men ordered me to go to the
next Afghan post and announce his appointment to Tashkent. I
looked at him aghast. The Russian government had solemnly declared to England that Russia would abstain from any relations
with Afghanistan. I knew that our Foreign Office would be greatly
incensed if they heard about my crossing the inviolable Afghan

border. But I had received the order from the commander in chief in the presence of all the officers, with the garrison standing at attention, pale with malaria and patriotic emotion. It was impossible to question an order in the strict military surroundings of the Kushk fortress.

I clicked my heels, put my fingers to the edge of my cap, and answered: "Yes, Your Excellency." In the prescribed Russian military form it sounded much longer—*Slushaius Vashe Vysokoprevoskhoditelstvo*—and had to be said in one breath, half the syllables swallowed in a gulp.

I felt like a man who was going to plunge in midwinter into a swift river. I took a carriage, an officer of the customs guard, and some mounted men and drove on a highway—clean, straight, and useless, as are all military things in peacetime. Two miles away the highway stopped at a small rivulet, the limit of the Russian Empire and its military and political power. In crossing it I had everything to risk and nothing to gain. But being a civilian I had to uphold the dignity of the civil service.

"I cannot go any farther," said the officer, "but you may take two of my men as guides." On the other side could be seen some scanty vegetable gardens, a few trees, and a small village of mud houses. I mounted a horse and splashed across the rivulet. We followed a path between the plantations, rode into the village, and reached a small square in the center of it. Afghan soldiers in brown jackets, baggy white trousers, and pointed turbans stood in ominous silence before a house larger than the others. In front of the door a tall officer, with cartridges across his chest and a sword at his side, looked fixedly at me. I said in Persian that I had been sent by the Russian governor-general. The officer motioned me to enter the house. We came in and sat on English iron camp chairs. I said that General Subotich sends his greetings to the governor of Herat and makes known his appointment to Tashkent. I asked the officer to transmit this message to its destination.

Now it was the turn of the Afghan to be perplexed. He looked at the ground and said something to the servants. Tea and sweets appeared on the round iron table and provided a welcome diversion. A few phrases were exchanged about the weather and the harvest. Again a painful silence. Finally the officer said that he would ask instructions from Herat. I rose, saluted, and rode back to Russia and freedom. I reported to General Subotich, who said briefly: "All right." That was all. I did not write to St. Petersburg, and nothing was ever heard about my mission.

Tashkent and the Election of the Second Duma

I was promoted to the position of political secretary to the governor-general in the beginning of 1906, and I had to leave Ashkhabad and move to Tashkent, the capital. The city was large, the country rich, and the population numerous, but I missed the brisk and dry Transcaspia. Tashkent was damp, its air heavy, its Russian colony and its natives fat, commercial, and prosperous. They disapproved of the Russo-Japanese war as a bad venture and showed it on their ballots.

The second parliamentary election of Russia was the great event of 1907. I was on the committee in charge of balloting. A progressive candidate was elected by an overwhelming vote. But the people of Tashkent overshot their mark. Their favorite son, instead of remaining a liberal, took his seat in the Duma as a Social Democrat, which meant the extreme left. Communism was still unknown in Russia in 1906, and Lenin also. Like Julius Caesar, Lenin had attained the age of thirty-six without the world being aware of his existence.

The elected representative was a retired vice-governor, V. P. Nalivkin, a brave, honest, and popular man and an expert on central Asia. Nalivkin came to St. Petersburg in an indignant mood. The ministers were still appointed by the tsar and responsible only to him. Personally, Nalivkin had never been a revolutionary; he had spent all his life in military and civil service in central Asia. But once the Duma was elected, according to Nalivkin, it was to be supreme, and the tsar could rule only by and with its consent. No conflict was possible. Nalivkin was a trained officer. His strict sense of military discipline moved him to an absolute allegiance to the Duma. A military mind cannot obey two chiefs at the same time. I believe that Cromwell's Puritan cavalry, the Ironsides, was composed of men like Nalivkin.

But the Russian Duma had no Cromwell and few Puritans. The Duma was dissolved, a new election ordered, and Russian Central Asia deprived of the right to send representatives. These repressive measures of the government were met by terrorist reprisals. Officials were murdered throughout Russia, including Ashkhabad and Tashkent. The peaceful people became frightened, and the opposition grew bolder. The year 1906 was dragging to its lugubrious end when I received an order to accompany the emir of Bokhara on his visit to the tsar.

Emir Seid Abdul Ahad of Bokhara

Emir Abdul Ahad of Bokhara was the only person in the whole Russian Empire who could call on the tsar and stay in his palace as his honored guest. Of the vast empire of Tamerlane only two native states—Bokhara and Khiva—remained. Khiva, a tiny state, owed its preservation to its remoteness in the desert north of Transcaspia. Bokhara, located on the railway line and surrounded by Russian dominions, maintained its semi-independence through the exertions of its ingenious ruler, Abdul Ahad, a personal friend of Nicholas II.

Abdul Ahad had acquired this extraordinary position by his own shrewd wits. As a second son of the old emir, he was not in the direct line of succession. But the crown prince of Bokhara, a fanatical Moslem, had declined to go to Russia to attend the coronation of Alexander III, and Abdul Ahad was sent in his place. This was the opportunity of a lifetime for Abdul Ahad. He already understood that the road to the throne of Bokhara lay through St. Petersburg, and he carefully prepared his plan.

The decisive moment came when he was asked if he was the Heir Apparent. He answered, as if bowing before the supreme authority of the emperor, that this depended entirely on the will of His Majesty. This answer highly pleased the tsar, who understood that it implied a request of the emir to have his heir accepted by Russia. The emir was informed that, in conformance with his wishes, Abdul Ahad was recognized as his heir by the Russian government. Consternation ensued in Bokhara, but nothing could be done. The eldest son refused to submit to the loss of his succession and fled to India. Abdul Ahad had won. At the death of his father he ascended the throne of Bokhara.

Beginning his reign as a Russian protégé, Abdul Ahad was unpopular with his fanatical subjects. His position was precarious. One petty Moslem state after another was annexed to the Russian possessions in central Asia. Abdul Ahad trembled that his turn would come. Realizing that resistance was impossible, he launched a policy of catering to Russia's interests.

He was supported by P. M. Lessar, then political agent at Bokhara, who wanted to preserve that state as a safety valve against Moslem discontent with Russian innovations in Tashkent. Natives displeased with Russian rule could migrate to Bokhara and there enjoy in full the privileges of medieval Moslem administration in conformity with the best traditions of orthodox Oriental despotism.

The emir agreed to the construction of a Russian railway across his dominions and their inclusion into the customs frontiers of the empire. Each concession of the emir was rewarded by some honorary distinction. He received the title of Highness from the tsar. The position of Abdul Ahad became firm, but it depended entirely on his personal relations with the Russian sovereign.

Abdul Ahad feared and admired Emperor Alexander III. The massive bulk of the tsar, his deep voice and imperious manners, his rough but sincere friendliness and plain common sense mixed with facetious humor impressed the emir, who felt him to be a real ruler in whom he could place his confidence.

The death of the emperor was a great shock to the emir and to Nicholas II, who sincerely loved his father and was not ambitious by nature. He created a medal in memory of Alexander III, and during the mourning period the ministers wore no other decorations when they called on the tsar. Abdul Ahad, with his infallible tact, was equal to the situation. He founded the order of Emperor Alexander III—*Iskender Salis*—the highest in Bokhara. He knew that it would please the tsar and induce him to wear the Bokharan order, a master stroke in the best Abdul Ahad manner.

Abdul Ahad went to St. Petersburg to offer his condolences and presented the tsar with the star of the new order, set with big diamonds, the most expensive order in the world. After that the emir waited for the day of the official dinner in his honor. In the morning a telephone call came to the emir.

"His Majesty desires to know over which shoulder, the right or the left, the ribbon of the new order is to be worn."

"In the same way as the St. Andrew [the highest Russian order]," answered Abdul Ahad.

Abdul Ahad felt more at ease with Nicholas II and allowed himself some liberties, but he trusted him less. The character of the young tsar was malleable and did not yet have the rigidity which it later acquired under the pressure of his stubborn wife.

In the beginning of his reign the tsar was under the influence of his mother, the Dowager Empress Mary. A Danish princess by birth, she disliked Germans in general and her daughter-in-law in particular, but otherwise she was not interested in politics. Though brought up under a very liberal regime at home, Empress Mary felt perfectly happy in autocratic Russia, ruthlessly ruled by her husband, Alexander III. But when the first revolution broke out in 1905, she realized that common sense made it imperative for her son to make the same political concessions which had been granted by all the other crowned heads in order to remain on their thrones. She was then in Copenhagen, and she wrote a letter with that message to the tsar and sent it to him with the Russian minister to Denmark, A. P. Izvolskii. The emperor listened to his mother's advice and made Izvolskii his minister of foreign affairs, giving Izvolskii the opportunity to say that his entry into the cabinet coincided with the advent of a constitutional regime in Russia. How constitutional the regime was he had yet to learn at his own expense.

This was the last victory of the dowager empress. The tsar regretted having granted the constitution, his wife supported him, and the breach between mother and son became complete. Izvolskii remained foreign minister, but he was never accepted into the intimacy of the tsar and the tsarina, the latter considering him a protégé of her mother-in-law.

Young Empress Alexandra came from one of the small German principalities, whose puppet kings and dukes were vassals of the German emperor. They were useless to their own lands and owed their existence to the endurance of ancient monarchic traditions. When the young empress arrived in Russia, she found the same obsolete traditions still alive. She grasped at them and stuck to them with all her strength, consummating the downfall of her weak husband.

In 1906 the dowager empress held her court at the castle of Gatchina, a large unwieldy building, the favorite residence of her late husband. The tsar and the tsarina stayed at the lovely palace of Tsarskoe Selo, the Versailles of the Russian monarchs. After the double defeat of the Japanese War and the revolution, there were no receptions, and gloom reigned at both courts. The impending visit of the emir came as welcome news, and everything started to stir again.

To St. Petersburg with the Emir

I left Tashkent by the evening train and on the following day saw the barren hills and cultivated lowlands of the Bokharan kingdom. The railway station was located in an arid desert, several miles away from the town of Kermineh, the residence of the emir. It had been expressly stipulated by the Bokharan authorities that the railway tracks must not pass too close to any inhabited place lest the whistle of the engine disturb the prayers and pious meditations of the Moslem population.

Next to the depot building stood a small house belonging to His Highness, with his special waiting rooms hung with chintz. This interesting decoration was a conception of the emir himself, who sought to imitate the silk tapestries and Gobelins of the Russian imperial palaces without too much strain on his private purse.

In the glaring sunlight a crowd of Bokharans in white turbans and long multicolored gowns was gathered around the house. The dignitaries could be easily distinguished by their gorgeous brocades, embossed velvets, silver belts, and curved scimitars. These worthies stroked their beards and lifted their eyes to heaven, expressing their concern at the departure of their beloved ruler for distant lands peopled by infidels. Their mournful looks showed their distress that their monarch should be exposed to unclean contacts among people ignorant of the elementary rules of the Moslem religion.

Courtiers bowed and admitted me into the illustrious presence. The emir was seated in a room that had good carpets and indifferent European furniture. The Bokharan sovereign was a tall, rather heavy, handsome man with a full face framed by a lustrous black beard. He wore a white turban of Indian muslin and a robe of checkered black and violet. The blending of the two dark colors produced a harmonious effect, as did his regular features, the thoughtful expression of his large eyes, and his measured, calm speech. An imposing personage whatever his attire, he had perfect command of himself. When nervous or shocked at something, he drummed slightly with his fingers; that was all. The tone of his voice remained unchanged.

The aim of his journey to St. Petersburg was to receive the order of St. Andrew, worn by the tsar and given to crowned heads. There was no greater distinction at the disposal of the emperor. The emir was firmly set on having this order, as he himself told me, and I knew that he would get it. He was bringing costly presents, selected personally with great care, and he had prepared himself for the journey to the imperial court by studying the official military gazette. He knew all the recent promotions, the rank of the important people, and their actual influence. That is why the emir moved so easily at court. He was accompanied by his only son, Crown Prince Seid Mir Alim, a short, fat youth, who looked quiet and inoffensive but in reality was keen and observant, unexpectedly making biting remarks with an innocent expression on his bland face. Twenty years old, cheerful, and sly, the young prince reminded me of a leopard's cub.

According to immutable custom, the prime minister had to remain in Bokhara during the absence of the monarch. There was much talk about the chief statesman in the retinue of the emir—Nasrullah Beg, a potential premier. Abdul Ahad showed him a marked favor. In general he treated all his attendants well, but his entire affection was concentrated on his son, whom he called *Nuri-Cheshm* (Light of My Eyes). The Emir's deep attachment to his son, a trait by no means common among Oriental rulers, was one of his most attractive qualities.

I remember once, while speaking with him, I expressed an opinion against the death penalty. As a representative of the Russian intelligentsia I was talking in a purely theoretical way. But the emir took it from a practical point of view. "Of course, it is dangerous," he said. I realized with a shudder that the life of each of the more than a million Bokharans hung on a single word of the man who was talking with me. During this hectic time the tsar, with his gentle temper, European education, and Christian upbringing, often took more human lives in a single month than this Oriental despot did in his whole reign.

As I entered the room, the emir graciously shook hands with me and asked about the health of the governor-general. Having satisfied the interest of His Highness in this respect, I took a seat. The emir inquired in a businesslike way how much time remained before the departure of the train. A courtier sadly informed him that only a few minutes were left. The emir lifted his eyebrows in a preoccupied manner and asked for a glass of water, which was presented to him by a "slave." Slavery had been abolished under the previous emir at the instance of the Russian government, but Bokharan courtiers still prided themselves on this honorary appellation.

The glass was full of yellowish water from the river Zarafshan, fresh and innocuous to health, but of objectionable appearance. The emir contentedly gulped it down, arranged his large belt of embossed gold and the scimitar attached to it, and rose. Seated, he could look mild and affable, but walking, he was always dominant and majestic. It seemed as if all the might of his state was moving with him.

It was only a short walk from the house to the station, but the emir mounted a carriage, and his dignitaries ran on foot after him, an obligatory expression of devotion at the departure of the sovereign. We entered the car, and the train moved. Through the windows the emir contemplated the plain and villages scattered in the distance. Suddenly he became interested. "Look, look," he said, pointing to a group of riders racing in a mad chase. It was a *baiga,* the favorite game of the Bokharans. A horseman seizes a sheep and gallops away, pursued by his mounted companions. A wild race ensues, each man trying to snatch the sheep. The rider who reaches the goal with the sheep across his saddle is proclaimed the winner. As a young man Abdul Ahad had a passion for this sport. Once he and the other riders collided and fell in a heap with their horses. Abdul Ahad did not break any bones, but he lost his front teeth and was later supplied with a new set in Russia. The emir eagerly followed the game with his eyes, until a turn of the railroad concealed it from us. "It is a good omen, a very good omen, to see a *baiga* when you start on a journey," the emir said gaily, still looking out the window.

Our train ran on imperial schedule. This meant that every other train was sidetracked on the 3,000-mile stretch from Bokhara to St. Petersburg. The train carried baggage cars with horses and other gifts for the tsar, a car with soldiers who mounted guard during the stops in the cities, other cars with the kitchen, the servants, the retinue, and the emir's own car, a present from the emperor. It was red on the outside, decorated with stars and crescents and gilded latticework. Inside there was a blue anteroom and next to it a salon upholstered in purple leather with crushed silver designs. Ingeniously placed mirrors gave the impression of space.

"See, I have twelve rooms," the emir said to me, pointing to the mirrors. They actually reflected about a dozen times. With his usual tact, the emir made no alterations in the imperial gift, adding only two small portraits of the tsar and the tsarina, painted on enamel. In the next compartment there was a comfortable bed of ordinary size. I heard that the emir, who was six foot six, found it too short and slept on the floor, in regular Oriental fashion.

Beside the guards, there were only four Russians with the emir: myself, representing the Ministry of Foreign Affairs; Colonel Beliaef, representing the Ministry of War; the emir's doctor; and the emir's interpreter. The rest were Bokharans: three important dignitaries and a numerous retinue of attendants, servants, and servants' servants

—a whole caravan of Orientals dressed in all the colors of the rainbow. The emir presented a sharp contrast to their gaudy appearance, uniformly dressed as he was in dark—almost black—violet. He wore Russian boots and a Russian general's blue trousers with a large red stripe running down each side. On his shoulders were silver epaulets with the monogram of Tsar Nicholas II, indicating the rank of aide de camp general and general of cavalry. I believe the emir imagined his attire might pass for a uniform, though the boots and trousers were hardly visible under his long robe. He introduced uniforms in the Bokharan army but permitted his ministers and attendants to wear any hue they chose. None of the Bokharans, however, ever dared wear anything approaching the emir's dress in color. The crown prince usually wore a bright orange robe with a large sun embroidered in gold on the back and looked like an orange himself. He was educated in Russia at the Military School, where he had private tutors and did not follow the regular curriculum. He was a dignitary at the Russian court and as such once attended a breakfast en famille with the sovereigns.

Abdul Ahad received the governors of the provinces on our way and distributed gold and silver stars of the Bokharan order. We left a whole galaxy of them in our trail.

At last our train thundered through the suburbs of St. Petersburg. The engineer stopped the engine with masterly accuracy. The ponderous train continued to glide smoothly and noiselessly till without a jerk it came to a stop before the railway platform. I saw, passing in succession before the windows of the car, the red faces of the policemen with tight collars and bulging eyes, tense with attention, the various shakos and helmets of the stiff military officers, and the matchless silk hats and bright smiling eyes of my colleagues from the Foreign Office. A man in a gold-trimmed cocked hat with white plumage stood in front of them and was the first to enter the car. As the emir rose and listened to the marshal of the court welcoming him in the name of the emperor, people filled the car. I shook hands with my friends; we were in St. Petersburg.

We were taken directly to the Winter Palace, where a residence was prepared for the emir and his suite. By some mistake, the Foreign Office interpreter and I, who were under orders never to leave the emir, were placed in the last of a long train of court carriages. When we reached the palace, the emir had already been taken upstairs to his apartment, the welcoming group had departed, and we had to walk up the marble staircase alone. We passed a long line of splendid rooms, brilliantly lit and perfectly empty, and reached a magnificent hall.

At the end of it two grenadiers stood on guard on both sides of a closed door. We were perplexed. Would they bar our way with their bayonets if we tried to enter? There was nobody else in the vast hall from whom we could seek advice. At last we dared. Nothing happened. The grenadiers remained as still as statues and let us pass.

In the next room the emir, comfortably seated at a round table, was taking refreshments. He motioned amiably to us. A lackey in a red livery with green velvet breeches and white silk stockings moved silently about, offering tea on a silver tray. The room was quiet and peaceful; the fire flickered in the fireplace. We took tea and felt at ease. I had imagined that the palace would be filled with people, movement, and perhaps military music. Nothing of the kind. The emperor was at Tsarskoe Selo, and the Winter Palace was as deserted and silent as the wastes of Bokhara. The emir finished his tea and sat gazing thoughtfully in front of him. We took our leave and retired to the quarters assigned to us in the wing of the Winter Palace occupied by the emir.

The next few days were spent in preparation for the formal audience with the tsar. Abdul Ahad was a vassal approaching his sovereign. Etiquette demanded that upon his arrival to the capital he wait until it pleased His Majesty to appoint the time of the audience; also, that he be given a few days to rest, as if he had come from his distant kingdom on the back of a camel and not in a luxurious railway car. Meanwhile the presents brought by Abdul Ahad were conveyed to Tsarskoe Selo to be offered personally by the emir to the emperor of Russia as a token of loyalty. There was no need to hurry, as the emir's visit was to last about a month. It would have been a sign of imperial disfavor if he were to be dispatched back to his country in a few days.

The Foreign Minister Izvolskii

The emir of Bokhara depended on two agencies in his relations with Russia: the Foreign Office, represented by the political agent in Bokhara; and the War Office, in the person of the military governor-general of Russian Central Asia. As political secretary at Tashkent, I was at the disposal of both ministries, which gave me a large amount of freedom as long as I was on good personal terms with the Asian Department and the governor-general. But in St. Petersburg, where a certain coolness normally existed between the Ministry of Foreign Affairs and the Ministry of War, I ran the risk of being torn in two, as both ministries had equal claims on me. The minister of foreign affairs, Izvolskii, was new to his office, as was A. F. Roediger, the minister of war. Both demanded that I report to them immediately and, what made matters worse, chose the same hour of the same day. Luckily I received Izvolskii's order first, as I had looked in at the Foreign Office at once. When an officer from the War Ministry came to me with a summons to appear at two o'clock, I answered that I already had an order from Izvolskii to present myself at that time. The officer gasped. His sense of discipline admitted no refusal, but he realized that I was in the same predicament.

"I am ordered to inform you that you have to report to the War Office," he said coldly. "I am not to discuss the order."

The deadlock could have been easily avoided by mutual concessions, but there was already a tempest brewing concerning which minister would entertain the emir first. The incident of my presentation to the two ministers was still being discussed at the Winter Palace by the respective representatives as I hurried to the Foreign Office to call on Izvolskii, my direct chief. As a result, I was not invited to the lunch given by the minister of war on the next day, and, in quick retaliation, none of the military received an invitation to accompany the minister of war to the lunch at the Foreign Office a few days later.

Izvolskii would have been called a conservative in England; in Russia he was not only a liberal but actually represented the left wing of the cabinet and was the only minister under the new parliamentary regime who could appear before the Duma without raising a storm of protest. He was much maligned by foreign and Russian conservative writers later on and received little praise for his remarkable achievements. It is only fair to do him justice and present the facts as they stood.

The diplomatic position of Russia offered a ghastly sight after the Japanese War. Japan was victorious, and England was her virtual ally. France's confidence in the value of the Russian army was badly shaken. Austria and Germany enjoyed the situation and were preparing a move toward Belgrade and Constantinople. Russia was practically defenseless, almost friendless, and further incapacitated by the first revolution of 1905. Such was her condition when Izvolskii stepped in.

His creative, energetic mind started to work at once, and with extraordinary rapidity he restored Russia's position in Europe and Asia. The Asian Department had taken all the blame and was considered a pitiful wreck. Izvolskii reorganized it entirely. He divided it into three independent sections, each under his immediate supervision. One section dealt with the Far East—its object was to maintain a friendly attitude toward Japan. Another was concerned with Persian and central Asian affairs, which meant close collaboration with England. The activities of these two sections received Izvolskii's attention first. The success of the treaties concluded by him was demonstrated in 1914. In fact, only during his term of office were relations with England and Japan thoroughly satisfactory.

It was his policy with reference to the third, the Balkan section, that proved fatal first to Izvolskii in 1909 and then to Russia in 1914. In both cases mistakes were made by the Russian foreign ministers, and Austria and Germany tore at the thin web of European peace. It survived the strain of 1909 but went to pieces in 1914.

At the appointed hour I presented myself to the Foreign Office, passed through the office of the private secretary, and entered the large room chosen by Izvolskii for his study; it was bright and spacious, without too much furniture or decoration. Everything looked comfortable and elegant, reflecting the master's taste.

Izvolskii sat at his desk to the right of the door—tall, well built, and well fed, rather an ultrafashionable than an ultrahandsome man. His short nose and monocle gave him a slightly supercilious appearance, which was mitigated by the courtesy of his manners. He rose, pointed to an armchair, screwed his glass into his eye, and looked ready to listen to my report.

I spoke about the situation in Bokhara and Tashkent and finished by saying that the emir was aide-de-camp general to the emperor, whereas the governor-general of Tashkent was not. This made him appear the emir's inferior.

"That can easily be remedied," said Izvolskii, intimating that the head of the Russian dominions in central Asia could be promoted to the same distinction.

"But the emir would still be his senior by promotion."

"Does he know it?"

"Yes, of course," I answered. Izvolskii smiled.

"That cannot be helped," he said.

I started to speak about the respective positions of England and Russia in the Middle East. There was no major conflict of interests, and the existing friction was groundless and detrimental to both sides. Izvolskii listened attentively. His monocle had fallen down during our talk, and he looked serious and likable. I felt that he was in sympathy with what I said, although I did not know that he was in favor of a general agreement with England on Asia that would give both nations a free hand in Europe.

He was not well informed on the problems of central Asia but quickly grasped the main points, as was evident from his questions. I had to enter into some details concerning the Indian frontier, and our conversation became protracted. It was the first time in my life that I was speaking with a Russian statesman who had broad views, and I was greatly impressed. I saw Izvolskii several times, for he was very accessible to his subordinates, who referred directly to him.

One day in 1906, Izvolskii received a letter from the German embassy informing him that the noted revolutionary Rosa Luxemburg had been arrested in Warsaw, then a Russian city. The embassy requested that, as a German subject, she be deported to Germany. The police department was advised accordingly. Shortly after, a discreet telephone call came from that department inquiring whether the answer to the German embassy could be delayed for three days, the time needed for the trial and hanging of Rosa Luxemburg. After that the police authorities would be willing to present their sincere apologies. The request was granted. In some mysterious way the news spread in the Foreign Office. Izvolskii knew nothing about the telephone call and the answer to it. The next day there was some whispering, and people began to look gloomy. The younger men in the Asian Department became excited and consulted one another in hushed voices, condemning participation in what they considered a judicial murder. It was resolved, as a last recourse, to speak to M. G. Priklonskii, a conservative man of honor.

"Infamous!" exclaimed Priklonskii, jumping from his seat. He went straight to the minister and laid the case before him. Izvolskii wrote a telegram in his own hand to the governor-general of Warsaw, requesting the immediate delivery of Rosa Luxemburg to the German authorities. She was saved for the time being, only to be killed by the German police in Berlin during a so-called attempt to escape in 1919.

I greatly admired Izvolskii. He offered to Nicholas II the last chance of reconciliation with the Duma, which alone might have prevented the collapse of the empire. Izvolskii was necessary for the stability of the government. His presence gave a constitutional coloring to the cabinet, and this impressed the Duma, the people, and the foreign governments. As such Izvolskii was irreplaceable. Even Prime Minister P.A. Stolypin, who was purely dictatorial in his activity, was under the moderating influence of Izvolskii. Left alone after the latter's departure, Stolypin ceased to tolerate any opposition and antagonized everyone.

A friend of mine, a diplomat and a liberal monarchist, told me once: "Stolypin can do anything. I can be arrested by his order this very night, and not a single voice will be raised in my defense. There is no safety from Stolypin in Russia." He laughed bitterly. But my friend exaggerated. Stolypin was by no means a tyrant; he was neither vindictive nor suspicious. He was simply a very resolute man —honest, patriotic, and disinterested, loyal to the tsar and Russia. But he came too late, at least twenty years too late. He wanted to continue the strong monarchic rule of Alexander III. This regime had already been undermined by the irresolution of Nicholas II and the hapless Japanese war. Autocratic monarchy had become a broken reed, and the Russian people became restive under it. They would have accepted only a dictatorship of the masses, which Lenin was to promote later. Stolypin's mistake was that he recognized no opinions except his own and that of the tsar. He did not take into consideration the psychology of the masses, and he stood openly for the privileged class, including the well-to-do farmers.

A poor man can easily accept the superiority of the man who is richer and more fortunate than he, but you cannot force a poor man to respect a richer one. The self-esteem of the poor man will revolt. Russia in 1907 was already in a state of potential rebellion. Such a condition is highly dangerous in case of a protracted foreign war. Izvolskii was heading toward difficulties with Austria and was to leave a very uncomfortable diplomatic situation to his successor S. D. Sazonov, not the type of man who could weather a storm.

Luncheon at the Foreign Office

The duties of the foreign minister included considerable enter-taining, which was costly in time and money. Izvolskii decided to invite the emir and all the cabinet and thus discharge at one and the same time his obligations toward his colleagues and His Serene Highness.

The main question was to assure the presence of Prime Minister Stolypin, who lived in constant dread of assassination. The terrorists were more bent on murdering him than on killing even the tsar, con-sidering that of the two Stolypin was the more detrimental. Every time the prime minister went out, he risked his life. Since the at-tempt of the previous summer, when his villa had been wrecked by an explosion, Stolypin lived in the Winter Palace by special invita-tion of the tsar. The Foreign Office stood on the same plaza as the palace, and Stolypin accepted the invitation.

The emir arrived very punctually, but all the ministers were already there. There was only one lady, the hostess. The Bokharan dignitaries were not invited, and from the Russian suite of the emir I alone was present.

We went almost immediately into the dining room; a corner room, it had windows on two sides which filled it with sunshine, a rare occurrence in St. Petersburg. As the room was not very large, the party had an air of intimacy, and the presence of the emir gave an exotic tinge to the formal assembly. I had the impression that the ministers enjoyed it. They quietly conversed and observed His High-ness, who looked slightly ridiculous, handicapped by the proximity of the hostess, who sat next to him. She tried to engage him in con-versation, but the Bokharan potentate rolled his big black eyes and spoke little. He dreaded that she would ask him questions about his wives, whom he disliked to discuss in public. The emir had already had such an experience with the young empress. She in-quired how many daughters he had. For the first time in his life Abdul Ahad was caught unaware. He did not know their exact num-ber, for sons alone mattered in Bokhara. Izvolskii also attempted to divert the emir without much success, and he ordered champagne. Abdul Ahad took a glass of mineral water and drank nothing else.

In the meantime I examined the ministers. They were a well-assorted team under the guidance of Stolypin. They looked rather young; few of them had graying hair. The tsar had already dismissed the old counselors of his father and preferred people of his own age, keeping in reserve only the septuagenarian I. L. Goremykin, who personified the immortality of the Russian bureaucracy. I wonder who has taken his place under the Soviets. Russia is unthinkable without a bureaucracy, which is proliferating in the USSR. Probably the Goremykins will multiply also.

There has been so much talk about the corruption of the tsarist ministers that I feel obliged to correct this impression. A dishonest minister was an exception during the reign of Nicholas II, up to the time of World War I. The ministers of the prewar period were competent and efficient. They lived as it were in a glass case, surrounded by rivals who coveted their places. They could not risk a scandal. There were accusations of graft in the artillery, supply, and transportation departments, concerning subordinates who took advantage of the confidence of the grand dukes, their official chiefs. It was not the men themselves who were wrong but the system they tried to maintain.

Three ministers attracted my particular attention: Premier Stolypin; the minister of finance, V. N. Kokovtsov; and the minister of war, General A. F. Roediger. The mastermind of them all was Stolypin, prime minister and minister of the interior; in his hands was concentrated the administration of the empire, and he practically ruled Russia. He sat, calm and haughty, among the members of his cabinet and looked in the pink of health—rosy, smooth, and elegant. He had nothing of the air of a person burdened with dignities and cares of state, a pose which some statesmen like to assume. I noticed a kind of cold, disdainful challenge in his eyes. He reminded me of the Persian grand vizier, Amin os-Soltān, who had the same fearless expression of a man resolved to die fighting at his post. Stolypin had many enemies even in the party of the Right. He understood the tsar and Russia well, and he knew that he could place his confidence in neither. The tsar was secretive and unreliable, and Russia labored under a deep agrarian discontent.

The plight of Russia was its mass of impoverished peasants. Stolypin wanted to eliminate them altogether by forcing them to leave the land or become hired men. Their land was to be acquired by conservative, well-to-do farmers who would firmly support the state and property rights. Stolypin might be called a progressive, as far as this term could be applied to an aristocrat, a landowner, and a minister of the interior in the reign of Nicholas II.

The other interesting person among the guests of Izvolskii was Minister of Finance Kokovtsov, who was to succeed Stolypin in the premiership. He looked quick, impulsive, and expansive, like a promising college professor, with a political career ahead assured by safe, conservative opinions. He frankly despised the Duma, something Stolypin never did. His point of view was well expressed by his famous phrase: "Thank God, we have no Parliament."

The minister of war, Roediger, a bespectacled general with a bulging waist, was a voracious reader of books and papers, more learned than intelligent and more active than efficient. I never heard of a thoroughly satisfactory Russian minister of war. Perhaps this is impossible in Russia under any régime.

We rose. Our hostess expected that the emir would offer her his arm, but Abdul Ahad moved straight ahead. She shrugged her shoulders slightly and followed him. In the drawing room she sat on the sofa and again tried in vain to enter into conversation with the Bokharan ruler. Stolypin went to a window and stayed there, looking somewhat annoyed. He wanted to leave but decided that it would not be proper as long as the emir remained and reconciled himself to the situation.

The minister of public works, General N. K. Schaufuss, took hold of me and started to ask questions about Bokhara. There were no public works in Bokhara except mosques and irrigation canals. Such conditions did not seem to satisfy the general, and he kept talking, looking sternly at me. My chief, the foreign minister, came to my rescue, offering his colleague a box of cigars wrapped in fine straw and a special cutter—a complicated affair. This gave me an opportunity to slip away. I retreated into a corner, but my chief discovered me there and offered a cigar as a consolation. I declined.

"Extraordinary," said Izvolskii mockingly. "It seems that young men in St. Petersburg have ceased to smoke cigars altogether." He laughed and moved away with his box.

At last the huge bulk of the emir rose from the sofa, and the prime minister walked briskly after him.

Tsarskoe Selo
The Audience with the Tsar

Nicholas II was staying at Tsarskoe Selo. The name in Russian means "Village of the Tsar." It had been built as a country seat, a place where monarchs could retire to spend a holiday away from affairs of state. But it had become more than that. As the sovereigns formed the habit of passing the height of the season there, Tsarskoe Selo acquired the importance of a personal capital of the tsar, separate from the national one.

St. Petersburg was a great city with a large population, which led a life of its own. There was the Duma, odious to the tsar, and the university and technical schools, whose students held meetings of protest. There were numerous factories, with workmen who could strike or make street demonstrations. In Tsarskoe Selo there was nothing of the kind. It existed exclusively for the emperor and his court. Every person arriving there turned courtier as easily as a man entering a church assumes a devout attitude whatever his personal convictions.

As Nicholas II grew more and more estranged from his people, he stayed longer and longer at Tsarskoe until it became, like a lonely island, the last refuge of the monarchy, finally submerged by the rising tide of revolution. The little town was dwarfed by the imperial residence, which comprised a large park with stately alleys of trees leading to several palaces, the whole forming what the Chinese call in their picturesque language the forbidden city.

Access to it was elaborately protected. We were conveyed from St. Petersburg by a special train, running on a private branch of the railway to the tsar's own station at Tsarskoe Selo, where court carriages were waiting for us. The emir's carriage had a team of four white horses with outriders à la Daumont. We drove rapidly through the park and stopped before the Alexandrovskii Palace, the favorite residence of the emperor, a fine but less pretentious building than the great palace of Catherine II.

We were ushered into a square room with a picture on the wall representing the arrival of the Russian fleet under Admiral F. K. Avelan at the port of Toulouse, the only manifestation of the Franco-Russian alliance—the treaty itself had remained secret for several years. A circular table in the center of the room was covered with refreshments. The master of ceremonies escorted the emir to meet the tsar. The Bokharan dignitaries, the Russian attendants, and myself were to be called later. Left alone, we pulled some chairs and sat around the table. There was an artistically arranged fruit basket containing apples, oranges, grapes, and one pear, probably for the sake of the color scheme. We helped ourselves to the dainties on the table. The court lackeys standing by the walls looked at us with reproachful eyes. They were right. I had not finished peeling my pear when two aides appeared and invited us to follow them.

We passed through several lofty rooms that looked like libraries, with mahogany bookcases along the walls and newly published books displayed on tables. On top of the bookcases were numerous polychrome, foot-high statuettes of soldiers dressed in different styles. Every tsar took a special interest in introducing new uniforms and comparing them with the old ones. The rooms seemed very homelike and comfortable, notwithstanding their large size. Everything looked solid and unadorned, in accordance with the personal taste of the emperor, who disliked pomp and ostentation in familiar surroundings.

We came into a hall where a few people were assembled. The minister of the imperial household, Baron V. B. Fredericks, an old beau, still kept a gallant appearance with his big whiskers and smart waist. We waited. Some more uniformed men came in. They stood or moved around easily, addressing each other in a familiar or deferential tone, according to rank relation, and looked with indifference on us and with curiosity on the strange Bokharans.

A flash of color was provided by a Negro servant in gorgeous Oriental attire of crimson, green, and yellow, wearing a silk turban on his head. These "Arabs"—as they were called in Russia—had been fashionable at court since Peter the Great. When they first appeared, common people shunned them, considering them infidels, if not devils incarnate.

We all stood in a semicircle before a closed door with the Negro servant in front of it. Every now and then he peeped through the narrow space between the two halves of the door, then turned to us and grinned. Nobody paid any attention to his grimaces. Suddenly he threw the door wide open and vanished. The emperor, the empress, and the emir appeared on the threshold. The emperor, a small, pale, blond man, with a pointed beard and soft moustache, was in a dark green uniform. He wore it extremely well; his steps were light and the sound of his voice gentle. He seemed pleasant but not impressive. He looked at us quietly as he passed, talking with the emir. But when he entered the next hall, full of people, he stiffened and turned his head right and left, lifting his chin in an attempt at a majestic bearing, evidently imposed on him by training. He did not possess the natural poise of his father nor the self-satisfied assurance of the kaiser.

The empress, much taller than her husband and a beautiful

woman, had something stiff, shy, and cold in her manner and entirely lacked the graciousness that makes a queen popular. People felt ill at ease in her presence. She made the tsar look small, soft, almost feminine, while she appeared tall, unfriendly, somewhat sullen.

The emir towered over the imperial pair in his snow-white turban and long Oriental robe of dark, almost black violet, splashed with bejeweled decorations. He looked magnificent, but his movements were guarded, and strain showed in his eyes as he watched the sovereigns.

All moved into the hall where the gifts were displayed, an exhibition of Bokharan products. Heavy red carpets with designs in black, blue, and white were arranged in small pyramidal tents. Silk embroideries were disposed in the same way. Among them lay lambskins, the famous karakul, the finest in the world. Chardzhui melons stood in piles like cannonballs. On the tables were gilded and enameled silver vases and dishes. In the center were placed objects for the personal use of Their Majesties—a writing pad of solid gold set with diamonds for the emperor and a diamond necklace representing the chain of the order of St. Andrew for the empress. The chain consisted of small, artistically wrought double-headed eagles connected by the x-shaped crosses of St. Andrew—a very appropriate gift, as the Russian sovereigns often wore the order of St. Andrew, the highest in Russia.

The emperor glanced at the offered treasures with polite indifference. He was not acquisitive by nature. But the empress blushed with pleasure as she viewed the necklace. She also carefully examined the precious picture frames, dishes, and vases made by Bokharan goldsmiths. A German princess from a small, provincial, impecunious court, she was visibly moved at the sight of the big jewels to which she was unaccustomed by virtue of her upbringing in traditions of rigid economy and good housekeeping.

The emir looked anxiously at the monarchs. They moved on to a window. Turkoman horses from Bokhara in gorgeous trappings were promenaded outside for their inspection. The emperor turned gently to his wife indicating that he had had enough of the show, and the sovereigns walked out with the emir.

We were conducted to the square room and served refreshments. After a while the emir reappeared in the company of the chamberlain and the master of ceremonies, and we all departed for the Winter Palace.

When we sat in the train on our return journey, Abdul Ahad beamed with satisfaction. He was certain now of obtaining the cross of St. Andrew and was particularly impressed by the conversation he had had with the tsar:

"Is everything quiet in your dominions, Your Highness?"

"Yes, Your Majesty," Abdul Ahad had answered.

The Emir kept repeating: " 'Your dominions!' The Tsar said, 'Your dominions!' " That assured the Bokharan ruler of continuing possession of his kingdom.

Interesting as was the huge Oriental ruler with his turban, his gold embossed belt, his glistening scimitar, his adroit manners, and his clever speech, he was reduced to insignificance before the slim figure and light steps of the all-powerful Russian monarch. The tsar spoke little. His pale face took on various expressions, from the assumed strained dignity when he walked in official processions, like a living symbol of Russian autocracy, to the ordinary calm of a human being, as he picked morsels from his plate during the long court dinners.

I saw much of the tsar, but always in the same atmosphere of state function. However, I spoke with people who had known him more intimately, and what they said complemented and confirmed my personal impression.

The life of the tsar was divided into three parts. The first aspect, his family life, was happy until his son developed Hemophilia and his wife became hysterical.

His second concern, governmental duties, involved the reports of the ministers and the council of state. The tsar read many official papers and made some notations on each with a pencil—a few words or a simple oblique stroke with a dot on each side. His remarks, as a rule, are not interesting. This reading was rather a mechanical habit with him. He listened attentively to verbal reports but disliked discussion. If he disagreed, he started fumbling with things on his table and said nothing to the contrary, but a few days later the minister was likely to be dismissed without warning. The tsar was extremely polite. I never heard of his having said a harsh word to anybody. He knew how to conceal his feelings. He liked to produce a pleasant impression on the man with whom he was talking, even if he hated him at that moment. This absolute lack of sincerity was the great defect of the tsar's character. Nicholas II was aware of his mental limitations, as he had to deal with talented or, in any case, highly trained and experienced counselors. But once inspired by the will of God, he became adamant, to the surprise and despair of his ministers, who vainly tried to oppose what they considered weak and poorly founded opinions. Often the tsar used his ingenuity to comment on some insignificant details and thereby gave the wrong impression of his having a real grasp of the matter under consideration. His meetings with the kaiser were particularly unfortunate. They usually ended in the tsar's discomfiture, which had to be redressed by his ministers. This made the kaiser furious. He assailed the tsar. Their last exchange of telegrams led to Russia's entry in World War I.

Finally, the third part of the tsar's life involved official receptions. The tsar assumed a certain automatic attitude and repeated the same, usually meaningless gestures and phrases, unless he had prepared beforehand what he was to say. This could go on for hours, until those present were more bored than the tsar himself. He impressed me as a trained but talentless actor who had learned a role by heart and played it without a single variation hundreds of times. He was like a mechanical toy that would move straight ahead until the spring either unwound or broke. Fear could stop him like a physical obstacle, but once the fear passed and the obstacle was removed, he would resume his progress in the same direction. He was taught by his father to be an autocrat, considered it his duty, and tried to be a ruler in fact. But this required independent thinking and adaptation to changing conditions, of which he was utterly incapable. In the first twelve years of his reign he lost a fortress, a fleet, and the war with Japan. In the next twelve he was to lose everything else, including his life and the lives of his family.

The Dinner at Tsarskoe Selo

A few days after the audience we were invited to a gala dinner in honor of the emir in the great palace of Catherine II at Tsarskoe Selo, the Russian Versailles. But the French château was built by a man, King Louis XIV, in his magnificent, imposing, and formal style. Tsarskoe Selo was the creation of a beautiful woman, the Empress Catherine, for her personal delight, in the amorous manner of the late rococo. It is the enchanted palace of a fairy queen without a consort and with a glittering crowd of admiring gallants. All the royal apartments are located on the first floor of the palace in a straight line of immense length.

We mounted the staircase and entered the reception rooms, which followed one another in endless succession. The rooms, in true Louis XV style, were very high but not very large. Each had two windows and could accommodate ten or twelve persons, just the right number for a pleasant, informal talk. I liked them better than the stupendous, cathedral-sized halls of the Winter Palace, where people had to stand at attention or break into groups as in a marketplace.

Each room of Tsarskoe Selo has a charm of its own, with an infinite variety of decoration. I can remember only the Amber and Jasper Rooms, with panels inlaid with these rare materials. We could not stop to admire them but had to move on with the other guests until we reached the large Silver Room, a kind of concentration point, where we all assembled. We did not have to wait long. Life in the palace was well regulated, ordained by the monarchs and obeyed by them. The room rapidly filled up. The sovereigns came in with the emir at the appointed time and, nodding rapidly to the bowing uniformed men and curtsying ladies, walked directly to the door of the Golden Dining Room, which opened at once.

The room was vast and of magnificently harmonious proportions. On two sides the rows of windows were separated by mirrors in gilt frames, with three pairs of sconces each, forming blazing walls of gold and light. The table of the tsar stood across the room, with two long wings at right angles—a gleaming array of crystal, silver, and china.

The guests were seated according to their rank, the amount of gold braid and decorations on their breasts increasing with their proximity to the emperor's table. A multitude of red lackeys added to the color scheme of the spectacle. The imperial table, the center of attraction, was adorned by the presence of the tsar, the frozen beauty of his wife, and the Arabian splendor of his guest. The tsar and the empress spoke with the emir through an interpreter standing behind the chair of the emperor, although the emir knew some Russian, which he skillfully used during private interviews with the tsar.

I sat at the far end of the table among young colonels, the aides of the tsar. Theirs were highly coveted positions. All careers were open to them. The fat Prince V. N. Orlov, a rising star who sat next to me, was chief of the field chancellery of the emperor.

A real Russian dinner was served, substantial and abundant, with some lighter dishes of French cuisine. There were no *zakuski* (hors d'oeuvres), which are customary only at lunch or at late supper. A turbot from the Black Sea followed a light soup. Appropriate wines were offered after each dish. The venison roast made its solemn appearance at the end of a succession of courses, and champagne rose to the brim of the Baccarat glasses. The cupids on the painted ceiling seemed to dance and wave their garlands of roses.

The magnificent room, all lit up, warm, and full of the gay and carefree charm of the eighteenth century, exercised its spell on the guests. The meal proceeded rapidly, almost too rapidly for me, for I enjoyed it more than any other court function I had attended. The sovereigns rose and the hundred guests stood up at once. As I passed the table just left by the sovereigns, I saw on it an oval dish covered with flowers. I took some orchids and carried them home to my mother. They were splendid, but faded soon, like the monarchy itself.

We assembled again in the Silver Room. For a while the monarchs stood there, talking with the guests. Then the Tsar turned to the Emir and said with a twinkle in his eyes: [Let us have a smoke, Your Highness] *"Poidemte pokurim Vashe Vysochestvo."* They went out, and the stream of guests flowed to the stairs. Soon we were called to take our places in our carriages, and we followed the emir's white team of horses to the station.

The Parade on St. George's Day

Nicholas II, the most pious and the least military of the Russian emperors, attributed particular importance to the maintenance of a religious spirit in the army. The emperor considered it his strict duty to be present at military festivities, which implied a religious service and a parade. The clergy blessed the tsar and the soldiers, who later were congratulated by the tsar.

The three supreme, unimpeachable, and incontestable authorities —the church, the throne, and the armed forces—formed an integral whole in the mind of the tsar. The rest—the will of the people, public opinion, elected bodies, etc.—were bound to absolute obedience, and in case of need were to be forced into it. Autocracy in the hands of Alexander III was something to be shaped by him. To Nicholas II, it was a gift bestowed on him from above, which had to be recognized as such by all reasonable people. It would have been useless to argue about this principle with the tsar, and nobody did.

Given this conviction of Nicholas, the revolution of 1905 created

an indescribable confusion in his mind. He was frightened into sub-
mission and granted a constitution. The he repented, tried to restore
his autocracy, and displayed an even more pronounced devotion to
the church. Of special significance to him was the celebration of the
day of St. George, the patron of the Russian army. That this Army
had just sorely suffered at the hands of the Japanese was considered
by the Tsar a trial imposed by Providence which would be compen-
sated in due time.

When we came to Tsarskoe the church service was not yet over,
and Abdul Ahad, a Moslem, could not attend it. We had to wait
until the end of the religious ceremony and were directed to the
officers' mess of the Red Hussars, the tsar's own regiment. These
hussars had no rivals in the fascination they held for boys and girls
of the upper classes. Almost every schoolboy of old Russia had a
period of military infatuation when he dreamed of joining the colors,
naturally as a cavalry officer, and of course as a hussar. The Horse
Guards looked showy and aristocratic, but nothing could beat the
popularity of the hussars, who represented cavalry at its best. Of a
well-established type, consecrated by tradition, they were smart,
brave, gay, companionable, perfect dancers, and very handsome. Of
course, not every hussar was handsome, but he appeared to be. The
tsar often wore their uniform, which fitted his slim figure to perfection. The Red Hussars were a very expensive regiment and led a
fast life. The mothers preferred Horse Guards at a ball, but the
daughters wanted hussars. We took tea with the officers delegated
to entertain us, which they did with good grace, although tea cannot
be called a hussar's drink.

As the weather at St. Petersburg could not be relied upon in
November, the troops were to be reviewed by the emperor in the
riding school. When we arrived there, the parade was in full progress. The tsarina was on the reviewing stand, and the tsar stood on
the ground in front of it. Since the building was large but low and
the bands were playing full blast, the noise was deafening. We stood
in the front row, quite close to the marching troops. They moved
with extraordinary rapidity. The music was playing much too fast,
making it difficult for even the tall guardsmen to keep time. A short
officer risked being split in two as he made enormous strides. I felt
bewildered.

The tsar greeted the regiments as they passed him, but his voice
could not be heard over the fury of the brass instruments. An aide

signaled to the soldiers with his arm to answer the emperor, but their voices sounded weak, drowned in the noise. The music stopped only when the tsar addressed his final thanks, received with cheers.

I was particularly dissatisfied with the end of the parade, the ceremonial march. Its very name implies dignity and solemnity. There was none. Military attachés next to us exchanged puzzled glances and assumed ironical expressions. If we could not conduct a peacetime parade properly, what a mess our generals would make of their troops in case of war! Parades should give the soldiers an opportunity to see the emperor, to hear his voice, to carry away with them the impression of his personality, the center of everything. Instead of that their attention was distracted by the gesticulations of the aide and the commanding officer, signaling the moment when the soldiers had to answer the words of the tsar, which they did not hear. The direct contact between the tsar and the soldiers, the only thing of real importance in the whole parade, was lost.

I liked our modest reviews in central Asia better. The short, sturdy, perspiring Ashkhabad soldiers could not be compared in drill and appearance to the showy giants of the guard, but our parades were conducted amid the general excitement of an enthusiastic public, children included. Soldiers marched gaily, at a moderate pace. The music was thrilling, notwithstanding the occasional shriek of a trumpet. The men could see the commander as he passed along their ranks. His every word was heard, quoted after the parade, discussed, and keenly appreciated.

After the parade, we drove to the palace. The reception was exclusively for the military and included all the knights of St. George* present in the capital. I heard muttering among the officers, as a short, thickset admiral, the former viceroy of the Russian Far East, E. I. Alekseev, who had lost Port Arthur, wriggled his way through the crowd, followed by astonished and indignant glances. His very presence seemed to me tactless and outrageous to the brave people who had fought the war.

Quite different was the attitude of the officers who hovered around a handsome young priest wearing the cross of St. George. He had led the counterattack at Tiurenchen, the only success of Russian arms. There was really something of a St. George about him. I wondered whether things would have gone better if he had continued to lead

* The cross of St. George was the highest Russian military decoration given for valor. *Ed.*

the soldiers, leaving it to the generals to sing chorales in the church.

We moved into the Gold Dining Room for lunch. The guests were seated in groups of six at individual tables and could talk freely. Liberated from my party of Bokharans I found myself in the company of five knights of St. George. One of them, a lieutenant in the navy, leaned over to me and said: "You quite resemble an acquaintance of mine whom I met in Siam. His name is Kalmykow. Do you know him?"

"Yes," I replied. "I know him well, and I think he too knows Lieutenant Veselago."

We both laughed. This was an unexpected reunion after seven years. Fate had tossed us all over the world and then brought us together at Tsarskoe Selo. Our conversation continued till we were summoned to the Silver Salon.

The reception was resumed after luncheon and lasted a long time. The monarchs could not relax for a moment. In the dense crowd three open spaces, like magnetic fields, attracted the people—one around the emperor and the other two around the empress and the dowager empress. The tsar stood in the same place, changing only the position of his feet, speaking continuously with the officers presented to him. He nodded his head mechanically and occasionally stroked his moustache with his lean white hand. The empresses moved slowly but constantly, stopping to exchange a few words with a guest, then resuming their course. This continued for hours.

The young empress, uncertain of her Russian, looked tensely into the faces of the guests, trying to ascertain whether she could address them in French, English, or, as a last resort, German. Her hesitation left a sense of disappointment in her wake. Sometimes she stood still, with her arms hanging hopelessly on both sides of her shapely figure.

The dowager empress appeared sure of herself in her dignified progress around the hall. She was making her circuit like a planet round the sun, the sun being in this case the luster hanging from the center of the ceiling. She was a small woman, very straight and stately. All her movements looked natural, although very restrained. She allowed herself only to clasp her hands in front of her, keeping the elbows close to her body. She presented a complete contrast to her daughter-in-law.

The dowager empress looked quietly at the persons who receded before her, chose someone to speak to, addressed a few words, and proceeded further. I wondered how she succeeded in never making the mistake of addressing the same person twice. She really had a royal memory for faces. She managed the language difficulty very well. During the twenty years of her stay in Russia, she had acquired about that many Russian phrases, and a few more which, according to her, were Russian. But she used them freely, had a charming smile, and produced a pleasant impression.

I stood modestly aside and seemed to be far from the orbit of her march when I noticed with dismay that the celestial course had turned its path toward my humble self. I was pressed in on all sides except in front, and the empress's eyes met mine. I imagined that I saw a small mental process going on in her mind. She recognized my uniform as that of the Foreign Office, realized that I must speak French, and made the calculation that I must have some relation to the Bokharans. All this offered the necessary prospect for a bit of conversation. The mental process finished, the empress moved toward me.

I bowed and touched with my lips the fingers of the graciously extended little hand. The empress asked me in French what was the language of the Bokharans, as if she was seeing them for the first time in her life. The subject of the Bokharans being rapidly exhausted, the empress inquired in what countries I had served before. When she heard that I had recently come from Siam, she became interested and inquired about the Siamese Prince Shira, who had been educated in Copenhagen at the court of her father. She asked some other appropriate questions, then moved away in the same calm and dignified way.

All that I heard about her indicated that she had mastered well the by no means easy task of royal duties. While visiting an exhibition of Russian paintings, she acquired pictures representing the homes of poor peasants, little orphan children, and the like. The pictures remained there for the duration of the exhibition, with the label: "Bought by H. I. Majesty the Empress Mary." That produced a favorable impression.

The young empress was not popular at all. Once she went to an international exhibition of ceramics at St. Petersburg, the first attempt of the Russian industrialists to compete in this field with the artistic productions of other lands. The empress carefully examined the foreign stands, talked with the people in charge of them in various languages, then shot a frightened look at the Moscow stand and fled. All the Russian section was aroused by this lack of interest in native products, amounting to an open contempt of Russian industry. The Russians are expansive, affable, and sensitive. The lack of response from the cold and tactless tsarina soon made her an object of resentment. The tsar needed help, but he did not get it from his consort. On the contrary, she estranged him from his mother and his people.

I waited for the great reception on St. Nicholas' Day to form my final impression of the sovereigns in public.

St. Nicholas Day

Every Russian bears the name of a saint and used to celebrate the day dedicated to him. With the accession of the new tsar, the day of St. Nicholas became a national holiday for all Russia. The reception at Tsarskoe Selo on this occasion was the greatest of all.

But when we arrived at the great palace of Tsarskoe, we saw only empty rooms. The Bokharans sat down and remained silent in their ceremonial robes, like so many idols. I felt bored, got up, walked through several rooms, came to the anteroom, and saw a closed door. I opened it and unexpectedly found myself on the upper gallery of the palace chapel. I retreated and then, moved by curiosity, looked down.

At first sight the church seemed to be almost empty, with a large open space in the center and a single man standing there on a red carpet. It was the tsar. Along the walls I saw a multitude of people in uniform. The air was warm and impregnated with the smell of incense and hot wax, peculiar to Russian churches because of the number of burning candles. A deacon stood in front, swinging a censer. He finished a prayer and moved away. A side door opened, and a procession of clergy appeared, with the officiating priest carrying the Holy Host. The people bowed, and the deacon, in a powerful voice, rolling like thunder, invoked the blessings of God on the most pious and autocratic sovereign of Russia. The tsar kneeled. He was once more confirmed in his divine right to rule alone his empire—the people and the land.

The service continued with an awe-inspiring solemnity, as the choir started—slowly as though from a distance—the sacred hymn of the cherubims. The rich full voices rose, fell, and rose again in a triumphant glorification of God. Amid the floating incense the tsar moved toward the priest and kissed the gold cross offered to him. In a moment the church was crowded by a multitude of people, congratulating the emperor on his name day. Then the crowd opened, the tsar walked toward the entrance, and I rushed to my Bokharans.

I collected my Oriental flock and hastened to the great staircase. But the Tsar had already passed. We saw only the grand dukes and followed after them. The reception took place in the great Golden Room. Like Versailles, Tsarskoe Selo has no throne room. The king was king wherever he trod. I felt that something was needed, a crown or a throne under a dais. There was none. The tsar was, as usual, in his colonel's uniform, given to him by his father. Nicholas II never wore a general's dress, as he would then be obliged to change the initials "A III" of Alexander III for his own "N II." A gentle thought, but reminiscent of the twilight of the gods in German mythology.

But the empresses were up to the occasion, looking like the queens in children's picture books. The young Empress Alexandra had a long red velvet train with a large border of sable, carried by two pages in Hessian boots, white deerskin breeches, and gold-striped uniforms. Strings of diamonds round the neck of the tsarina descended to her waist, like flashing rivulets of light. The Dowager Empress Mary wore the same number of crown jewels and a violet train. She had no widow's veil. The empresses kept carefully apart. Once the young empress came close to her mother-in-law and hastily withdrew.

I saw no representatives of the Duma. Probably there were some, but they were not conspicuous. The doors of the palace remained closed to the Russian people, and the tsar did not greet them. The only time he was to make a public address was on the day of the declaration of World War I. He appeared on the balcony of the Winter Palace and was received with delirious applause. For a few moments he was really popular and held complete sway over the hearts of his people, for he impersonated Russia in peril. But these moments did not last. The weak personality of the tsar fell more and more under the domination of his wife, who hated all those with a liberal and independent turn of mind.

Two years before her downfall, the tsarina said: "I hate Rodzianko more than Chkheidze, because I can hang Chkheidze, and I cannot hang Rodzianko."

N. S. Chkheidze was the leader of the Social Democrats. M. V. Rodzianko was the president of the Duma, a huge man of imposing appearance and loud voice, a wealthy landowner who had served in the Horse Guards and was a chamberlain of the emperor. An honest, decent fellow, he was considered a nonentity by both his friends and foes and owed his election to the unanimity of this opinion. The idea of hanging Rodzianko was typical of the hysterical tsarina, who completed the ruin of the monarchy, dragging with her her obedient little husband.

The reception seemed endless. Everybody had to remain standing. The long, narrow stream of those to be presented trickled toward the emperor. Finally the rivulet dried up. The tsar looked around, approached the empress and the emir, and all three walked out. The dowager empress was also gone. The crowd dispersed with a sense of relief. We were glad to reach the haven of a drawing room and sit down. But we were not at the end of our experiences of the day.

Time passed. A strange silence spread over the palace. I became apprehensive and asked the officers delegated by the Ministry of War to attend on us what we were to do. They knew no more than a corps commander during a big maneuver gone wrong. We started to wander through empty salons. Not a soul was there. The innumerable court flunkeys had all disappeared. In distress we descended a staircase and found some guards. Our coats were brought to us, but not our carriages. We dressed and waited.

After a time, a pair of court runners, with ostrich feathers on their caps and particularly solemn expressions on their flat faces, appeared on the landing. Then two more court lackeys entered, all in red and gold lace. I wondered about the meaning of this night promenade in an apparently empty palace. Then came the court marshal, Prince A. S. Dolgorukii, with his ebony staff, and immediately after him the tsar and the empress descending the stairs.

The emperor saw the Bokharans, who, in their warm wrappings, looked like silkworms in their cocoons. He laughed and showed them to the empress, who smiled also. That was the only time I saw the monarchs in a human mood. The tsar put on a gray military overcoat and stood waiting while the empress, in her coat of black fox, wrapped a fleecy Orenburg shawl round her head. They left. Carriages were brought to us also and we left, but without the Emir. The fact was, we had lost him.

The chief Bokharan dignitary, Nasrullah Beg, who expected to be confirmed prime minister, was livid. At the station, I jumped out and saw the white horses of the emir's carriage rapidly approaching. He went straight into the railway car and sat there without paying attention to the distressed looks of his retinue. He had taken tea alone with Their Majesties, and nothing mattered after that.

The Grand Dukes

Whenever I went to a reception with the emir, we met grand dukes. The Russian imperial family, which had been on the verge of extinction in the eighteenth century, as had those of England, France, Austria, and Spain, later expanded into full bloom and, at the time of the accession of Nicholas II, was the most numerous dynasty of Europe. Were this prolific progress to continue unabated, an epoch could be envisaged when the whole empire would be populated exclusively by grand dukes and their official and morganatic descendants.

If the grandeur of a grand duke be taken literally and measured in feet and inches, then the Grand Duke Nicholas would easily be first, for he was the tallest of them all. The uniform he chose to wear accentuated his height. The vertical plume of his shako, his lean face, his short cavalry jacket—which looked even shorter on him—his long legs in tight breeches and small narrow boots, all gave him the appearance of a man of one dimension. In his fifties, the grand duke preserved the sprightly vivacity of youth and, alas, its mentality as well.

I saw him in the morning drilling a cavalry regiment on a plaza. This innocent occupation seemed to give him utmost satisfaction. He enjoyed riding and cavalry training. He undoubtedly returned home to lunch in high spirits and with a good appetite. Was this all that was needed to command an army? And the grand duke was made commander in chief of all the Russian forces in World War I, with the longest frontier to defend, with a few obsolete fortresses which it was decided to abandon, with a single plan of mobilization and no partial ones, with one-dimensional strategy—toward the enemy and back—and hardly a plan at all for the conduct of war operations. It seems that the grand duke never bothered about war plans, which had to be prepared on the spot by the general staff and served fresh, like an omelet by his cook.

The other grand dukes looked very insignificant. The only exception was Michael, the brother of the tsar, a friendly young man. When the emir called on the dowager empress at Gatchina, I happened to be between her and Grand Duke Michael, who approached his mother from behind me. I turned my head by chance, saw him,

and stepped aside. Michael looked at me, smiled slightly, and remained where he was. I do not know if he did it purposely, in order
not to increase my confusion, but I know that he was kind and very
unconventional. His marriage was also unconventional. His wife was
not accepted at court, although he personally was much liked by the
tsar, who finally abdicated in his favor. He was not allowed to ascend
the throne and perished, a gentle victim of a merciless revolution.

Back to Bokhara

The emir was received in a final audience, and the Russian and
Bokharan autocrats, after a happy meeting, parted with complete
mutual satisfaction. Abdul Ahad had received all that he desired, and
the tsar could only regret that Russia was not Bokhara, and the Russians were not like the obedient Bokharans whom he saw bowing
before him.

After the keen, intelligent eyes of the leading statesmen of Russia,
it was strange to see before me the fat, placid faces of the Bokharan
dignitaries. They showed me the large jeweled rings they had received from the tsar as mementos of their visit and spoke with satisfaction of the high Russian decorations bestowed on them in recognition of the successful management of their state.

The Bokharans, who had remained mute in St. Petersburg or
produced only some unrecognizable Russian sounds, started to talk
freely again in their Persian dialect. Oriental pilafs appeared on the
table in the dining car. As I passed through a corridor, I smelled the
sickening odor of opium from behind a closed door. I found myself
back in Asia before I had reached its borders. Our train slowed down
before the station of Kermineh and was welcomed by the discordant
sounds of a Bokharan band. The emir was particularly proud that
his band played everything by ear, without bothering about printed
music.

I longed to go to Tashkent to see my family, but according to
etiquette I had to accompany the emir to his residence, stay there for
a while, and swallow some more pilafs prior to recovering my freedom. I was again surrounded by native life, so different from ours
and, I must say, often extremely offensive in its manifestations. I
came in contact with it in three places: Bokhara, Kermineh, and
Atchin.

The old city of Bokhara was the seat of the emir's administration,
headed by a cabinet of three ministers. The town had a long and

glorious past. Before the coming of Russia it had been the capital of the strongest state in central Asia, and in still older times the center of high learning. The world listened with respect to the voice of the great Bokharan physician Avicenna, whose medical works, written in Arabic and translated into Latin, were considered in Europe second only to those of Hippocrates.

All that was gone, and what remained was degenerate and harmful. Science was reduced to a bigoted explanation of the Koran. The wide and beneficial influence of the state shrank to the narrow limits of graft and extortion. Despotism and fanaticism became the characteristics of Bokhara and were benevolently looked upon by the Russian monarchy, which considered them merely excesses of a laudable zeal.

Abdul Ahad knew the situation well but could not help it. He had already gone to the limits of his power in permitting such civilizing innovations as the railway, and he could not go further without meeting open revolt. The position of the Bokharan ruler was no more secure than that of the Russian tsar. However, by an irony of fate, the Oriental potentate was hated because of his progressive attitude. During the latter part of his reign the emir stayed in the town of Kermineh; he never visited the city of Bokhara, the capital of his realm, for fear of an attempt on his life.

In 1901, as acting political agent, I had to open a small railway branch constructed by the emir and linking the main line with the old city. For years this extension had been opposed by the Moslem clergy lest it affect the sanctity of the town. At last they agreed to it. The population seemed quiet, but a personal appearance of the emir was out of the question. I had no military escort as I rode on the first train of civilization to the grim walls of the ancient capital. A few armed men would have spoiled all the effect and would have been of no avail against an angry mob. Before the walls, awaiting the train, stood a multicolored crowd of Bokharans with the *kushbegi* (prime minister) in the center. He looked like the son of Abraham before the sacrifice. I walked to him, shook hands, and greeted the others. The Bokharans bowed in a salaam. The kushbegi beamed. The Moslems were as gentle as a flock of lambs.

But you can never tell. A few years later, when I was in Tashkent, disorders broke out during a religious ceremony arranged by the Persians, who are considered heretics by the Bokharans. Streets turned into pandemonium. The venerable Moslem priests led the turmoil. Russian troops with machine guns were called, and quiet was restored without bloodshed. The political agent asked the emir why the people did not obey his officials. "Because I am the servant of the Russian tsar," answered Abdul Ahad. He knew his subjects.

The emir had a brother who lived in honorary exile as governor of a remote province of Bokhara. Abdul Ahad never mentioned his name to me but was constantly informed about every particular of his life. The ruler of Bokhara was remarkably well posted on whatever happened in his kingdom. Ministers came from the old city, presented their reports, and went back. Spies were plentiful. The emir was by no means a tyrant by policy or natural inclination, but everybody lived in constant awe of him. It was a fundamental part of Oriental despotism.

As acting political agent I had visited Bokhara several times and had lived for months in the little Russian town of New Bokhara, close to the station of the Central Asian Railroad. The political agent, exercising the powers of a governor, administered the Russian settlements scattered over Bokhara. These duties were far from complicated. Much to my amusement I found that the chief clerk of the police, in whom was vested the surveillance of political exiles, was a political exile himself. He was a pleasant, well-read man, and he kept a circulating library of mildly radical books. But he found few readers among the members of the colony, who were chiefly interested in gossip, cards, and cotton prices.

A much more difficult problem—an unsolvable one—was the enlightened civilizing control which I was supposed to exercise over the native administration and the people of Bokhara. The old city itself was appalling, the most unsanitary Oriental town I have ever visited, although it possessed a European hospital founded by the emir. The only supply of "fresh" water was from open reservoirs polluted with various germs, some known to science and some yet to be classified. Bokhara had been enlightened by the loftiest teachings of mankind—from the tenets of Zoroaster, the philosophy of Aristotle during the conquest of Alexander the Great, and the religion of Buddha, up to the words of Christ, brought by migrating Nestorians, and the faith of Islam—but no one had taught the Bokharans the value of pure, clean water.

And that was not all. Lepers lived inside the walls of the city, freely mixing with the population and soliciting alms from passersby. These unhappy people were allowed to intermarry, a Moslem priest giving his blessing to the perpetuation of the disease among the coming generation. Girls are married young, before they show any clear sign of the hereditary illness. But the marriage of a healthy Christian with a Moslem would be considered a horrible crime, punishable by death. I asked an educated Bokharan why marriage is not forbidden among lepers. "But they are good Moslems," he answered with astonishment. Once, as I was riding to the citadel I was assailed by a leper. Clamoring and gesticulating, he ran after my carriage, trying to take hold of it with his hands. My escort of cossacks was needed to chase him away.

Smallpox often ravaged the city, as the women in the harems could not be subjected to compulsory vaccination. Thus the seclusion of their women made the homes of the Bokharans centers of disease. At night, as I lay in my bed, I dreamed of bounding lepers and test tubes adorned with Latin labels. Alas, I had no means of improving the hygienic conditions of Bokhara. One of the few practical results of my stay there was an ordinance prohibiting the exportation of archaeological remains. The removal from ancient buildings of dated inscriptions on marble slabs, often artistically decorated, made difficult if not impossible the identification of the structure, its date, and the names of its builders. This ordinance was posted at railway stations and continued in force till the outbreak of the revolution.

The antiquated Moslem clergy was the chief obstacle to progress. Bokhara, a holy city, was for hundreds of years a center of Moslem fanaticism. Its religious influence extended far beyond its frontiers over all Russian Central Asia. The part of the Moslem population which was under Russian rule had become somewhat less fanatical, but many superstitions were kept alive by the mullahs. Not only did the faith in old miracles remain absolute, but new ones were a daily occurrence in central Asia. I once saw a funeral monument of unusual length over the grave of a saint near Ashkhabad. A mullah assured me that the cenotaph corresponded to the actual length of the saint's body. The holy man, he claimed, continued to grow in his tomb, and they had to lengthen the monument accordingly. How they managed to ascertain the progress of the growth of the buried divine was not explained, but the monument attracted pilgrims and increased the donations.

During a visit to Baga Eddin, a holy place not far from the city of Bokhara, I witnessed the sacrifice of a ram, which was slaughtered as an offering at the shrine. Sacrifices mentioned in the Old Testament were still practiced in Bokhara and Persia. In this respect, as

well as in some others, these countries were two thousand years behind our time.

In spite of its squalor, Bokhara still possessed some monuments.
The most ancient was the citadel, built on an artificial mound,
possibly of Buddhist origin (a *stupa*). In it were located the infamous
"bug cells," underground dungeons originally intended to serve as
water cisterns but later used as prisons. At that time they were full
of bedbugs, which made life intolerable for prisoners. I was assured
by a respectable native that the bugs were specially fed on raw meat
to keep them fierce and in good shape. I laughed at him, but he remained convinced of the veracity of the legend and proudly considered the bug cells a kind of national monument. It seems that
several Russian and English travelers who had vanished in Bokhara
early in the nineteenth century finished their days in the underground dungeons. Once firm, friendly relations with Russia were
established, this old prison was no longer used and was replaced by
a more humane one. But prisoners continued to be attached by iron
collars and chains of the type used in slave-owning lands.

The highest building in the city was a lofty tower or minaret from
which political criminals were thrown down, so that the people of
Bokhara could sometimes actually see the change of a cabinet by the
fall of its members. These abominations were abolished by Abdul
Ahad.

Racially, the Bokharans, as well as the population of Russian
Turkestan, are of two types: the Iranians (*Tadjik*) and the Turkish
(*Uzbek*). The Iranians have delicate oval faces and beautiful eyes; the
Uzbeks have flat Mongolian faces and bridled eyes. There were also
two languages—Iranian and Turkish.

The following verses of an unknown poet, told to me by an old
Moslem, throws some light on the feelings of the people concerning
their mode of life. Freely translated they read:

> The world is a mill as cruel as the flood.
> Its stones are mov'd by a stream of blood.
> You are like grain, and the stones are low:
> Above is heaven, and the earth is below.
> You shall be crush'd, unless you flee.
> You must be hard, or cease to be.

To avoid the dangers and hostility of the old city, Abdul Ahad
transferred his residence to the little town of Kermineh, where the
political agent and the ministers went to visit him. In Kermineh

there were few mosques and less restraint. I saw people gathered around a public dancer on the marketplace at the popular festival of Now Ruz, celebrated throughout the country except in the old capital whose rigid devotion allowed only religious ceremonies inside its sacred walls.

Even more liberty was enjoyed by Abdul Ahad in his favorite country seat, Atchin, up the Zerafshan River. Here there was little pretense at European furnishings—just splendid carpets and two or three armchairs, used exclusively for the reception of the political agent. The hall was light and airy; slim wooden columns—painted, gilded, and sculptured—separated it on both sides from the other rooms. The walls were decorated with brightly colored plaster work and fanciful Bokhara-style designs, set off by the deep red of the carpets on the floor. Instead of windows, there were doors opening directly onto the park, with a large lake farther down and a wide, open space beyond.

But for me, Atchin's chief attraction was the falcon hunt. Abdul Ahad graciously placed all his hunting equipment at my disposal, and I started off in the morning in true medieval fashion, with dogs leaping and mounted attendants carrying falcons on their wrists. The meeting place was a lake, well known for its waterfowl, chiefly coots. Horsemen galloped on the shore, chasing the birds in my direction. While trotting, I found the curved beak of the falcon inconveniently close to my eyes. I dismounted and stood on the bank, with the bird perched on my right hand, protected by a heavy falcon glove.

The falcons were extraordinarily well trained, the best-educated beings in all of Bokhara, humans not excepted. The lake was long, my hand became weary, and I had just given the bird to a falconer when I saw a coot flying. I signaled to the falconer. He freed the bird, which settled on my naked hand. I became apprehensive when I saw my wrist in the grip of the falcon's enormous talons. But he rested so gently that he did not even scratch my skin. He kept his balance with half-outstretched wings, then straightened himself and sat erect and proud, truly a royal bird.

He took a rapid survey of the surroundings, then looked at me with his beautiful, intelligent eyes as if asking what to do next. The waterfowl was still too far away, and we had to wait. The coot came flying low above the water. The falcon became alert, bent forward, glanced rapidly at me, then leaned forward again, fixing all his attention on the coming bird. The coot was nearing, flying parallel to the shore. I thrust my hand forward, loosing the little straps of leather attached to the falcon's legs. He glided off without the slightest jerk and went straight as an arrow, aiming without any deviation a little ahead and at a right angle to the course of the coot.

The stupid bird saw the danger when it was too late to change the direction of its flight to avoid the fatal collision. The falcon grasped his prey and turned toward the shore. Both came flying together and fell to the ground at my feet. The falcon killed the coot, then flew to me and sat on my hand. It was a masterful performance, but not in the regular style, as the coot had been flying too close to the water. Usually the falcon ascends high in the sky, then falls like a stone on the bird and strikes it with his chest, never with his claws. Only a well-trained falcon can do this. Ordinary hawks pursue their prey like hounds and seize it. But such a chase is below the dignity of a falcon, who often strikes down several birds before coming to rest.

The flight of a falcon is a marvel to see and is not an easy achievement for a young bird. I saw a falcon fall on a coot, miss it, and tumble down into the water. He swam to the shore and was rescued by his falconer but was too ashamed to take any further part in the hunt.

The falcon is remarkably obedient but also has his whims. Sometimes, when released, he flies to a tree and sits there, refusing to hunt. If the falcon belongs to the emir, the falconer has to stay under the tree, repeating in a desperate voice the usual falconer's call. This may last for half a day or more. The falconer cannot return without his ward. Eventually the falcon flies down to the falconer without offering any explanation for his conduct. It is useless to try climbing the tree, for the falcon would wait until the man got within reach of him and then fly off to the next tree. Once a falconer of Ivan the Terrible lost the tsar's favorite falcon in the woods. When he finally found the bird, he built a church on that spot.

The Bokharans are passionately in love with their falcons, and it will be granted that a really good bird deserves the affection bestowed on him. The title of the prime minister, *kushbegi*, is literally Chief Falconer.

The education of a falcon is quite a pedagogical problem. A young bird has all the fierce, proud, indomitable courage of its kind. Punishment will not change his temper; it will only make a valuable bird worthless and dangerous. The trainer must win by his patience the confidence, respect, and attachment of his pupil. The rest is easy. The falcon will return the friendship and trust shown to him. If the training is unsuccessful, the fault may rest with the man as much as with the bird.

Falcon hunting was my only diversion during my sojourns with the emir. The time not taken by audiences I passed in seclusion, according to the Bokharan etiquette. I knew nothing about the private life of the emir. The Bokharans I saw did not dare to speak about anything except the weather and the excellent state of health of their ruler. His son was the only member of his family I was allowed to meet. The rest was veiled in mystery.

I was not empowered to change the Bokharan system of government. My chief duty was to harmonize as far as possible the divergent conceptions of the Russian and Bokharan administrations.

Vastly different as they were, the Russian and Bokharan nations had one thing in common: Russia and Bokhara were governed by autocracies, and both autocracies were irremediably doomed. The Russian monarchy was supported by a state church which openly proclaimed that the authority of the tsar was a divine institution. In the gymnasium I was made to memorize abundant texts from the scriptures prescribing—according to the opinion of my teachers—a reverent obedience to the tsar as one of the first duties of a good Christian. The same monarchical principle was taught in Bokharan mosques regarding the emir, but with much less enthusiasm, for among themselves the mullahs considered the emir a very unreliable believer.

But the opposition in Russia and in Bokhara started from different directions. In Russia the liberal and radical parties united in an attack on unlimited monarchy. In Bokhara the old mullahs and the fanatical population were defending the medieval principles of Islam against Russian—in this case, Western—innovations. The Bokharans as a whole realized the overwhelming superiority of the Russian army and bowed before it. In final reckoning the Russian monarchy also depended on its army, and when the latter was demolished by German artillery, both the Russian and the Bokharan sovereigns were dethroned.

Emir Abdul Ahad died before the revolution, and it was his son, the young Emir Seid Mir Alim, who had to face the storm. He wisely realized the futility of resistance and, taking with him the contents of the Bokharan treasury, fled to Afghanistan.

Tashkent
A Political Trial

Finally I took leave of the emir and returned to Tashkent. It was a great relief to be back home, to see my wife and my daughter, and to resume my ordinary work and mode of life. A whole month of attendance on His Highness was a great strain. It is true that our trip had been very interesting. I had formed a fairly good idea of the imperial capital, the tsar, the court, and the government. I saw them living in an atmosphere of unlimited power and dread of assassination. Several people I had met were killed within a few months. We had been surrounded by detectives, and I heard them talk. One morning they were discussing how Stolypin should go out in the afternoon.

"No, not in a closed carriage. I would prefer to whisk him away in a light fly with a single fast horse." That was how the prime minister had to ride in the Russian capital.

There were plenty of executions throughout the empire, but not in Tashkent. Even when the public prosecutor was killed in his office, there was no death sentence. They always brought reprisals —a vicious circle. Tashkent kept out of it.

As an honorary justice of the peace I had to sit in court in the capacity of a supplementary member representing the participation of the people in judicial proceedings; there were no juries in Russian Central Asia. In 1910 a conspiracy of railroad workers was discovered at Samarkand. They had started to prepare bombs but were arrested before they had time to make use of them. There were a few young boys and their leader. The judgment of the Samarkand court had been contested by the prosecutor as too lenient, and the minister of justice ordered a review of the case by the court of Tashkent, which was instructed to go to Samarkand and hold a new trial. To my acute discomfort, I had been summoned to take part in it.

The judges of Tashkent were in a difficult position. They considered that the case had been tried fairly. Nevertheless, it was necessary to increase the severity of the penalty; otherwise our sentence would also be set aside, and the defendants would fare even worse. At the same time we could not make the sentence too hard, as it would discredit our colleagues of Samarkand, who were already under suspicion. In short, both courts were in a serious quandary, and I with them. We were reinforced by a second supplementary member,

a retired general who had been president of the court martial, a bad
omen.

We arrived at Samarkand. The beautiful capital of Tamerlane
looked ugly to me on that winter morning. We went straight to court
and sat till late in the evening in a low, poorly lit hall. There was
sufficient lighting in the foreground only, and the rest of the room
was in a sinister semiobscurity. I saw the accused. Their leader, a
skilled worker, about thirty-five years old, sat in a deep soft armchair;
he was seriously ill. The rest were mere youths.

The presiding judge asked the general to read the indictment. The
defendants were accused of forming a revolutionary society. A brief
outline of its objectives followed. The retired general started to read
in a clear and sonorous voice, emphasizing every phrase with gusto.
He was evidently pleased to be again taking part in a trial. But when
he reached the denunciation of the abuses of the imperial government made by the accused, the general became red and his voice
hoarse. With increasing irritation, he continued the enumeration of
the aims of the society: the dethronement of the tsar and the proclamation of a socialist republic in Russia. Here the general's voice
broke; he turned violet and mumbled the last words with difficulty.
The accused were listening with assumed indifference.

"Is that what you wanted to do?" asked the president of the court.

"Yes," answered the chief defendant. The others nodded.

The president declared a recess. All of us except the general
hurriedly assembled in a private conference. "I propose to give the
maximum term to the chief accused," said the president. "It will not
make any difference to him, since he has cancer of the kidneys and
but three or four months to live. Only the other sentences matter.
We can leave them as they are or even reduce them. That will protect the Samarkand judges."

We agreed. When we assembled in the consultation room, the
general assented. "Yes, yes, make it harder for the chief culprit. He
deserves it," he said.

I do not know what became of the young accused deported to
Siberia. Possibly they are now at the head of the Russian government.

The Generals

Central Asia had been conquered by Russian generals and had
since remained under military administration. Most of the Russians
residing there were or had been army officers. They gave a special

character to the entire community. The generals still represented the salt of the earth in the eyes of the local society and in their own opinion. I saw many of them, for the governors-general were constantly changed at that time. Twice a week I presented my report to the governor-general, which gave me the occasion to talk with him, and I was often detained for lunch.

I remember the gruff veteran, General P. I. Mishchenko. He was born in a fort in the Caucasus, had seen much fighting during the rebellion of the mountaineers, and had recently taken part in the Japanese war. He was an old warrior, outspoken, rough, and sincere, with simple manners and a kind heart but extremely irritable. One needed training in handling him. I lacked it and often uncautiously ran the risk of trouble.

"Why did we lose the Japanese war?" I asked once. Fortunately, he was in a good mood that day.

"Because the Japs won it," he answered. I saw that it would be dangerous to press further and desisted. Besides, it was the best explanation of any I had heard at that time.

Another governor-general, N. I. Grodekov, was also elderly but had received an excellent education in the sixties, a period of reform and enlightenment in Russia. He had traveled and read a great deal and had written books on ethnography and geography, one of which was translated and attracted attention in England. He treated me with favor—a great advantage, as I could not refrain from making inopportune observations. Once during lunch, in the presence of other guests, I attacked vigorously our way of colonizing eastern Siberia.

"Our settlers there are cramped around the railway stations and river ports. They receive, according to the latest law, ridiculously small allotments of land, although there are millions of unoccupied acres. In Canada immigrants are treated much better. No wonder our Far East remains an uncultivated forest."

"I initiated this law when I was governor-general there," said Grodekov. People at the table looked at me and then turned their heads in the opposite direction. I felt I was in deep water, in an utterly hopeless situation.

"There is a distinction between administration and colonization," continued Grodekov, "and the aims of both have to be taken into consideration. Settlers used to disperse in the forests. There was no possibility of collecting taxes or drawing statistics. Sometimes the location of their villages remained unknown and unmarked on the maps. In fact they were entirely out of contact with the administration. I had to establish definite regions where I could keep some kind of control over them."

I saw no good in keeping control over people settling in a virgin forest. Let them first establish themselves and make a living. Then you can impose taxes and draw statistics. But I could not say this. The governor-general was carrying out the policy of the government. It was not for him to change its narrow and bureaucratic course.

I was deeply touched by the way Grodekov spoke to me. He remained calm, and his voice was gentle and serious while he explained the situation, without the slightest indication of a rebuke. He knew how to respect a frank opinion. The tension was relieved, and the conversation turned to other topics.

At times, however, Grodekov was difficult to deal with. In 1907 the Russian consul at Kashgar wrote that the Chinese governor wanted to visit Russian Central Asia and call on General Grodekov. It seems that the latter had had some experience with Chinese officials in the Far East and could not stand them after that. When I reported the proposed visit to Grodekov, he said curtly: "I won't receive him."

Nonplussed, I asked what reply I should send to Kashgar.

"Do as you like," said my chief. That was the worst possible answer. Whatever I should do would not be to his liking. "What else do you have to report?"

"Nothing," I said disconcertedly. The governor-general moved his eyebrows slightly, intimating I should retire.

One of Grodekov's aides, to whom I turned for advice, was more explicit. "For God's sake, stop the Chinaman from coming and don't mention him any more or you'll put the chief into a rage. That's all you'll gain by it."

I composed a negative reply to our consul in Kashgar who, fortunately, did not insist.

The last of the governors-general whom I knew was A. V. Samsonov, a splendid, brave man, much maligned after his defeat at Tannenberg. I shall speak in his defense in a later chapter.

Samsonov was fifty when I met him in Tashkent in 1909; his advancement to commander in chief had been rapid. Active and intelligent, he was considered one of our best fighting generals. He was from the south, and my mother remembered him as a small and very handsome boy. He had finished at cavalry school during the Russo-Turkish war of 1877–78 and had gone straight to the front.

I once spoke with him about the prospects of a future war. It was summer, and his family and mine were staying in the mountains some distance from Tashkent. The trip generally took me a whole day, since there were no post horses and no automobiles. When I finished my usual report, Samsonov said: "I am going to the mountains this afternoon. Won't you come with me?" I accepted gladly. The governor-general had the use of excellent horses with fresh relays on the road. When I called on him later in the day, he put a small automatic in his pocket. I wonder if it was the same bluish black pistol that ended his life at Tannenberg.

"There is no danger," he said, "but I always like to be armed."

We drove rapidly. There was only one cossack seated next to the driver, and we could talk freely.

"In a few years," I said, "Russia will have a population of two hundred million. What we need is peace till then. Any war would be premature now, and we have nothing to gain by it."

"Yes," he answered, "and moreover, with Sukhomlinov as war minister, we cannot make war. He is a lazy, vain, presumptuous fellow, nothwithstanding all his apparent brilliance."

Samsonov was often rash in his judgments, but in this case he was right; he knew V. A. Sukhomlinov, who had been his chief in the cavalry school. I wondered later why Samsonov, a hussar and a typical military man, was able to realize the necessity of peace and remain calm, whereas the people of our Foreign Office could not.

When Lord Charles Hardinge was appointed viceroy of India in 1910, I thought it would be a good idea for Samsonov to congratulate the new viceroy. My chief agreed. There was no time to consult our Foreign Office; moreover, I dreaded its red tape. There had never been any exchange of telegrams between the Russian authorities in central Asia and the government of India, and, to my knowledge, none have taken place since. I knew, however, that Hardinge had been very popular as ambassador in St. Petersburg, a post he had left only recently, and decided to act on my own responsibility. I carefully figured out the day of Hardinge's arrival in Bombay, prepared a telegram of good wishes, had it signed by the governor-general, and sent it out. Two days passed. I was becoming perplexed. "No answer yet?" asked Samsonov when I came to him with my usual semiweekly report. I had to say no. A few hours later a cossack brought me an envelope from the governor-general containing a very amicable reply from Lord Hardinge. He had received our message on his way from Bombay to Calcutta and had answered in the friendliest terms from the nearest telegraph office. Samsonov was very pleased. Copies of both telegrams were sent to the minister of foreign affairs and presented to the tsar. Nicholas II noted: *"Khoroshii pochin* [A good beginning]."

One of the advantages of my position as political secretary in Tashkent was that I could go to St. Petersburg for instructions. After the dismissal of the foreign minister, V. N. Lamsdorf, I often availed myself of this privilege to call on his successor, Izvolskii, who brought new life into our Foreign Office and broke the stalemate caused by the defeat in the Japanese war.

The Russian Foreign Office in 1907
The Anglo-Russian Agreement on Persia

Izvolskii's great achievement, with which his name will be forever associated in Russian history, was the agreement with England concerning Persia and central Asia. As long as these lands were a cause of friction, Russia and England could not work together in Europe. Through Sir Arthur Nicolson, the British ambassador at St. Petersburg, Izvolskii arranged a complete understanding with Sir Edward Grey, the English foreign minister, and persuaded the tsar to ratify it. Grey and Izvolskii did not prevent World War I, but they created the entente which made possible a victory over the Germans.

Their task was not easy. There had always been a Germanophile party both in England and in Russia. As late as 1912 Grey's hand was forced, and Viscount Richard Burton Haldane, the British Lord Chancellor, was sent to Berlin on a friendly mission. There was a desire in England to arrive at a lasting accord with Germany, but it did not materialize. Only a temporary truce was possible between states with antagonistic interests. The Anglo-Russian agreement was firm because it was based on a common desire to be free from entanglements in Asia in order to face the rising menace of Germany in Europe.

I was on leave in a summer resort in Germany in 1907 when the agreement was signed. On my way back to Russia, I stopped at Berlin to call on my brother-in-law, Colonel A. A. Michelson, who was military attaché at the Russian Embassy. I asked him how the Germans were treating us after the Japanese war. "With contempt, like impoverished relatives," he answered.

I also stopped at St. Petersburg and went to the Foreign Office. As I entered the corridor of the Asian Department, I heard rapid footsteps behind me, and a hand touched my elbow. It was K. A. Gubastov, acting foreign minister in the absence of Izvolskii.

"Come to my office at twelve and lunch with me," he said, rapidly passing ahead.

Punctually at noon I entered his study. Gubastov rose and locked his desk, and we went out. Our way lay along the Moika Canal. Of all the appointments made by Izvolskii, that of Gubastov as assistant minister was the most fortunate. He was a small man of about sixty, still quick and active, cheerful and friendly, with simple manners and without pretense or affectation. He was popular both at the Foreign Office and in high society, including that of the grand dukes. He was at ease everywhere and with everyone. I saw him in the palace in the presence of the tsar, and, although in full uniform, he looked just as unconcerned as ever in the imposing and oppressive imperial precincts. Izvolskii was temperamental and impulsive; Gubastov, calm and sedate. In short, he was Izvolskii's guardian angel and made everything smooth for him. A man without ambition or enemies, he moved forward by the sheer attraction of his personality.

We exchanged some desultory remarks. I wondered what would come next. The agreement about Persia and central Asia had just been signed, but I could not be the first to speak about it.

"Well, what do you think of our convention with England?" he asked.

"I consider it so advantageous for us that I would never have signed it if I were an Englishman," I answered jokingly. We both laughed. Gubastov was very pleased with the agreement, as was Izvolskii. It completed the entente of Russia, England, and France.

Here I must make an observation. Incredible as it may seem, Sir Edward Grey thought that all the advantage was for England only. He wrote: "The gain was equal—on paper. In practice we gave up nothing. . . . What we gained by it was real—what Russia gained was apparent.*

As a matter of fact, the agreement was a masterful piece of statesmanship. It was wrongly called a partition of Persia. On the contrary,

* Viscount Grey of Fallodon, *Twenty-Five Years, 1892–1916* (New York, 1925), *1*, 154–55. *Ed.*

it assured her integrity by eliminating the conflicts on concessions. It withstood for years the blunders of various diplomats. Although abrogated by the Soviets, the agreement still survives in Persia in practice and is the only safe policy there. Every trespass brings a speedy retreat of the offender. It is the law and the prophets, which can be supplemented but not destroyed.

We entered Gubastov's house. He left me in the library and went out to give orders to the servants, as he was unmarried. I looked at the bookcases. A long row of new books extended along a shelf, all dealing with the French Revolution. Gubastov evidently realized how closely the situation of the Russian monarchy resembled that of the French on the eve of the great upheaval.

At lunch we spoke about the relations of America with Japan. An American fleet had been sent into Japanese waters.

"They won't fight," said Gubastov. "Rosen [Russian ambassador at Washington] wrote me so." The conversation soon swerved to the home situation, the usual topic at that time. Gubastov was a moderate conservative; I, a liberal. He was anxious about the rift in Russian society, with a large number of young people taking a leftist position. He tried to excuse the excesses of the right. Finally he said in a sad voice: "You know, the people I meet are so utterly conservative." It was true, and we both realized that it was the stubbornness of the rightists that made conciliation difficult. Liberals are always meek by their very nature.

Our convention glided without break over the dangerous surface of political discussion. Gubastov did not try to convert me. He merely wanted to ascertain my opinion, and I made it clear. I could trust him, and to be frank was the only way to be friendly with him. Gubastov, with the sure tact of a diplomat, changed the subject as soon as he was sufficiently informed.

"Try these French plums," he said as the dessert was served. "They are excellent." We finished lunch in gay spirits, and I took my leave. A few days later I boarded the express for central Asia.

The Russian Foreign Office in 1908–09
The Austrian Crisis and the Downfall of Izvolskii

When I came to St. Petersburg in 1909, the atmosphere of the Foreign Office was gloomy. Gubastov had resigned and was replaced as assistant minister by S. D. Sazonov, who was to bring Russia into World War I. Sazonov's previous career had not been particularly remarkable. Ministers usually chose for their assistants inconspicuous persons who would provide a dull background for their own shining selves. There was also another consideration. Sazonov's brother-in-law, Stolypin, was prime minister.

As I was talking with Izvolskii, who seemed nervous and out of sorts, the door opend slightly—a shadow fell into the room, and a sharp nose peeped in. Izvolskii saw it but purposely paid no attention. After a moment of hesitation, the shadow retreated and the door closed. The shadow was Sazonov. The following year he succeeded Izvolskii as foreign minister of Russia.

Izvolskii's downfall was the work of his own hands. He was much concerned over freedom of navigation through the Dardanelles. It was a vital question for Russia. It was just the proper moment during the negotiations with England to ask her consent for a change in the status of the Dardanelles. Sir Edward Grey expected such a demand from Izvolskii, was ready to discuss it, and had addressed detailed instruction in this sense to the British ambassador at St. Petersburg, Nicolson. "But," wrote Grey, "it is not for us to propose changes with regard to the treaty conditions of the Dardanelles." * Grey thought that Russia had received practically nothing in Persia, was willing to give some other compensation, and had even discussed the question of the Dardanelles with the Russian ambassador in London, Count A. K. Benckendorf.

But Izvolskii was under the fatal impression that Russia was the privileged party in the Persian agreement. He did not dare raise with Grey the question of the Dardanelles, lest the whole agreement fall through in case England should refuse his request. Instead, he waited a year and then went to visit Austrian foreign minister, Alois Aehrenthal, and discussed with him the question of the Balkans and that of the Straits. It was a deviation from the policy that every serious step had to be examined beforehand by the three members of the entente. Nothing was signed during the interview between the Russian and Austrian ministers. That much is certain; the rest is a matter of controversy.

Aehrenthal immediately proclaimed the annexation of Bosnia, a Turkish province under Austrian occupation. Izvolskii protested. Aehrenthal answered that he had Izvolskii's oral assent, which the latter hotly denied. Relations became extremely strained between Austria and Russia, the latter supported by France and England. German Chancellor von Bülow cautiously declined to interfere. Then suddenly, in April 1909, Izvolskii, without notifying his part-

*Grey, *Twenty-Five Years, 1,* 157. *Ed.*

ners of the Entente, yielded to the Austrian demands. There was a
general commotion about this inexplicable retreat. The story I heard
from a Russian Foreign Office source was as follows.

During an audience with the tsar, when Izvolskii triumphantly
declared that all the Great Powers were indignant with Austria,
Nicholas II, in his quiet manner, handed him a private letter from
the German kaiser requesting an immediate acceptance of the Austrian annexation of Bosnia and his own (the tsar's) order to agree to
it. Izvolskii had to bow before the will of the tsar and left the palace
a broken man. Because of personal considerations, he did not resign;
he dragged on for a few wretched months until he was appointed
ambassador to Paris.

The Russian Foreign Office in 1910–11
Sazonov and the Balkans

The year 1910 was an important one for Russia and, incidentally,
for the rest of Europe. It was a year of respite, not fully utilized
to advantage and followed by a turn for the worse. The Russian
revolution of 1905 had been finally and definitely liquidated by
Stolypin, and Russia entered a period of industrial prosperity. The
Duma was composed of a majority of moderate, timid, well-to-do
people, subservient to the government. A small, clamorous opposition in the Duma, finding no immediate response from the mass of
the people, had abandoned any hope of entering the cabinet and
coming to power. There was no prospect of a change originating
inside Russia, who relapsed into her previous passive state. There
was only one possible danger—a war with a great power. And this
danger was just around the corner.

The chances of war depended on the head of the Foreign Office,
but Foreign Minister Izvolskii was slated to become ambassador to
France, and the modest, well-meaning, sensitive, and touchy Sazonov,
lacking in talent and experience, was to be his successor. Izvolskii
had energy, character, and initiative; Sazonov had none. But Sazonov
pleased the tsar, who had taken a liking to him. There was an
essential similarity in their characters. Both were weak, sensitive, and
compliant to a certain degree, but when offended they became resentful and obstinate. Their tempers affected the conduct of the
foreign policy of Russia.

The situation was not pleasant. The kaiser had achieved a resounding victory over Izovlskii, the Russian Foreign Office, and the
tsar himself. The German emperor took advantage of it to drive

a sharp wedge into the rapprochement between the Russian and English governments. He wanted an extension of the Baghdad railway into Persia, a German concession. The extension had to be built with Russian money. The Baghdad railway, still far from completion, strengthened the German position in Turkey. The proposed line was detrimental to Russia and injurious to England, violating the spirit if not the letter of the Anglo-Russian agreement.

Sazonov had not yet been appointed minister of foreign affairs when, in October 1910, he accompanied the tsar on a trip to Germany. The young empress wished to visit her brother, the duke of Darmstadt, a small German state, and Nicholas II had to make a courtesy call on the German emperor at Potsdam. The kaiser seized this occasion for a confidential talk with the prospective foreign minister of Russia, and both the tsar and Sazonov fell victim to the insistence of the kaiser. I cannot say to what extent they gave promises to him, but undoubtedly they did not confront him with a flat refusal. This gave a new impetus to German penetration into the Near East. At the same time France was hard pressed in Morocco. Germany seemed to be threatening on all sides at once. Sazonov and the tsar tried to conciliate Germany, retreating before her and acceding to her demands. That alarmed England, who followed an identical policy but did not like us to do the same, especially at her expense, as was the case with the extension of the Baghdad railway. Here the responsibility of the Asian Department comes in.

The Asian Department had suffered much as a result of the Japanese War. N. G. Hartwig, its director, was sent as minister to Persia, and the department was divided into three independent sections. The section chiefs, entirely subdued, had no opinions of their own about the situation in the East. That could suffice under Izvolskii but not under Sazonov, who lacked information and needed advice. He received from his subordinates only obsequious obedience, mixed with an egotistical desire for personal promotion. After the Potsdam meeting the chief of the Middle East section immediately turned Germanophile and Anglophobe. I was against such a policy, feeling that once an agreement had been contracted, it was to be adhered to strictly. Persia was in the throes of a revolution, and common action on the part of Russia and England was an absolute necessity. I felt no desire to remain under the orders of the Middle East section and, in 1911, went to St. Petersburg and asked to be transferred to the Balkan section.

I was told there was no opening, the usual answer. I spoke about this with my mother-in-law, who had known Stolypin as a young man, the estates of their parents being not far apart. He was still at the head of the government but had only a few months to live. She wrote him a letter. Shortly thereafter I was called to the Foreign Office and offered the position of consul general in Uskub (Skopje), the capital of Turkish Northern Macedonia, bordering on Austria, Serbia, and Bulgaria, all of whom had an eye on it. The post did not look comfortable or easy—two Russian consuls had been murdered in Macedonia in the last few years—but I accepted it, as there was no choice. Foreign Minister Sazonov told me that Balkan affairs were entirely new to him. In fact, Sazonov himself knew nothing about the Balkans, as I understood from my talk with him, and had only an instinctive feeling of distrust. The new assistant foreign minister, A. A. Neratov, had the Balkan files at his fingertips but had spent all his life at his desk in the Foreign Office and never served abroad.

Sazonov went on leave, and before my departure I spoke with Acting Foreign Minister Neratov. I asked him why I was being sent to Uskub.

"To maintain peace there," he answered.

I felt little reassured by this explanation. During my stay at the legations I had become well aware of the exposed situation and limited resources of a political consul.

"I understand that Uskub, as the center of Northern Macedonia, is the scene of the conflicting interests of Serbs, Bulgarians, Turks, and Albanians. What support can I have?" I said.

"None whatever. You are to be a mere observer. Until now we had only consuls there. You will be the first consul general in Uskub. That is all."

"I suppose I can rely on the friendly feelings of the Balkan Slavs toward Russia?"

My distinguished chief cut me short. "They hate us," he said curtly.

As a matter of fact, there was a pro-Russian feeling among the Balkan Slavs, but each nation wanted Russia's exclusive support and was resentful when that support was extended to her neighbors. Certainly in 1911 there was no particular Panslavism in the Russian Foreign Office or in the Balkan states themselves.

6 The Balkans

Uskub

My appointment to Uskub launched me into the turmoil of the Balkans, a place full of dynamite, figuratively and literally speaking. And Macedonia was its worst part. A Turkish province soon to be wrested from the Turkish Empire, full of conflicting nationalities— Serbs, Bulgarians, Albanians, Turks—with revolutionary bands committing bomb outrages, it was surrounded by Balkan nations— Serbia, Bulgaria, Montenegro, and Greece—each striving to snatch a piece of territory from the Turks. In the background loomed the ominous presence of Austria and Italy, ever ready to step in; farther north was Russia, with no interests of her own in Macedonia, but firmly set on opposing an Austrian advance. Russian policy was dictated by historical traditions, the community of race and religion, prestige—a word void of any exact meaning but full of implications —and last of all by an illusory hope of obtaining some practical advantages or preventing others from getting them.

Pending further instructions, my own task was to be an observer, friendly to all. The unfortunate thing was that all these friends were bent on mutual destruction, and I risked being caught in the scramble. There were no Turks in Northern Macedonia except soldiers and functionaries. The local Moslem population consisted of Albanians, bitter foes of the Turks, and Christians, the so-called Macedonians who called themselves Serbs or Bulgarians according to the church they attended on Sundays. The Albanians, Serbs, and

Bulgarians disliked one another but were united in a sincere hatred
of the Turks. In short, Macedonia was a powder magazine with all its
people carrying explosives in their pockets.

I left my family in a little villa near Moscow, with flowerbeds in
front of the veranda and tall pine trees all around. It was the beginning of September, and my second son had been born in July. My
mother was to take care of my wife and children and bring them to
Turkey later, if the hornets' nest of Uskub proved to be fit for habitation.

Once in the express bound for Vienna, I felt like a war horse going
into battle. Danger or no danger, Uskub was certain to be an
interesting place. I knew that relations between Russia and Austria
were the worst possible. I had experienced the tension between
Russia and Great Britain and had seen it happily ended. But there
was no hope of betterment in respect to Austria. The only man who
could be called friendly to Russia, the Heir Apparent Francis Ferdinand, was surrounded by domestic and foreign foes. At the same time
the Austrian Foreign Office was full of vast schemes and tried, not
without success, to circumvent and use Berlin. In a word, the Austrian Foreign Office seemed to be doing a mad dance on top of a
volcano without having a clear idea of the inherent danger to
Austria herself and to the rest of Europe.

I stopped in Vienna, one of the most attractive capitals of Europe.
Good God, why could the Austrians not keep quiet and thank
Providence for the blessings showered on them? Each man is prone to
laud his own country. I am not an Austrian; officially, I was their
political enemy. That gives me the right to say that Austria was
one of the choicest places of Europe, if not of the world.

I saw our vice-consul in Vienna. He was in love with Austria. "A
paradise for a sportsman, or rather for everyone," he said. I heard
the same comments from the Austrians. However, this paradise was
unstable. In spite of the country's large trade, flourishing industry,
and vast resources, the banking situation was none too strong. Why
this was so I leave to the economists to explain, if there still are
people willing to believe the economists and not the facts. The lack
of stability was Austria's misfortune. Its government, its policies, its
army—very brave indeed—were all deprived of a solid foundation.
The smallest state in Europe has something firm in it; the Austro-
Hungarian monarchy had nothing. It existed for the benefit of a
dynasty and a bureaucracy. The population benefited from the large

expanse of customless territory, but its prosperity was hanging on a hair. To use a German expression, Austria was a *credit anstalt* (an institution based on credit).

In Vienna I purchased the furniture for our new residence in Uskub, listened to some enchanting music—the gayest in Europe— enjoyed a few excellent meals, and left for the Balkans. My next stop was Belgrade. The entire staff of the Russian legation was at Herculesbad, a resort in Hungary across the border. That looked very reassuring. I proceeded to Constantinople. At the frontier of Bulgaria and Turkey I changed from the Orient Express to a Turkish train dimly lit by candles. There was a strong outbreak of cholera in Constantinople. Dark railway cars and the threat of a deadly disease were my first impression of Turkey. However, the next day was better—a radiant sun, the beautiful sight of Constantinople, the marvelous Bosphorus, with embassies in splendid villas.

The Russian ambassador was on leave. The chargé, a refined, punctilious man, invited me to dinner. "In tuxedo, please," he said, "and mind, no white tie." These were the only instructions I received from the embassy, and I became perplexed. I carried very little luggage with me and had only a tailcoat. I asked the advice of a secretary, newly arrived from Paris. "A tailcoat with a black bow tie will do," he said. It did. I mentioned to the embassy people that I would like to see the sultan going to the mosque on Friday, but they said that was not interesting. Nothing seemed to interest them in Turkey. They looked bored. However, they did their utmost to be friendly to the Turks.

Aboard the steamer taking me to Salonika I met a colleague. "Look at this," he said, pointing to a newspaper he held in his hand. "The Turkish press is full of attacks on Russia, notwithstanding the friendliness of our embassy. And not a word about Italy, which is going to occupy Tripoli."

"Is that so?" I exclaimed.

"Yes. The orders have been given to the Italian troops to embark. Everybody knows it except the Turks, who are recalling the few troops they had in Tripoli." He laughed.

I disembarked at Salonika, the terminus of the Macedonian railways and their chief port. The northern railway, like a long spear whose handle was at Vienna, passed through Serbia and pierced the western part of Turkey, the spearhead emerging at Salonika. Austrian influence flowed down this line like an electric current. Serbia was an impediment to this flow, and Austria had planned to build a parallel branch, going around Serbia and running exclusively on Turkish territory from the Austrian frontier down to Uskub. Russia was against this plan and wanted as compensation a line connecting Serbia with the Adriatic Sea, across the projected Austrian line. After some bickering both projects were safely shelved.

The train I took traveled over the unattractive, marshy lowlands of Macedonia, the birthplace of Alexander the Great, who was able to recruit here, for his conquest of the world, less than one army corps. He had to be sparing with the lives of his men, and it was useless for him to try to exterminate his innumerable adversaries. He won the most decisive victories with the smallest losses, an example for all time. What would he think of the modern battles with their tremendous bloodshed and indecisive results?

In the afternoon the train reached Uskub, the last Turkish city before the Serbian frontier. A few miles south, in a miserable village still extant, Justinian had been born—Slav by birth, Latin by name, and emperor of Byzantium by the will of fate. A short distance north, on the bloody field of Kossovo, the Turks defeated the Serbs in the fourteenth century and became their masters for five hundred years. Uskub lies on both sides of the River Vardar. On the east side is the old town; on the west side, the new settlement created by the railway and extending from the station to the river. A substantial bridge connects them. There is an embankment on the western shore where my consulate stood.

I was greeted at its entrance by Bukovich, the interpreter, a highly respectable Serb, and two *cavasses* (armed consular servants acting as messengers and guards).

"Where is the third cavass?" I asked.

"He is not well and is staying home. But he will be back soon. He has cholera."

"Let him stay home, don't hurry him," I said, entering the consulate.

I made calls on my colleagues and was elected by them dean of the consular body as the only consul general in this interesting but modest city. The first to return my visit was the Italian consul. He entered my office quickly and sat down with a dejected expression. I looked at him.

"We are at war with Turkey," he said by way of explanation.

I expressed a sympathetic concern for his personal situation and that of the world in general, and after a pause I inquired: "Who is to take over the protection of your interests?"

"Germany," he answered. "But having no consulate here, she is represented by Austria and . . ." He stopped, swallowed the rest of the intended sentence, and stared at me in mute dismay. Relations with Albanian chiefs were particularly delicate at that time.

"I see," I answered. "There is the question of your archives. Well, send them to me or to some other colleague." He nodded. The archives were transferred, over the garden wall, to the adjoining house and disposed of according to his instructions.

The Italo-Turkish war became the center of attention. One day I was discussing it with a Frenchman of Uskub. "We weathered a much harder time in July during the Agadir crisis," he said. "I had received papers to be ready to join the army at the first summons."

"Are you in favor of a war with Germany?" I asked.

"We won't stand repeated provocations," replied the Frenchman. "If Germany considers herself stronger than we, well and good—let us fight and have it over." That was my first intimation of the immediate dangers of the European situation.

Uskub itself was not a healthy place to stay. Macedonian revolutionaries were committing dynamite outrages in order to discredit Turkish rule and achieve local autonomy, the first step toward the secession of a Christian province.

In October 1911 my mother brought my family from Russia and left in a few days. About two hours after her departure, Bukovich entered my study and stood hesitant.

"A bomb exploded under a freight train close to Uskub," he said, naming the exact hour and locality. I felt stunned. Only with a great effort of will did I succeed in figuring that the passenger train had passed the place of the explosion more than an hour before the freight train and that my mother ought by now to be in safety beyond the Serbian frontier.

One morning I found a letter in my mail. Its author wrote that, being obliged to hide in the mountains, he felt lonely and wanted to communicate to me his hopes of a better future for his native land. The letter, written by a young and famous *Comitadzhi* (*chetnik*, revolutionary), had a poetic tinge. There was no return address, of course, and I could send no answer. These revolutionaries carried poison with them, since they preferred not to fall into Turkish hands alive.

A secret, relentless war was going on around me between the revolutionaries and the Turks. But the attempts at murder were directed against others, not against me. I had a strange, instinctive feeling of absolute security, a feeling I had experienced several times in dangerous situations. True, two Russian consuls had recently been murdered in Macedonia, but they had incurred the enmity of the Albanians and the Turks. I had no enemies.

One day I went for information to the *konak* (government building). It was late, and the rooms were empty and dark. A lamp was lit only in the office of the *Mektubchi* (chief clerk). He was rolling cigarettes from a heap of smuggled tobacco spread on his desk. This detail at once gave our conversation a character of friendly intimacy.

"The *vali* (governor) will be late today. Why wait for him? I can tell you right now that we have received a telegram that a bomb was thrown in the bazaar of Ketchana. A riot followed. There are nine victims."

This was fresh news. I wanted to find out how long it would take to spread, so I called on the Austrian consul. He knew nothing as yet, but I had hardly sat down when a clerk entered and stopped short at my sight.

"You can speak," said the consul. The clerk told about the massacre at Ketchana.

"Correct," I said, rising from my place. "Allow me to retire, as we both have to prepare our reports."

This was our main task. The consuls had to keep the embassies informed of the progress of revolutionary activities. From time to time the ambassadors wrote to us that they were planning reforms for Macedonia. What kind of reforms were projected we did not know, as they were never communicated to us. No one took them seriously. The neighboring states—Serbia, Bulgaria, and Greece—were only waiting for a favorable occasion to invade Macedonia. The opportunity came with the Italian declaration of war on Turkey.

The year 1911 came to its end, but the Italo-Turkish war dragged on into 1912. The telegraph started to hum between Belgrade, Sofia, and Athens. Our Balkan colleagues were undoubtedly informed of what was going on, but the representatives of England, France, Austria, and Russia in Uskub remained ignorant of the accumulation of warclouds in the Balkan sky.

The relations between the consuls were very friendly. We used to meet twice a week and play bridge. But politics could be discussed

only among the English, French, and Russian representatives. My
wife had receptions every Sunday, attended by a rather large number
of people for a city like Uskub. Once a chocolate cake was placed
on the table. It was uncut, and a few moments passed in expectation.
"Well," said the Greek consul, taking a large knife, "I shall divide
this Macedonia." And amid general laughter he successfully accomplished the feat.

With the coming of spring I often went driving with my family in
the afternoon. The environs of Uskub were pretty with fresh green
vegetation. Frequently the cavass who accompanied us would volun-
teer explanations: "Here, on this very spot, a rich Albanian was
killed. He was shot through the back. The man who shot him was
well concealed behind the flat rock over there. A little farther up I
shall show you the place where three men were killed. They were
coming from . . ."

"Can't you tell us something more cheerful?" asked my wife.

"But there is nothing else to tell," answered the cavass.

As the weather grew warmer we moved to the hills above Uskub,
where I had rented a Bulgarian schoolhouse, empty during vacations.
The air was cool there, the scenery glorious and looking perfectly
peaceful, but soon I was to know better.

The trouble started among Albanians in a spectacular but harmless way. All northern Albania, adjoining Uskub, rose in revolt
against the Turks and marched on Uskub. They heartily disliked the
Young Turk government which had dethroned the Sultan Abdul
Hamid, very popular among the Albanians. Usually the Young
Turks had recourse to force in such cases, but now they were so dis-
heartened by the war with Italy that orders were given not to interfere with the Albanian movement. Eighteen thousand armed mountaineers joyfully entered Uskub. The invasion, meeting with no resistance, was peaceful. The Albanians dispersed, taking quarters in
Moslem houses. First of all they decided to do a bit of washing. The
balconies and windows of Uskub were adorned with shirts, trousers,
and other picturesque objects of Albanian attire. Since they had no
change, they had to stay indoors while their laundry was drying. That
contributed much to the tranquility of the town.

The next day witnessed their appearance, smart and clean, in the
streets of Uskub, and the Turkish officers were their first victims. It
was the month of Ramazan, the Moslem Lent, when they do not eat
until sunset. A copious meal was prepared in the garden of the

Military Club on the embankment. The Albanians came first and cleaned up everything—plates, dishes, cauldrons, and frying pans. Not a morsel of food was left when the Turkish officers made their belated appearance.

After that the club was guarded by armed soldiers at dinner-time. As I passed along the low iron garden fence, my eyes met the muzzles of loaded rifles pointed toward the sidewalk, with soldiers kneeling in a double row, an unexpected spectacle.

The Albanians behaved well but continued to linger in Uskub, whose population was greatly annoyed by their presence. I personally liked the valiant mountaineers, although I knew they could be very dangerous. Once in a solitary lane I was accosted by an armed warrior who asked me for money. The situation was delicate. I resolved to be firm and answered that he must accompany me to my home. He accepted willingly. Only when we reached the consulate, with the guards at its door, did I give him some coins, and we parted with expressions of mutual goodwill.

But the Christians were in a state of panic, and wild rumors circulated in the town. It was reported that the Turkish commander was going to eject the Albanians by force. As there is nothing fiercer than a fighting Albanian, the Christian population assailed the consulates with requests for help. The consuls met at my house. I was delegated to call on the angry commander and to dissuade him from taking rash steps. Unfortunately, a new general had assumed command of the army corps, and our friend Javid Pasha had left the city.

When I arrived at the military headquarters, I was told that because of the Ramazan the general was asleep and would receive no one. I returned to my house and told the consuls that my mission had fallen flat.

Now it was our turn to become excited. We hurried to our carriages and dashed to the commander's house. To increase the confusion, the coachmen stopped at the lower gate of the garden. We stormed the undefended entrance and rushed up the steep ascent. The commander could see from his window the British, Russian, French, Austrian, Serbian, Bulgarian, and Greek consuls running up to his porch at full speed. We arrived out of breath. An orderly opened the door, and the old general came smiling and proffered his hand. "Sweet as a lump of sugar," the Serbian consul said later.

The commander explained that the inhabitants of Uskub were

not in the least danger. He personally had nothing to do with the Albanians. They did not concern him at all. There was much truth in what he said, and we retreated after an exchange of compliments.

The Turkish government resorted to spiritual means and sent to the Albanians the Mui-Mubarek—a hair of the prophet Mohammed. The Albanians retorted that it was only a hair from the beard of Mehmet Shefket, the war minister, and wanted to test it by throwing it into a fire, for a sacred hair would not burn. The Turks refused, and the hair vanished from the scene. The Albanians moved toward Salonika, where the Sultan Abdul Hamid was kept a prisoner after his deposition. They were told that the sultan had been removed to an unknown destination, and they returned to their mountains.

There were complaints from the Christians inhabiting the secluded valley of Kalkandelen on the fringe of the Albanian mountains, and we decided to make an investigation. The English, French, Russian, and Bulgarian consuls went together in the second half of September.

The Albanians resented this intrusion. There was talk among them of an attack on us, but the idea was abandoned after it was decided that simultaneous murder of the representatives of four powers would not be safe. We always acted together, and this close union made our position more secure and influential.

We reached Kalkandelen in the evening and stopped in a large Orthodox monastery that served as a popular place of pilgrimage but had only one monk. A monastic community cannot exist with fewer than that. After dinner I walked in the courtyard with the French consul, Pierre Léon Carlier, admiring the buildings surrounded by splendid walnut trees.

"Aren't they beautiful?" I said to my colleague.

"Fine," he answered pensively. "I was apprehensive," he added, "about the Turkish maneuvers at Adrianople: much too close to the Bulgarian frontier. Yet they are in full progress, and nothing untoward has happened."

"Yes," I answered, "but they are not finished yet." I felt a cold shiver run down my back. In a flash I realized the proximity, nay the certainty, of war should the Bulgarians consider these maneuvers to be a Turkish provocation. I hated the idea that I had brought my family into an exposed frontier town. Would there be time enough to send them back to Russia? I hurried to the Bulgarian consul, who was enjoying the peaceful landscape, and told him of my anxieties. The Bulgarian answered calmly: "You see I am with you on your trip. That shows that all is quiet." He was silent for a few minutes. "If something happens, we shall know it and shall at once return to Uskub. So don't be disturbed."

His words reassured me, and we continued our tour. Tense as the situation was, hostilities could not start suddenly in the slow little Balkan states. The standing armies were small. It was necessary to mobilize the entire population, consisting chiefly of peasants dispersed in hamlets all over the country. That would take time. We decided to continue our investigation.

Our visit relieved the fears of the Christians who had been threatened by the Moslems. No murders had actually been committed. It was I who nearly became a victim of the excited passions. My coachman passed a carriage with an Albanian going in the same direction. The Albanian's driver became furious and aimed his pistol at my coachman. Since my carriage was ahead, going at full speed, I could easily be hit instead of my coachman. Our guards seized the frenzied driver, who happened to be an Austrian Moslem. That was too much of a complication. I agreed with my Austrian colleagues that the driver should be deported to Austria and that the Turkish authorities should close the case. None of us wanted to create a new incident. We had enough of them as it was.

The First Balkan War

We returned to Uskub highly pleased with an exciting and interesting excursion across a wild country. But when I reached my home and saw my family, I was again oppressed with anxiety. I consulted at once with friends, who offered to inform me immediately if war was decided upon. These Balkan friends are still dear to me and were my only hope, as I could not place any reliance on the embassy, which made a secret of all it knew.

Scarcely a few days had passed since my return when, one morning, a man entered my office and looked fixedly at me. He was a Macedonian. I did not remember seeing him before but understood at first glance that his coming meant mobilization of the Balkan states. He told me who had sent him and added that he was warning me.

"All right," I answered. He nodded and left at once. I rushed upstairs.

"Pack up quickly," I said to my wife. "You will leave by the two o'clock train." My wife gasped. I expained to her that there was no time to lose. I drove to the bank, had a hurried meal with my family, saw them off at the railway station, and sighed with relief. They were out of danger—the rest would take care of itself.

Two hours later, when the train reached the frontier, Serbian soldiers were already removing the tracks. Only the car with my wife, the three children, their governess and nurse, and two cars with refugees were allowed to pass—the last Turkish train to cross into Serbia. The next day a general mobilization in Serbia, Bulgaria, Montenegro, and Greece was officially declared.

Relieved from anxiety about my family, I was free to face the situation. The only official information I had consisted of a recent letter from the embassy concerning projected reforms in Macedonia. As if anyone cared for or believed in them! Things had already gone much too far. I had to rely on my wits to disentangle myself from the impending complications. There was little doubt that Serbia would strike at once at Uskub. It is true that the Turks also planned an attack. But the Turks are slow, and the Serbs are quick. The chances were that the Serbs would be the first to appear on the scene. That made probable the collision of the two armies close to Uskub, if not at its very gates.

"War?" I asked a Balkan colleague.

"Certainly," he answered. "The country would not allow the government to retreat after a mobilization. You know what it means for us—the entire male population called to arms."

Every day the consuls, except the Austrian, assembled at someone's house and sat silently together, like a pack of partridges at the beginning of a hunt. We tried to play bridge or talk but could not. Our official activity had stopped altogether, as I had received a friendly hint from the Turks that my letters and telegrams would be accepted but not forwarded until the end of the war scare. There was no declaration of war yet, only a feverish movement of troops and a tense feeling in the city.

One day we were sitting motionless at the Bulgarian consulate. Only the Greek consul was walking about until he stumbled over an entering servant and snatched a telegram from the latter's hand.

"For you," he cried, rushing to me. "What is it about?"

"Coded," I answered. I went to my consulate, decoded the telegram, and returned at once.

"Anything concerning me?" asked the Greek.

"Yes, sir," I said. "You are recalled. And you also," I added, addressing my Bulgarian and Serbian colleagues, "and I am taking over the protection of your interests."

A few more days, and war was declared. Gloom fell on Uskub; people ceased to laugh, and voices became serious and often subdued. My situation was particularly difficult, as I had received orders from the embassy to take charge of the interests of the Serbs, Bulgarians, Greeks, and Montenegrins. In other Turkish towns France took over the protection of the Greeks. The Christian population of Uskub was stricken with fear. I visited churches, schools, and private houses, comforting the people. They appreciated my calls and recovered their spirits. I wondered why, as I risked as much if not more than they.

Three Turkish army corps were being concentrated at Kumanovo, twenty miles from Uskub, for an attack on Serbia. According to pre-World War I strategy, an attack was obligatory at the outset of a war. It took millions of lives during World War I to realize the fallacy of this conception.

My first duty was to send away the remaining belligerent nationals as quickly as possible. The station was crowded—a train was leaving for the front. The platform was thronged with a dense mass of Moslem women, forgetting in their dismay to veil their faces streaming with tears. As the train moved on, a wail arose. The women lifted their babies, who stretched their little hands toward the soldiers. These leaned out of the windows and waved in answer, trying to suppress the grief on their hardy faces.

News came and spread with lightning rapidity that the Serbs had crossed the Turkish frontier. This meant they were marching on Uskub.

Arms were distributed to the Moslem population, who remained quiet.

Kumanovo

"They are fighting," said Bukovich, entering my room in the morning.

"Where?" I exclaimed.

"At Kumanovo."

That sounded bad for the Turks. A single ridge separated the plain of Kumanovo from Uskub. The Turks had to face the Serbs on this plain or else lose Uskub. The initiative was no longer theirs.

Both sides avoided taking risks, and the fighting brought no decisive results. After a long day of suspense without reliable news, I decided to see the *vali* (governor). I was told at his office that he was at the telegraph station, and I drove there. The room was lighted. The governor came from another room, pale with emotion.

"We have beaten the Serbs," he said. "The telegram from the commander in chief has just passed Uskub on the way to Constantinople."

I went home and wearily sat down on my chair. "Now," I thought, "at least we shall be safe in Uskub, for the war will move farther north."

The next morning I heard the same news—i.e., that the Serbs had lost. I sat sulkily at my empty desk. No mail. No work. Again the prospect of a dull day. In the afternoon I would go to my French colleague, a brave and cheerful fellow. I knew that he would treat me to some excellent French preserves, talk about his family estate, and show me its picture on a postcard.

"A real Louis XVI château," he used to say, "acquired by my great grandfather during the Napoleonic wars. What victories, what triumphs! Money flowing like water." These words were accompannied by a tender look at the picture of the château.

At this moment I was recalled to reality. The door opened, and a magnificent Albanian appeared in full war attire. It was the owner of my house.

"What a hero you look!" I said, admiring his martial figure.

"A hero indeed," he answered grimly, seizing his khaki coat as if he wished to tear it to pieces. "I am going to throw away all that."

"What is the matter?" I asked, astonished at his fury.

But the Albanian had recovered all his composure. "We are beaten," he said coldly. "I come straight from Kumanovo."

"Is it possible! How did it happen?"

My guest shook his head negatively, intimating that he would not enter into any explanations. "I have no time," he said curtly. "Take this and keep it for me." He threw on my desk a heavy bundle wrapped in red cloth.

"What is it?"

"Gold," he answered.

"For God's sake, let me count it and give you a receipt."

But he lifted his hand in a kind of farewell and was out of the room in the twinkling of an eye. I opened the bundle. A heap of gold coins glimmered before me. I started to count them, became mixed up, took a sheet of paper, wrote that this money belonged to such a one, with his name in full, and placed it in my safe. Albanians are like that. If they trust you, they trust you for good. In about a fortnight the Albanian came again and took back his gold without counting it.

I hardly had time to recover from my amazement when I heard a carriage rolling up to my door, and my Austrian colleague, Heimroth, came in. He sat down in an armchair with a friendly smile. I liked him. He was a Pole by origin, a perfect gentleman and a charming colleague, correct, intelligent, and tactful in the midst of the difficult situation we all had to live through.

I saw that he was going to speak about the Serbian defeat, which implied a defeat of the traditional Russian policy. He wanted to know my reaction to the news and wished to broach the delicate question without hurting my feelings.

"Well," he said, "the Serbs are beaten." He was speaking French with me, as usual, and his mild voice was in itself a kind of apology for his words.

"No," I answered, "they are victorious."

He gasped. "Are you certain?"

"Absolutely." *"Donnerwetter!"* That was German, and came from the bottom of his heart—an exclamation of consternation difficult to translate in one word.

He sprang from his seat and rushed out as fast as my Albanian. I heard the thunder of his carriage. My room seemed to be full of electricity; after all these shocks I could not remain in it. I went to the station and met the district manager of the railroad, Swiss by birth, and a reserve officer.

"What about the Turks?"

"In full retreat, as we call it. I left Kumanovo with the last train at 11 A.M. Shells were falling on the station."

A little later my French colleague came to see me. He was also a reserve officer. All the city seemed to turn military. "I shall dig a trench in my garden," he said. "If the Turks decide to make a last stand in Uskub, the Serbs will have to bombard the town."

I had an instinctive aversion to trenches and said so.

"Then keep away from crumbling walls," he answered.

I resolved to stay in my consulate and let the blessed thing crumble on my head.

Turkish soldiers started to pour into the city. There was talk of resistance. I became indifferent to everything as I sat down to lunch. But I was not to be left in peace that day. The Christians under my protection came to the consulate, asking my assistance. I forgot my own troubles and started to work again.

Next to my house was an empty Serbian school. It was put at my disposal. I placed an inscription on the door that it was the chancellery of the consulate, and the refugees were transferred to it, with a cavass guarding the entrance. They were relieved of their anxiety and felt safe. I did not share their confidence. I was not sure that my activity would be covered by international law, which, as a rule, favors the stronger party, and I was far from feeling strong.

A young Serb, about thirty years old, looking intelligent but rather unpleasant, came to see me and began an interminable discourse. I grew impatient. He saw this and said that the Turkish police were after him and he could not leave the consulate.

I told him to wait and went out to consult with my servants. These humble folk were invaluable: they knew the psychology of the masses, were very well posted on the situation, and were my best guides, next to Bukovich. Woe to the consul or diplomat who disregards public opinion. They said that the visitor was a very dangerous man, the chief agent of the Serbian propaganda, a man dreaded by the Christians and pursued by the Turks. It was impossible to keep him in the consulate, open to everyone, where his presence would soon be know to all. The only way was to smuggle him into the new chancellery. That was done.

"Shall I use my gun if the Turks try to enter?" asked the Albanian cavass guarding the chancellery door. A single man, he was ready to fight the whole town. The Albanians are the best guardians in the world.

"No," I said. "Let them in, if they insist. But they won't come."

The agent stayed till the danger was over, then left without a word of thanks.

The situation, although not critical yet, was decidedly unpleasant. My nerves became tense. A priest who called on me told me with emphasis that the Turks would surely be destroyed, because God was with the Christians. I replied that the ways of Providence were inscrutable. My answer did not please him much, but I never liked religious feelings that obliterate moral sense in the human soul.

In the evening it started to drizzle. I was told that the lane in back of the consulate was full of Turkish women who had fled from the villages. In the darkness I dimly saw a mass of crouching figures sitting on the wet pavement, mute with fear and trying to protect their babies from the rain. They could not stay there all night, but Moslem fanaticism made it impossible for me to offer them the hospitality of my house. I sent for the mullah of the nearest mosque, who took charge of them. I went to bed late, thoroughly tired, and fell soundly asleep, thank God.

I awoke next morning with the disagreeable sensation that a sea of trouble, dangers, and complications was in store for me. I was in a maze of political difficulties, with a general slaughter the most probable outcome. I wished I could stay in bed all day and forget about Uskub, the war, and all that it implied. It was not my war. Why should I be mixed up in it? There was not a single Russian in the city. If Serbia chose to fight Turkey, what did a consul have to do with it? I had been told that a man is under obligation to sacrifice himself for the sake of his country. But what about a foreign country? The question remained unsolved when a cavass peeped into the door. I had to get up, dress, and start the usual—in this case unusual—day's work. Are the Turks still here? Yes, and more of them. All the army is here, back from Kumanovo. Well, this is no concern of mine. I am only a civilian servant overloaded with responsibilities, a consul in a town under martial law or no law at all. This was my conception. Then came the reality. In the office I met a distressed Bukovich.

"There are disorders in the prison," he said. "People say that Christians are being murdered there." He wanted to add something and could not. His voice faltered. I suddenly became calm.

"Bring a carriage," I said to the cavass. My words sounded as strange to my ears as if another person were speaking in the room. I drove along the embankment, crossed the bridge, and turned up a long street leading to the marketplace. The prison stood there facing the plaza, which was overflowing with Moslems. The gaping entrance to the prison was closed by an iron railing. The excited faces of prisoners were peeping through it. A detachment of soldiers stood in front of the gate, aiming at it with their rifles. A command was heard, then the crash of a volley, and a cloud of smoke covered all. I ran into the smoke, shouting: "Stop firing."

It was a mad action, contrary to all military regulations, but

I had no time to think about them. An officer, sword in hand, barred my way. He looked sternly at me and said in a firm voice: "There is a revolt in the prison. I am acting on orders."

A European officer would have killed me on the spot for interfering with his orders, but the Turk did not. Certainly he had the right to do it. He saw my cavass and knew who I was. Still it was a gallant act on his part not to strike an unarmed man.

"Where is the warden? I want to see the warden," I said.

"Wait here," answered the officer. "I shall call him." He sent a man, and the warden came.

"Why this mutiny?" I asked.

"It is the second day that the prisoners have been without food. All the bread has been requisitioned for the army."

"Let the prisoners free if you cannot feed them."

"I need an order from the governor to do it."

"Telephone him."

The warden complied with my request. He was glad to get rid of his famished flock. The prisoners I saw behind the railing were Moslems, and the crowd outside sympathized with them. The volley had been fired above their heads. A few tense minutes passed. If a second volley to kill was ordered, some stray bullet might be in store for me, as I stood rather close to the gate and could not move away. The soldiers looked at me, and the officer stood by with his naked sword.

An order came to release the prisoners. It was received with a hum of approbation. The officer put his sword into the scabbard and ordered the soldiers to move aside. The crowd heaved when the railing was opened. As the Moslem prisoners issued from the gate, they were embraced, taken to cafés, and treated there. The warden asked me to follow him into his office.

"I cannot release the Christians," he said. "They would be massacred."

"What shall we do, then?"

"Let us wait till the crowd disperses. Then I shall release the Christians gradually, in batches. They will be conducted under guard of soldiers through the Turkish quarters and set free in the Christian part of the city. Nobody will harm them there."

That sounded reasonable, and it was a very decent suggestion on the part of the Moslem warden. It took us more than an hour until

all were safely freed. In the meantime I entered the prison, talked
with the Christians, and assured myself that all the cells were empty.
The warden grinned and rubbed his hands.

"Now I am free to leave also," he said.

I entered my carriage. The street was a stream of soldiers: two
cavalry regiments, artillery, infantry. The big stone bridge was impassable. I left the carriage, walked across the narrow wooden bridge
for pedestrians, and reached my home none too soon. The troops I
saw were still in military formation. But somebody shouted: *"Ghiaur
ghelior* [The infidels are coming]!" and all became confusion.
Artillerymen cut the traces of the gun carriages with their swords and
galloped away. There was not a single Serbian soldier in view, but
it took time until order was reestablished.

"What a day," I thought, entering my study. The room was quiet
and very comfortable with its Bokhara carpets, mahogany furniture,
bronzes, and pictures in gilt frames. I felt soothed and sat down.
Prison, prisoners, Turkish soldiers, and distressed Moslems seemed a
distant dream.

There was a knock at the door; it was the vali (Governor-General),
Galib Pasha, on foot, with a single policeman, the faithful soul,
all that remained of Turkish rule in Uskub.

"What can I do for you?" I asked, grasping his hand.

The governor was an honest, humane, and straightforward man.
We were friends, and I deeply sympathized with his misfortune,
which he did not deserve.

"The commander in chief left the town without even informing
me of his departure. Some officers took my carriage. Can you find me
one, as I want to leave also?" asked the vali.

"Certainly," I answered. "It will be ready in a moment."

I had a carriage reserved for me. All other vehicles had been
requisitioned. The vali took my carriage and drove to his house,
close by on the embankment, to take his secretary and his luggage.

Only a few minutes had passed when shots were heard in the street.
I seized my revolver and rushed out. The first man I met was the
vali, pale, with blood on his hands.

"Oh, God!" I exclaimed.

"I am not hurt," he said. "But my secretary, who sat next to me,
is killed, and your coachman is wounded."

It appeared that an Albanian had started to shoot at the vali,
missed him, killed his secretary, and wounded my driver in the arm.

The Albanian was killed on the spot by some passing soldiers. Things moved quickly in Uskub on that day. I invited the vali into my house, and rushed to the rescue of my coachman. I saw him walking back with his arm hanging limp and dripping blood, which left a winding trail in the dust. The horses with the empty carriage followed the wounded driver. A doctor was summoned to attend him.

I took the vali upstairs, and he washed the blood off his hands in my children's nursery. A servant brought two elegant leather bags belonging to the governor and deposited them in a corner.

"Can I leave them here?" said the vali. "There is money in them."

"Of course, you can," I answered. "Nobody will touch them."

I had become as indifferent as a bank cashier to the sight of gold in the consulate. We sat down to lunch. The vali decided to go by train to Salonika. But the cavasses said that no policemen and no carriages could be found in the city and warned that it would be too dangerous to go on foot now, since the Albanians were growing desperate with the departure of the troops.

We talked a while. The governor said: "There was a Serbian revolutionary in Uskub. My police looked for him all over the town, but we could not catch him."

I remained silent, as I could not very well tell the vali that the revolutionary was eating his lunch in the house next door. What did it matter now? There was no revolution any more, no Turkish administration, nothing but a dismal city in the grip of anarchy. The vali retired upstairs to take a rest.

The cavasses started to close the shutters. I understood that it had become known in town that the vali was in the consulate. They turned to me and said: "Give us guns. It is time to be armed."

I delivered to them the seven regulation rifles that the Russian government supplied to the consulates in Macedonia. Heavy cartridge boxes were brought into the dining room and opened. I loaded my rifle and sat in an armchair. The darkened room looked as grim and solemn as the faces of my attendants.

They suggested that it would be possible to walk to the railway station after sunset, when the streets would be empty. At night I accompanied the vali to the station, and he left by the last train for Salonika. I felt sad and lonely as I walked back through the deserted streets. I saw a battery of heavy field howitzers, magnificent guns, close to the station. As I learned later, the Turks had shipped the horses first, and there were no freight cars left to take the guns. We next ran into two men: the French consul and a cavass.

"Where are you going, Carlier?" I exclaimed.

"I am patrolling the streets of the Christian quarter," answered my brave colleague. "There are no police, and I am disarming the people I meet." He pointed to some objects carried by his cavass and indistinguishable in the darkness.

"And where is our Englishman?"

"Peckham is at home developing some photograps. He is all right."

"Good gracious!" I exclaimed. "Why don't you go home also? Let things take care of themselves. You will be murdered if you stay out all night." Carlier had no sense of fear. I wished I were like him as I walked my long way home.

At the consulate I found the mayor of Uskub, Albanian by birth, with delegates from the Moslem community. They said that they wanted to speak to me. I invited them to sit down and waited.

"Will the Serbs bombard the city?" they asked.

"I hope not," I said. "Certainly not, if it is not defended."

A silence.

"Will you go with us tomorrow morning to meet the Serbs and tell them that the army is gone?"

"I will," I said, They left.

The Serbs

In the morning the mayor came alone. I asked him where the other delegates who had promised to go with us were. The Albanian answered that it would be useless to wait for them and that we might as well start at once. This was an extremely unpleasant development. If a considerable part of the population disapproved of our mission, they might make short work of us. Only the day before, several murders had been committed for no other reason than that of excited nerves and plenty of arms.

On the other hand the nonappearance of the delegates could be the result of their despair. In a critical situation Moslems are apt to place their lives in the hands of God and accept their fate, whatever it might be.

I bit my lips. The cavasses looked perplexed and ventured no advice. The Albanian sat motionless, with the calm indifference of a red Indian, silent and inscrutable. The carriage was waiting at the door. It was too late for hesitation. I resolved to go.

There was nothing left to do except to don my dress uniform. After that I came down and entered my study for a moment. Suddenly the door opened and all the consuls of Uskub, three to be exact, made an unexpected appearance.

"Is it true that you are going to . . . Oh!" My uniform was an answer in itself.

"I am going with you," said Carlier, the Frenchman, quick as usual to make a decision.

"I think I'd better go also," said Peckham, the Englishman.

"Can you wait for us while we go home to put on our uniforms?" asked Heimroth, the Austrian, who also represented the German interests.

"Most assuredly," I answered.

The concert of nations was complete, with Italy absent fighting an African war, in Tripoli in this case. I felt greatly relieved by the offer of my colleagues, as it considerably diminished the risks of the whole enterprise. The cavasses prepared a white flag and a trumpet. We could not think of anything to add to these emblems of truce. The French and English consuls came with loaded rifles.

"Take a gun with you," said my French friend. "You may need it on the way." The Austrian had none, and I supplied him with a rifle.

The procession started. A man with a flag and the trumpet rode first, then an escort of mounted cavasses of the four nations, and finally the carriages. A Serbian priest on horseback appeared from nowhere and joined us.

The city was as dead as a cemetery, with windows closed, although all the people knew about our departure and looked through peepholes. When we issued into the fields, we were practically out of danger. At our left was the mountain ridge separating the valley of Uskub from the plain of Kumanovo. The road we were following ran diagonally to the ridge and crossed it seven or eight miles away, in the direction of Kumanovo. As we approached the ridge, we saw a deserted whitewashed building at the beginning of the ascent.

"There are men behind the house," said a cavass to me. "Look at that," cried another cavass, pointing back. A cavalry detachment was descending the slope in a long file, cutting off our retreat.

"This is Serbian cavalry," said the French consul.

They were Serbs indeed, and we were in their hands after traveling all morning in no-man's-land. We were surrounded. An officer came to us, and we explained our errand to him. He ordered us to step out of our carriages. We realized that any protest to the Serbs in the intoxicating atmosphere of war and victory would be useless and decided to submit to whatever indignities were in store for us. The soldiers took our rifles, which were never returned to us. The French consul was deprived of his elegant sword with its mother-of-pearl hilt. They bound our eyes. We were offered horses, but we declined to ride blindfolded. Somebody commanded us to march, and we heard the stamping of hoofs around us as we moved, holding each other's hands in order not to be separated. It was evident that we were out of the diplomatic sphere and in purely military surroundings.

We slowly walked up a mountain road. It started to drizzle, and the road became slippery. Our overcoats had remained in the carriages, and we felt that in our wet uniforms we were losing the last traces of our former prestige. The situation was decidedly unpleasant.

At last we were ordered to stop and take off our blindfolds. We were on the top of the pass. The crest of the mountain and the slope behind were full of soldiers, swarming like ants.

A general came. He was short, with white whiskers, brusque in speech and manner, considering us to be undesirable interlopers. I explained that Uskub was defenseless.

"Guarantees," snapped the general. We could offer none, except to state that we had left the city, which could be dimly seen in the distance, that very morning. The general shrugged his shoulders. "I shall report to the commander in chief, Crown Prince Alexander. Wait." He turned his back on us and strode away. With our civilian mentalities we were slow to realize that we were depriving him of the chance of a glorious combat for Uskub.

Obviously the headquarters were very close, for we soon heard a clatter of hoofs. A detachment of cavalry came galloping toward us; at its head was a very young officer on a fine charger. He alighted and came to me, extending his hand. It was Crown Prince Alexander, the future king of Yugoslavia. He understood at once that Uskub was his without firing a shot and that new glory was thus being added to his victory at Kumanovo. He was all smiles.

I presented to him the consuls of France, England, and Austria, and the mayor of Uskub, who was offering to surrender the city. The prince listened to him attentively and acquiesced with a movement of his head.

The Serbs had spent several anxious days at Kumanovo. It was necessary to give the troops a rest after the battle. At the same time nobody knew the exact extent of the Turkish defeat. Their army had not been captured, and its retreat had come so rapidly that it looked more like a strategic withdrawal to a stronger position than a flight, as it was in reality. The Serbs expected the Turks to take a new stand at Uskub and were making their preparations accordingly. That explained their delay.

But the Turkish commanders were thoroughly demoralized. They had been so sure of victory that they had no second line of defense to fall back on. The entire western Turkish front collapsed at once.

Our coming was a complete surprise for the Serbs, who had been full of apprehension about the fate of the Christians. As soon as we told them that the town remained without rule, they decided to move to its rescue immediately.

"Gentlemen, take places in my car. We shall move presently," said the prince in his pleasant, even voice, as he rode away. I heard his command, distinct but not loud. Echoed by someone in a hoarse, jerky tone, it rolled down, repeated, shouted, barked, yelled, till it grew fainter and fainter, reaching the farthest ranks in a kind of yelp.

Most of the Serbian cavalry had been sent to the south in a strategic but prefectly useless attempt to intercept the retreat of the Turks.

Our car, opening the way, moved slowly forward. On both sides marched two lines of scouts, who spread out as the narrow mountain road reached the level plain. Some cavalry rode a little farther on our right flank, and the mighty stream of forty thousand armed men flowed behind us. Their footsteps were light and almost noiseless when compared to those of our soldiers. They wore native shoes resembling moccasins, the only Serbian-made part of their equipment. All the rest was imported; even the horses were Hungarian.

"How well posted you were on the movement of the Serbian army," said Heimroth to me. As a matter of fact, I knew no more than he, possibly less.

We were offered excellent Serbian wine from the personal flask of the prince. There was nothing else in the car, and we remained without food all day. The troops on foot moved very slowly in battle formation, but no resistance was encountered on the way.

The sun was setting as we reached Uskub. An open field stretched

as far as the first houses of the city. Suddenly a flood of humanity
burst out of the town. People wild with joy were running, shouting,
and throwing their hats in the air. It was the Christian population
of Uskub welcoming the prince and the army. A page in the history
of Uskub was over.

Serbian administration was introduced, and Serbian documents
replaced Turkish ones in official transactions. A telegram from St.
Petersburg placed me under the orders of the Russian minister at
Belgrade, severing forever the previous relations with the embassy
in Constantinople. In this instance the Russian bureaucracy—this
slow, quarrelsome, peevish old lady—acted with truly youthful
alacrity and greeted the new development with a genteel smile. The
Austrian bureaucracy did not smile but accepted the situation with
a mental reservation to settle her account with Serbia later on.

The crown prince remained in Uskub until the occupation of the
entire province was completed. I saw him several times, and he
called on me. He was very young, slightly over twenty, had charming
manners, and looked intelligent. He was popular with the soldiers,
as I could see by the way they cheered him spontaneously when they
passed him on the road. I spoke to him about the difficulties of a
small state fighting the large Turkish empire.

"Yes," he said, *"La Serbie est un petit royaume qui désire être
grand* [Serbia is a small kingdom which wants to be great]."

I was preoccupied with the idea that Austria might declare war on
the Serbs, and I warned the latter not to provoke the Austrians by
some rash act. As a matter of fact, Austria was about to mobilize
when Italy's refusal to support her against the Serbs prevented the
outbreak of a world war in 1912.

I was advised that N. Pashich, the Serbian premier, would visit
Uskub. I went to meet him at the railway station, was told by his
personal secretary that he would not come by this train, returned
home, and heard a knock at the door—there was Pashich, accompanied by the same secretary.

There is something indescribable in the bearing of a prime minister, something like a radiation of power. This radiation may be very
mild, but it is always present. The premier need not look pretentious, and he usually is not. That could be detrimental to his
popularity. Pashich, with his white beard and the benevolence of a
grandfather, was perfect. The bounty that flowed from his eyes and
lips seemed limitless, like the clemency of Providence.

I had heard much about this great man. As a youth he had been a favorite disciple of the famous Russian anarchist M. A. Bakunin. Now he was the head of the government and the richest man in Serbia. Wasn't it marvelous? He knew how kings were overthrown and others placed on the throne. His cabinets, composed of his friends, were displaced, but he appeared again on top with a new cabinet and sometimes new friends. Like a submarine, he could navigate above and below the water. Submarines had been called "submersibles," but this name had to be abandoned—they sank too often. Pashich was even better than a submarine—he never sank for good.

He soon left for Belgrade and returned with the king. This time Pashich was in the uniform of a veteran soldier. He looked extremely patriotic. We all stood on the railway platform when the royal train arrived. King Peter stepped briskly out of his car, and spoke gaily with the people assembled to greet him.

"I hope to see you in Belgrade," he told me.

Surrounded by his Horse Guards, he made a state entrance into Uskub and attended a brief service at the cathedral. But when he came out of the church, he sat down in his car with a half-suppressed moan, almost fainting from exhaustion. He was at the end of his physical reserves, but he had achieved the dream of his life: a greater Serbia and the old capital, Uskub, restored to the realm.

With Uskub taken by the Serbs and the Turkish army retreating to the south, it was evident that Turkey had lost Macedonia. The war no longer held any interest for me. The issue at present depended on the attitude of the Great Powers. Only two of them, Austria and Russia, were concerned with the way the Balkan allies would divide among themselves the Turkish possessions which fell into their hands. Austria and Russia were left face to face, their interests sharply opposed. That augured bad for the future.

Fortunately the Serbs created a diversion by occupying the Albanian town of Durazzo on the Adriatic Sea. That immediately spurred both Italy and Austria against one another. An armed conflict between them was out of the question at that time. A diplomatic conference was the only solution. That meant long arguments but no threat of war. For me it was the right time to ask for a leave of absence. I went to Belgrade, which I found quite empty. All the male population had gone to war. Austria could have occupied the city without firing a single shot. But she did not stir.

I called on N. G. Hartwig, the most successful minister Russia ever had in Belgrade. He was elated at the Serbian victories but was in poor health, with only two years to live. Later on there was some gratuitous talk connecting his name and that of the Serbian Prime Minister Pashich with the murder of the Austrian Heir Apparent. Hartwig was a convinced monarchist and had an instinctive aversion to revolutionaries. Moreover, Archduke Franz Ferdinand, a sympathizer with the autocratic tsarist regime, was "the only friend Russia had in Austria," as Kaiser Wilhelm called him. Pashich, of course, was aware of the existence of the terrorists, but he was opposed to them.

As we were sitting together in the evening after dinner, I saw no evidence of Hartwig's splendid library that I had known so well in St. Petersburg. "Where are your books?" I asked him.

"They are still packed up in boxes," he answered. "Oh, I want to show you something," he said with animation and rapidly walked out of the room. Until then he had moved slowly and seemed to breathe with difficulty. He came back with what looked to me like a cake of brown soap, which he handled with loving fingers. There were signs engraved on it.

"This is a Babylonian book," he said. "It is four thousand years old."

A servant brought a coded telegram from Russia.

"The secretary is out and took the keys of the safe with him. We have to wait," said Hartwig with a sad smile.

Hartwig was a hard worker. I knew, however, that his work was little appreciated in the Foreign Office, the work of a man who sacrificed his life for the sake of his country. He died from a heart attack at the Austrian legation in Belgrade when he called there on July 10, 1914.

The Russian Foreign Office
Sazonov at the end of 1912

I rushed to Moscow to see my wife and children, and then to St. Petersburg, where I arrived on a frosty morning at the end of November 1912. I spent the day with my mother, who had been very anxious about me, and called at the Foreign Office late in the afternoon.

"Can I see the minister?" I asked the private secretary.

"He is expecting the British ambassador," was the answer. "Oh, you are from Uskub! Wait a moment. I shall speak to Mr. Sazonov. Perhaps he will see you at once."

The secretary returned and nodded to me. I entered the room I had known so well under Izvolskii. It had been well lighted then, but now it was almost dark. By the light of the lamp standing on the desk, which had been moved far away to the back wall, I could at first glance distinguish only the minister's face and the papers he was looking at. It seemed as if the vast room had shrunk to the little pool of light and the small man bent over his work.

Sazonov saw me and rose from his chair. "Safe out of the war," he said smiling. "Well, sit down and tell me about the Serbs. What were they doing when you saw them last?" I started to speak. Sazonov was in general well posted about the situation. He had presented to the tsar my report about the taking of Uskub.* It had been returned with the penciled mark of the emperor that he had read it. Sazonov looked satisfied with the march of events and showed no apprehension of complications on the part of Austria. His relations with Germany were still friendly. He looked composed and peacefully minded.

I told him that the Serbian war was practically over and that the Serbs would occupy without difficulty all the territory assigned to them by the treaties with Bulgaria and Greece. Now everything depended on the attitude of Austria.

"And what about Hartwig?" asked Sazonov. "How does he feel?"

Sazonov was still smiling, but I sensed a veiled tone of hostility toward my old chief and spoke in the highest terms of his great popularity among the Serbs and of his relentless energy. Sazonov nodded in agreement but without enthusiasm and turned to another topic. The conversation was rather long, as the British ambassador had not yet come.

"We are well satisfied with you," said Sazonov, as I took my leave.

At this time Sazonov had already been directing the foreign policy of Russia for three years. He had felt confused at the beginning, but he gradually gained confidence. The position of foreign minister did not seem as difficult as he had thought at first. The new champion of the Russian Foreign Office had even scored some successes. His

---

* Ministerstvo Inostrannykh Del, *Sbornik Diplomaticheskikh Dokumentov Kasaiushch-ikhsia Sobytii na Balkanskom Poluostrove* (Avgust 1912 g.–Iul 1913 g.) [Ministry of Foreign Affairs, *Collection of Diplomatic Documents Concerning Events on the Balkan Peninsula* (August 1912–July 1913)] (St. Petersburg, 1914), pp. 28–32. *Ed.*

MEMOIRS OF A RUSSIAN DIPLOMAT

policy of uniting the Balkan Slavs resulted in a Serbian and Bulgarian victory over the Turks, which was also a setback to Austrian and German influence. These two powers had done nothing to counteract this and remained strangely inactive. England, after some sharp remonstrances over Russian policy in Persia, became friendly again after the failure of the Haldane mission. Sir Edward Grey called a conference in London to settle the Serbian dispute over the frontier of Albania and helped Sazonov out of an embarrassing situation. The Russian Foreign Minister looked highly satisfied with himself and with the march of events.

But it was a lull before the storm. Austria had been prevented from attacking Serbia only by the unexpected opposition of Italy. Germany was hastening to consolidate her position in Turkey by sending a military mission to Constantinople, and Russian diplomacy was particularly vulnerable there. Sazonov had lost invaluable time by not making an agreement with England and France about further eventualities in the Turkish capital. The French and English policies in Turkey were not in accord with the Russian. Germany was getting ready to deliver a shattering blow to Russian interests in Constantinople, and Sazonov was to receive it unprepared and unprotected.

The Russian Foreign Office itself was in poor shape, being undermanned and consisting chiefly of young men, some of them ambitious, all incompetent. Sazonov was weak and needed expert guidance and advice, but he did not know how to get it. Such was the man who was to play a leading role in the forthcoming European crisis. England and France, with their much stronger statesmen, were, by the force of events, obliged to follow the policy of Russia, which dragged her foes and friends into the vortex of World War I.

St. Petersburg
December 1912

I received a Russian and a French Cross and was promoted to Crete. It was my last stay in Russia and the happiest time I ever spent in St. Petersburg.

Papers started to publish articles about me in connection with Uskub. Previously, telegrams sent by Russian correspondents from Uskub had been garbled on the way. Instead of a "Russian," a "Serbian" consul was active in Uskub, preventing looting and massacre after the retreat of the Turkish forces, although all Serbian representatives in Turkey had been recalled weeks earlier.

I had long talks with my mother. She became reconciled to my career in the Foreign Office, which she had formerly considered a perfectly useless and ridiculous institution. She promised to visit me in Crete. This picturesque island with its memories of Minos and the Minotaur had a strange appeal to my mother's practical mind.

As far as my personal life was concerned, everything looked bright and promising, but I was alarmed at the bellicose tendency of the press and the public. People spoke a great deal about a conflict with Austria, the ultimate fate of Constantinople, and Russia's historic mission in the Near East, although nobody knew exactly what this meant or where it would lead. There was the traditional point of view that Constantinople must be either Turkish or Russian and nobody else's. The Foreign Office preserved its calm, but it was doubtful how long it would be able to continue its cautious policy. And besides, the home situation was far from satisfactory.

One day I called on a former schoolmate, V. V. Nikitin, who held a highly confidential position as secretary of the council of ministers, the very workshop of the Russian government. My friend was a hard and efficient worker, endowed with an excellent memory but no ideas of his own—the perfect type of bureaucratic functionary of the old regime. Our conversation turned to the project of a small railway extension in the Crimea, which would connect the main line from St. Peterburg with the port of Yalta. As Yalta was the most fashionable sea resort in Russia, invaluable for invalids in winter and open all year round, no one doubted the utility of the extension. The last stage of the journey, in a horse-drawn carriage, cost as much as the railroad fare from St. Peterburg to the Crimea. Yet the extension had been under consideration for thirty-five years. I asked my friend whether it would be constructed soon.

"We are working on it just now," he answered, taking out of a drawer a voluminous portfolio of papers. He started to explain the various propositions, handling with deferential care the originals signed by ministers and other important people of Russia. It seemed that they all disagreed among themselves.

"Well, what is the net result of all this?" I asked.

Nikitin looked at me in blank amazement. "I told you that the minister of war had presented objections to the last project," he said, reverently holding a sheet of paper signed by the objecting general.

"Is he against the construction of the extension?"

"Of course not. The tsar desires it, but . . . ," and the impeccable memory of my bureaucratic friend evoked again the chain of arguments I had just heard.

"What are you doing now?"

"I? I am preparing a memorandum for the prime minister."

"And what will be the final decision?"

Nikitin's astonishment knew no bounds. "How can I tell?" he answered with a gesture of complete despondency.

After Stolypin's death, the confusion at the meetings of the council of ministers was to increase. The opinions of the ministers clashed, while the tsar sat there looking august and small like a Broadway church among towering skyscrapers.

We changed the subject of our conversation. My friend had recovered his presence of mind and started to tease me about our diplomacy. "It is all your fault," he said, "You never speak to Austria as you ought to do."

"And what about a war with Austria?" I asked.

"Why not?" he said.

It was my turn to attack. "Can you guarantee that there will be no revolutionary movement inside Russia?" I retorted.

My friend remained silent a few moments. "No, we cannot," he said.

As in the case of the Yalta extension, the question of who would command in the eventuality of a war was discussed but not settled.

One day on my way to the Foreign Office, I happened to see Samsonov, governor general of Turkestan, driving in an automobile. I was astonished to meet him in St. Petersburg and called on a colleague from the Foreign Office who was well informed about what was going on in high spheres.

"Yes," he said. "Samsonov is here, and there is a big intrigue at the court. The commander in chief in Russian Poland, General G. A. Skalon, is quite old and unfit for service. He was to be replaced by Samsonov, but there is a strong party against Samsonov. They say that Skalon must be left in Warsaw for another year so that he may celebrate his jubilee of promotion to officer rank fifty years ago. Samsonov is slated to command an army against Germany, but in the meantime he will be sent back to Turkestan."

I called on Samsonov the next day and had a talk with him and his charming wife. Samsonov was very gay and had no inkling of the opposition he was to meet. A chivalrous, dashing cavalry officer, of a frank and open disposition, he was absolutely incapable of fighting intrigues. He was to be appointed to command an army against Germany on August 8, 1914, less than a month before his defeat and death.

Samsonov was not the only person involved in sharp competition for responsible positions in the army in case of war. The most important was that of commander in chief. The Grand Duke Nicholas wanted it, as did the minister of war, V. A. Sukhomlinov, and the tsar was reserving it for himself but said nothing. Only after the declaration of war did the tsar announce his decision to the council of state, but he was overwhelmed by the unanimous opposition. The grand duke won the appointment. From that moment the tsar and he became estranged. The discord in Russia started at the very commencement of the war and began at the top.

Crete

With my appointment to Crete I reached the climax of my career. Crete was administered by a Greek governor-general but was nominally an independent state protected by Russia, France, Great Britain, and Italy, whose consulates had the status of legations. I could not wish for a better place.

When I left St. Petersburg in January 1913, all my prospects looked brilliant. I could not know that soon everything was to be submerged in the deep abyss of the coming catastrophe, that it was the last time I was to see Russia, and that this Russia was fated to disappear forever.

I passed through Athens, reached Canea—the capital of Crete, the largest and most remarkable island of the Mediterranean—and found myself surrounded by the glorious atmosphere of ancient Greece. Its splendid skies, its sea, and its blue mountains are always the same, and today's Cretans represent the nearest approach to Homeric heroes. They are tall, strong, sturdy, extremely brave, resolute, warlike, and irascible.

There are no venomous snakes in Crete, by tradition a special gift of the Apostle Paul, who converted the island. St. Paul used very strong language to describe the Cretans when he appointed Titus first bishop of Crete, recommending his flock to him in the following words: "The Cretans are always liars, evil beasts, slow bellies" (Titus 1:12). The Cretans claim that the apostle later changed his opinion entirely, but undoubtedly he had some difficulties with his congregation in the beginning. I liked the Cretans, but they are not easy to deal with.

Crete has only one harbor, but a magnificent one, the Suda Bay. At its entrance there is a small island with the remains of an ancient church dedicated to St. Nicholas, the patron of the eastern Mediterranean. Every Greek steamer in these waters carries an image of the saint. In 1913 the Cretans decided to rebuild the church and dedicate it to St. George, since George I was then king of Greece.

The governor-general, S. Dragumis, invited me to attend the ceremony with him. It was to be a great festival, and a whole fleet of small boats sailed with us. Our boat, which could normally accommodate twenty persons, took thirty-seven, as is usual on holiday excursions. As soon as we reached the middle of the bay the wind dropped, and we slowly advanced under sails. The Cretans were gaily talking and laughing. They felt perfectly at home on the sea —they are reputed to be the most experienced sailors of all the Greeks. I was not at all at ease. The sky had assumed an unpleasant color, and, although we were heading north, I noticed that the dust on a road running high along the mountain was whirling in the opposite direction. I called this to the attention of Korkutis, the master of our skiff and captain of the port of Canea. Arrayed in full uniform, he sat squarely with his back to the bow, cracking jokes. He looked at the mountain, and his color changed as much as possible after fifty years of tanning under sun and sea breeze. He threw off his uniform with all its decorations, rolled up his sleeves, and seized the bar. We had to face a sudden change of wind from southern to northern, a regular and very unwelcome occurrence in these latitudes. We were too crowded to use the oars and had to change sails under a contrary wind, the only really dangerous maneuver on a sailing boat. The wind fell, and our sails flopped. Then the contrary wind started to blow in gusts of increasing violence. The overloaded boat creaked and pitched. All the Cretans sat still in a strained silence. In a hoarse voice, Korkutis ordered his crew to change the canvas. Our boat leaned port and refused to budge. We ceased to breathe; the captain grinded his teeth. The boat heavily rose and turned leeward. We were saved. After that we flew under small canvas but at full speed toward the shore and landed with great difficulty. I took a look at the scenery. The sea was covered with raging waves. Boats were flying in all directions. One boat capsized and all her crew went down. Another boat was wrecked on the rocks; fortunately her passengers were able to swim ashore. On the island the bishop and the clergy were standing with their hands upraised, imploring the mercy of the darkened heaven.

The Cretans told me later that St. Nicholas was angered because his church had been taken away from him. The bishop did not dare return to Canea and retired for some time into a remote monastery. Finally the church was dedicated to both St. Nicholas and St. George. We had no more storms for the rest of the season, but news came that King George I had been assassinated in Salonika.

It is interesting to note that in ancient times the sun god Helios was the patron of the sea, and the present churches of St. Nicholas sometimes stand on the site of a temple or statue of Helios. Such is notably the case on the island of Rhodes. The festival days of St. Nicholas coincide very closely with the summer and winter solstices, and the Greek mariners coordinate their longer journeys with these dates.

The Cretans are very religious. The archbishop of Crete told me that in a remote village he found a pagan bas-relief with mythological figures. The villagers worshipped them and burned candles in front of them. Some of the figures were naked, and the people thought they represented Adam and Eve before their fall.

Crete has magnificent ruins, which, according to Sir Arthur Evans, date back to the time of Minos. This so-called Minoan civilization was in many respects superior to that of modern Crete. On its frescoes carts are represented, and there are remains of roads for wheel traffic, a mode of communication later entirely unknown in Crete. The few existing roads were built in the twentieth century. I had to ride on horseback along mountain paths in order to visit the glorious ruins of Knossos.

My pleasant stay in Crete and study of Greek antiquities came brusquely to an end when the powers decided that there was no longer any need for consuls general in Crete, and in consequence I was transferred to Smyrna,* the chief port of Asia Minor. I owed my transfer to a less advantageous position to the hostility of the chief of the Near East Section, Prince G. N. Trubetskoi. We differed so much that I prefer not to express any personal opinion about his handling of Bulkan affairs. The result is known.

* Smyrna (Ionian Greek for myrrh) was called Izmir by the Ottoman Turks who occupied the city in 1425. The Turkish name came into universal usage after the Lausanne Convention of 1923. *Ed.*

7   The Near East and World War I

The Russian Ambassador at Constantinople
M. N. Giers

I became subordinated to the embassy at Constantinople and had to present myself to the new Russian ambassador, M. N. Giers, the son of the late foreign minister. Brought up in an atmosphere of bureaucratic adulation, this obstinate and rather narrow-minded new ambassador found German influence firmly established in Constantinople and was unable to overcome it. He remained in this unenviable situation, distrustful of the Turks and resentful toward them. The old muddle over Turkey was intensified by a new and highly dangerous German experiment—the Berlin-Vienna-Constantinople-Baghdad axis, following the railway line rapidly being built across the Near East by a German concession.

Giers was imbued with the idea of Russia's might and full of contempt for Turkey, which, according to the then prevailing notion, was soon to be divided into zones of influence or parceled among the Great Powers. This was a common misconception that lasted till after World War I. Giers realized the importance of his mission and was uncomfortably conscious that the results did not correspond to his expectations. This did not contribute to improve his mood. He looked suspiciously at me because I had been appointed by the Foreign Office without his being consulted, a procedure often practiced by the Asian Department and always unpleasant to an ambassador. I assured him that I had been much better off in Crete.

The ambassador was mollified and repeatedly told me that he considered Smyrna a very important place. The statement was not amplified. I could only suppose that the ambassador was apprehensive lest Smyrna be occupied by some European power. But what would that matter to Russia? Our chief, most vital interests were centered in Constantinople, and there Giers and Sazonov were pitifully at bay. Every day the Germans were becoming more arrogant and aggressive. The climax came with the arrival of the German general, Liman von Sanders, who had been appointed military commander of Constantinople and of the Straits of Bosphorus, which were the keys to the Black Sea and provided the southern Russian ports with their only waterway to the outside world. The seeds of World War I were already being sown at Constantinople.

Giers complained to St. Peterburg. Even the mild Sazonov, who had catered for years to the whims and caprices of the kaiser, felt slighted by this unprecedented provocation; he made protests to Berlin, which met with scant success. Sazonov became incensed and, by the end of 1913, had assumed an anti-German attitude.

Russia was satisfied to leave Constantinople in the hands of the Turks, who were no menace to her and the least troublesome of her neighbors. But the German predominance at Constantinople had shattered the entire Russian policy in the Near East. The Austrian pressure on Belgrade acquired a sinister character. The railway line from Serbia to Turkey, the only independent link between Berlin and Baghdad, was threatened. Germany was encircling Russia, leaving to her only one free outlet on the Arctic Ocean. Russia had never been at war with Austria and in 1806 had saved Prussia from utter destruction by Napoleon. Was the Russian Empire to be strangled by Austro-German expansion from the Baltic to the Persian Gulf? For the first time in history a war between Russia on one side and Austria and Germany on the other was impending and almost inevitable.

It seems doubtful that the German government ever realized how offensive and intolerably detrimental its activity in Constantinople was to Russia. Certainly the kaiser had no intention of provoking a breach with the Russian government. Contrary to an often expressed opinion, the German emperor was not warlike, only boastful. He was a hero of military parades, blank shots, and brass music. He would

have been a perfectly harmless man except for the fact that he was
the emperor of Germany.

The only thing left for Giers to do was to conciliate the Turkish
government—there was an anti-German feeling among the Turkish
leaders. Giers not only failed to do that, but, worse yet, he prejudiced
Sazonov against the Turks.

Life in Smyrna
The Eve of World War I

I returned to Smyrna and found myself among Germans, Young
Turks, Catholic Levantines, Orthodox Greeks, and the archeological
remains of classical times. Five different civilizations were represented in Asia Minor, although only marbles and mosaics remained
from the most ancient. They stirred my imagination with memories
of classical studies. I saw the ancient gods and heroes alive before me.

Achilles was sitting in his tent in a clean chiton after the morning
bath, and Briseis was combing his hair, reeking with sea water.

Hermes stood in the marketplace, looking with an amused smile
on the cheating crowd of noisy merchants.

Minerva, with academic vigilance, was watching young Telemachus,
who was only a sophomore after all.

Zeus, the father of gods and men, was ruling the universe, firmly
seated on Olympus.

Apollo was present everywhere, in the radiant sun, in the melodious music, and in the brilliant intelligence I saw in the sparkling
eyes of E. Venizelos.

Only Mars had a foreign appearance, with the Prussian helmet
and the stiff military bearing of the German generals.

Smyrna looked like a paradise, except that her inhabitants were
not and did not care to be particularly innocent. The people of
Smyrna, predominantly Christian, were born and lived under
Turkish rule, which they despised, mocked, and exploited to their
best advantage. There was no opportunity for them to display civic
virtues, and nobody seemed to deplore this fact.

But the Balkan wars struck a patriotic chord in the hearts of the
Smyrna Greeks. They became conscious of the glories of the past, the
duties of the present, and the promises of the future. This future
was to end in their total annihilation, but in the exultation of the
moment nobody was disposed to gloomy thoughts. The Greeks of

Smyrna became ardent nationalists, and, this state of mind being highly contagious, the Turks turned nationalistic also.

My situation between the Turks and the Greeks was extremely delicate. Traditionally the Russian representatives in Turkey had to protect all Orthodox Christians for religious and political reasons, an unholy combination that always proved detrimental to Russia in the long run. The seven seats of the churches of Asia, mentioned in the Apocalypse, were still occupied by Greek bishops who applied to me for protection. I had to listen to their complaints about Turkish administration and intervene for them before the Turks. According to another tradition, Russian diplomacy was to uphold the Turks, the only power in whose hands we could consent to leave the sovereignty of Constantinople and its straits. Several Russian consuls paid with their lives for the attempt to conciliate the irreconcilable.

Then there were the Levantines. Their orgin was very mixed, mostly Greek and Italian, but they were Catholics and as such enjoyed the protection of the French consulate, even though they were Turkish subjects. All commerce was in the hands of the Greeks and Levantines, with a few European and Armenian firms.

The Turks were masters of the land. It is curious to note that all the leading Turks at that time were from Salonika, where the Moslem population was of mixed Turkish, Slav, Jewish, and Gypsy blood. So much for the purity of race and stock. The Salonika Turks were all ardent nationalists and Turkish patriots. The Young Turk cabinet was formed of Salonika men, and Mustafa Kemal Pasha, the future president of Turkey, was born there. The governor-general of Smyrna, Rahmi Bei, was from Salonika, and so was his powerful friend and protector the Grand Vizier Talaat Pasha. Rahmi Bei was young, strong, and intelligent, and we soon became friends. This smoothed our personal relations, although we remained at loggerheads over the Christian question.

The last to come were the Germans. They were a direct challenge to Russia. A strong pro-German party was headed by the minister of war, Enver Pasha, an ambitious, presumptuous young man with the manners and mentality of a Prussian second lieutenant. At least such was my impression when I met him at a dinner given in his honor by the corps commander. Among the guests were two aged German colonels with the rank of generals in the Turkish army. The methodical, punctual Germans felt awkward in uncongenial Oriental surroundings. The Turkish officers chaffed at their intrusion, although the Germans I saw were kind, conscientious people. The German military mission eventually was to prove a failure. Turkey's only successes in World War I were won by Turkish generals fighting independently of foreign advisers.

When the Young Turk revolution started, Enver, who was then military attaché in Berlin, went to Constantinople, took part in the revolt against Sultan Abdul Hamid, the friend of the kaiser, and returned to Germany. "A strange attaché," said the kaiser, "who dethrones his sovereign and comes back to me." But Enver proved such a docile tool in German hands that this little breach of military discipline was quickly forgiven him.

The minister of the interior, Talaat Pasha, soon to be grand vizier, distrusted and feared Enver. Enver had already killed his own predecessor at the War office, Nazim Pasha, during an argument with him, and he was always ready to use his gun again. Here was an opening for diplomatic action, and Talaat made some approaches to Giers, who rebuked him and lost this unique opportunity.

November and December 1913 passed rapidly, the last cloudless months of my life. I made many acquaintances among the Turks, Greeks, and other residents of Smyrna and was looking with confidence to the coming year. With confidence! The year 1914!

What is the meaning of New Year's Day? I had already seen more than forty of them, and none had any meaning for me except one— that of 1889. My father was desperately ill; he still had strength enough to walk in the street, but I was told he would not live to the end of the year. We were alone as the clock struck twelve—father, mother, and myself. Father filled the glasses and touched mine, with a calm smile. I had barely the force to restrain my tears and swallow the champagne, the bitterest drink I ever had.

On New Year's Eve 1914 I did not wait for the coming of midnight. My wife felt tired, so we retired early, and I did not hear the strokes of the clock which sounded the approach of death to the unsuspecting millions merrily acclaiming the advent of 1914.

For me New Year's Day began with going to church. The cathedral was full of common folk, but I saw no members of the richer classes. They had gone to bed late the night before, after plenty of food, drink, talk, and laughter, and they needed rest. After the service I went to congratulate the Metropolitan Archbishop, Chrysostome, who was still boiling with exasperation after the prayer he was forced to make for the health of the sultan. The Most Reverend Chrysostome was a man of childish faith and burning Greek patriotism, a fountain of eloquence when he preached, a real Oriental bishop of the dawn of Christianity, addressing the pagan world with flaming eyes and fiery words.

The constrast was complete when I returned home and received the Turkish governor-general, a prince of this world, young and strong, full of the sense of his power, of unbelief in Christ, and of reliance on the might of the sword and the scaffold. His conversation was gay and his visit short, as is usual on New Year's Day.

There were other callers, but my wife did not stay with me and retired upstairs. As soon as the reception was over, I joined her and found her pale and sad, an ominous sign. I asked if something was wrong with her. She answered that she was not quite well and looked at me with big, strangely serious eyes. I became anxious and thought that she needed more exercise and fresh air. I reminded her that the official opening of the American college a few miles south of Smyrna was to take place in the afternoon and asked her to go with me, thinking that the drive would do her good. She had looked rather weak during the last month. She was nursing a baby, but that could only partly explain her depressed condition. I sent for a carriage, but my wife declined to go without giving any reason. For the first time in my married life I met with a refusal from her. I went alone deeply perturbed. After presenting my congratulations to the president of the college, I hurried home. My wife was still sitting in her bedroom.

"What is wrong with you?" I exclaimed. "Tell me."

There was something indescribable in the character of my wife. If it could be defined in words I would say that she was true in everything, saw the truth, and radiated it herself. Although gentle and kind in her behavior, her judgment of people was unfailing, and she could recognize a false man at first sight. I had met many more people than she had, and to read their thoughts through the veil of their words was part of my profession, but I could never approach her instinctive, unerring appraisal.

I waited. She looked at me, cast down her eyes, and her lips moved slightly. I could hardly hear her voice as she started to speak. "I am coughing," she answered, "and there is blood." She showed me her handkerchief with a small rosy spot. The room seemed to darken suddenly, and the floor swayed under my feet.

A doctor came, and then another. Their diagnoses were the same:
The lungs were affected. She had to stay in bed, and the baby was
weaned. I telegraphed my mother at St. Petersburg to come at once.
I sat by the bed of my wife, trying to calculate with some degree of
precision how long it would take my mother to come from St.
Petersburg—ten days at least, possibly more.

But hardly a week had passed when I heard her voice in the next
room and her rapid footsteps. She had left the day after receiving my
telegram, just in time to catch the weekly streamer from Odessa, and
here she was. For a moment I saw anxiety depicted on her features,
but she recovered her composure at once and responded cheerfully
to the weak smile of my wife.

My mother adored my wife. Our house revived; it seemed as if
the presence of my mother had banished with a magic spell all our
worries and sorrows. She took over the management of the household with her usual energy. Nature itself came to our rescue with
beautiful weather and an early spring, and my wife started on the
road to recovery. We took a summer house in Buja, a summer resort
close to Smyrna and connected with it by a railway branch.

I began to breathe freely. If need be, I would ask for a leave and
take my wife to Switzerland. My mother could take charge of the
children. The illness treated at its inception would present no danger. All that was not a dream but a perfectly realizable project in a
normal world—not in the world of 1914. My mother saw us settled
in Buja and left for Russia. I took her to the streamer and looked at
her for the last time. We were never to meet again.

The international atmosphere was absolutely serene. The latent
enmities between the nations were dormant. After ten years of
bickering the cabinets were enjoying a rest. I saw no disquieting
symptoms from the distinguished travelers who passed through
Smyrna. Grand Duke Constantine of Russia came on his way back
from Egypt. It was the last time that I had to take charge of royalty,
and, incidentally, this visit was the source of considerable annoyance
for me. The grand duke was traveling incognito. This meant that he
did not want any official receptions, but it did not imply that his
journey was to be kept secret from the consuls. Nevertheless, the
legation at Athens failed to inform me of his impending arrival.

The grand duke and duchess were met abroad their streamer by an
agent of Cook, who offered them a trip to Ephesus, well worth seeing
and easily accessible. They drove straight to the station and left by a

special train before I could be informed of it. When I came to the station, they were already gone. What was worse, there was no engine ready. It would take hours to put a locomotive under steam, and the grand duke would by then be on his way back. I had to wait for his return, keeping in touch by telegraph about the progress of his train. I was extremely annoyed. There were robbers in Asia Minor who could detain the grand duke and his wife. They would not harm Their Imperial Highnesses, but the scandal would be tremendous. Fortunately the robbers were as ignorant of the royal arrival as I myself had been, and the party returned without mishap.

In the meantime I had to provide the best victoria in the city to bring them from the station, a special permit to drive on the quay, which in the evening was reserved for pedestrians only, and a steam launch to convey them safely aboard the big ship on the roadstead far in the gulf. The launch proved to be a tug, and I had to decorate it with carpets and cushions—there was no lack of them in Smyrna.

I was on time to meet the train. The grand duke stepped out of his car. He was tall and lean and looked stiffly military in his gray overcoat and soft felt hat. The grand duke was well educated—a president of the Academy of Science—and kind at heart, but he considered it necessary to assume an overbearing countenance. I wondered what good it would do to him and to the monarchy.

He thawed somewhat at the sight of the victoria and the steam launch and expressed his satisfaction. His wife, a plump German princess, looked pleasant and motherly and was all smiles as I presented her with a bouquet of Marechal Niel roses. The steamer started to whistle, and I promptly jumped into my tug.

There were other visitors. The wife of the Russian minister of war, V. A. Sukhomlinov, came to Smyrna on her way to Egypt. She was a platinum blonde with wonderful blue eyes, a fascinating, intelligent, dangerous woman, divorced and remarried to the old, light-minded, intriguing Sukhomlinov, the evil genius of Russia.

There were American millionaires interested in the American college and the world in general. There were ministers going to and from their legations. Mediterranean tours were as popular before World War I as they are today. This affected even the movement of warships. Single dreadnaughts and whole squadrons would appear in the Gulf of Smyrna. The big ironclads seemed to exercise a magnetic influence on each other. After the visit of an Austrian warship, an Italian was sure to follow. They remined me of gladiators in a Roman arena, marching in a cold and ceremonious manner and viewing each other with an assumed indifference. Russian warships also came, and I had to act as host to the officers.

An unpleasant complication in local politics was the persecution of the Greeks by the Turks. The powers did not intervene in what they regarded internal affairs of a sovereign state. They cherished and praised peace above all and abhorred the very idea of war.

The Turkish government considered the Greeks an undersirable element and in 1914 ordered their expulsion from the province of Smyrna. The Greeks were expelled from the villages of the seacoast and of the interior; a few were murdered. There was no systematic killing of Armenians, but the persecution of the Greeks proceeded relentlessly. I did all I could, but it was clearly beyond my power to stem the tide of Turkish policy. My intervention could only moderate Turkish excesses. One day, the seven bishops assembled in a kind of council in my consulate. I told them I would lay the situation before the Russian ambassador. His answer was that the grand vizier would come personally to Smyrna and make an inquiry. All the embassies had stirred and entered a losing fight in defense of Christianity; only the Germans kept apart.

Grand Vizier Talaat Pasha came to Smyrna, as well as a delegation of representatives from the Great Powers. They looked impressive but accomplished nothing. I had a talk with Talaat Pasha in the presence of Rahmi Bei. "What can I do?" asked the vali with a smile. "We have sent Turkish farmers to colonize the coast, but the Greek peasants simply won't stay with them and move away of their own free will."

"No, Rahmi," said Talaat Pasha, "the Greeks cannot remain. They are forced to leave. They must go." The tone of the grand vizier was decisive, and so was the expression of his eyes as he looked at me. The grand vizier, a corpulent, jovial, very matter-of-fact man of rather dark complexion, remained silent for a moment. I had no illusion about the situation, and Talaat did not try to deceive me. On the contrary, once the immutable point of view of the Turkish government was explained, the prime minister became very friendly. The life of a Greek condemned for a political assassination was granted; no more condemnations to death were to be pronounced. The Turks were always liberal in dealing with me.

Then the grand vizier smiled good humoredly, "I have just been in Livadia," he said, "to pay a visit of courtesy to the tsar who came

to the Crimea for the summer. What a luncheon I had! Wonderful!"
His round face beamed with satisfaction. He evidently liked good
food.

Talaat had spoken with the Russian emperor and Sazonov! I was
reduced to ashes. Talaat knew it and enjoyed the situation. He continued to beam. What he did not tell me was that he had approached
Sazonov in Livadia proposing an understanding with Russia. Prejudiced as he was by Giers, Sazonov declined Talaat's overture. That
was a great mistake. The grand vizier meant business. He was apprehensive of the influence of Enver Pasha and the Germans, and in
order to counterbalance them he needed the support of Russia.
Sazonov refused. It was May 1914. Less than three months later,
Turkey signed a military convention with Germany. Sazonov never
missed a chance to make a mistake.

The Declaration of War
Summer 1914

Late in June I saw in the papers that Archduke Franz Ferdinand
had been killed in Bosnia, an Austrian province, by an Austrian subject. That seemed to exclude the possibility of international complications. A few days later came the news of the death in Belgrade of
the Russian minister, N. G. Hartwig, my dear old chief in the
Foreign Office, an enthusiastic slavophile. This looked ominous. He
had called on the Austrian legation and died there from a heart
attack. Hartwig knew the Serbs well and was extremely popular
with them.

The Russian ambassador in Vienna, concealing for the occasion
whatever talents and intelligence were bestowed on him by nature,
asked for a leave of absence and left Vienna at the moment when
the Austrian ultimatum was being dispatched to Serbia. Our ambassador in Berlin did the same. The government of France, the
brains and power of the country, was navigating on the high seas
on a return journey from Russia. The English press was publishing
attacks on the unfortunate Serbs for lack of any better material. The
German kaiser was on a pleasure sea trip. Everybody seemed bent
on relaxation, except the Austrian Foreign Office: they were working
full speed.

Sazonov, deaf and blind to the incoming danger and diplomatically
disarmed by the absence of his chief agents, sat at his desk in St.
Petersburg. Meantime in Smyrna I was continually harassed by the

systematic persecution and expulsion of the Greeks by the Turks. My chief trouble was that I happened to be on good terms with both nationalities. One day the metropolitan archbishop of Smyrna rushed to my consulate clamoring that the Turks wanted to expel him. He had been suddenly called to the government office close to the quay, detained there, and sent back without any apparent reason. I reassured the distinguished priest, although I was rather perplexed myself and went to see the vali, Rahmi Bei, who was always very frank and friendly with me. I told him what I had heard.

"It is perfectly true," said the vali. "Either the metropolitan or I must leave the city. I wanted to arrest the metropolitan and ordered a steamer to be ready to take him away. The metropolitan came; the steamer did not. I do not know why. I had to dismiss the metropolitan till the boat comes."

"Your Excellency," I said, "the case is too serious to be decided here. Will you kindly give me the promise that the metropolitan will remain free till we get instructions from Constantinople. I shall telegraph the ambassador, asking him to examine this question with the grant vizier, who will cable to you directly whatever orders he sees fit."

The vali agreed. A few days later the metropolitan left on a leave of absence granted by the sultan.

The persecution of the Greeks continued. The situation became too much for my nerves. One day I found small children sitting on the floor of my office, playing; their father had been murdered the same morning. Another day I was asked to see a man who was in a carriage in front of my door, wounded and unable to leave it. I went out to see him and, as he started to speak, blood gushed out of his mouth—his lung had been pierced by a bullet. But these matters were of local importance. A storm was brewing in Europe, soon to carry everything in a hurricane of war and death.

One morning early in August, when I had just finished signing the last papers before going to Buja, a telegram from Giers was laid before me, as clear and dazzling as a stroke of lightning: "Germany has declared war on us."

For a few seconds I sat dumbfounded. Then a thought flashed through my mind, and I exclaimed: "Surely they have blundered somehow."

"They" were our Foreign Office. It was unthinkable that Germany should declare war on us without some provocation on our part. To declare war on Russia was against the interests of Germany—against her war plan, the only plan she had. Germany had to attack France first.

The immediate reasons for the outbreak were soon made clear. Ultimatums were sent by Austria to Serbia and by Germany to Russia. A rejected ultimatum means war. But why these ultimatums were presented with a rapidity that precluded any exchange of views and a peaceful settlement remained unexplained. I shall present the facts and let the reader draw his own conclusions.

At the end of July the French president, Raymond Poincaré, accompained by the premier and the leading members of his cabinet, paid a visit to St. Petersburg. This was the time selected by Berchtold, the Austrian foreign minister, to hand to the Serbs an unacceptable ultimatium, which was bound to be rejected and would offer Austria a pretext for invading Serbia.

The ultimatum was delivered in Belgrade on July 23, the day when the French embarked in Russia on a long circumnavigation back to France. In the opinion of Berchtold, that would preclude an immediate intervention by Russia, which would not act without previous consultation with France, and this was physically impossible until the French statesmen arrived in Paris. Their voyage would take a week or so, time enough, according to Berchtold's calculation, for the Austrians to occupy Belgrade. Then Kaiser Wilhelm would address a sharp warning to the tsar, who would accept it as he had in 1909.

But Berchtold did not take into consideration the state of mind which prevailed in St. Petersburg in 1914. He still believed that Sazonov would meekly submit to Berlin's threat. The Austrian foreign minister did not realize how incensed the Russian government was against Germany, because of the control over Turkey by the German generals in Constantinople, and how highly it rated the Serbian successes during the recent Balkan wars.

Berchtold was not alone in his erroneous supposition that Sazonov was still in favor of a cautious treatment of Germany. The French also had their doubts about the attitude of the Russian foreign minister after he had accepted the German extension of the Baghdad railway toward Persia. They made representations at St. Petersburg. The French wanted to reaffirm the alliance with Russia, indispensable to France. Whatever apprehensions they may have had were soon dispersed—Sazonov was an avowed Germanophobe. On his

part Poincaré promised complete support of the Russian policy
against Germany and Austria. Both governments exchanged solemn
pledges. Berchtold could not have chosen a worse moment for his
Serbian adventure.

The Austrian ultimatum to Serbia reached Sazonov on the morning
of July 24, the day after the departure of the French president. For
the next twenty-four hours the fate of Europe was in the hands
of the Russian foreign minister. Sazonov telephoned to the British
ambassador that he had just received the text of the Austrian ultimatum to Serbia and arranged to meet him and the French ambassador at the French Embassy. Sazonov considered that it was the
Entente versus the Central Powers, not a mere collision between
Serbia and Austria.

The three men met. It was the first war conference of the three
Great Powers which within a week, were to be fighting as allies in
World War I. Sazonov stated that the Austrian threat to Serbia was
unacceptable to him. The French ambassador declared that France
would support Russia with all her might. The British ambassador
answered in the negative. He said that he had no hope that the
British government "would entail engagement to support France
and Russia by force of arms." The answer was categoric. He asked if
Russia proposed to declare war on Austria. Sazonov replied that this
would depend on the council of ministers. He was correct, but he
added that he personally thought that Russia at any rate would have
to mobilize against Austria.

That was Sazonov's fatal mistake. As a threat, the Russian mobilization proved ineffective, for it did not prevent the occupation of
Belgrade by the Austrians. At the same time it made the danger of
war imminent, for it was to be followed by a German mobilization,
which meant war. The two ambassadors telegraphed the result of
their conference to their goverments. The council of Russian
ministers met in the afternoon of the same day, but no decision was
taken. A second meeting was to be held on the next day under the
presidency of the tsar.

The next day July 25, the situation was hanging on the action
of the English cabinet, which had received by wire from their
ambassador in St. Petersburg a full statement of Sazonov's position,
which was supported by the French. The situation was excellently
summed up by the English undersecretary E.A. Crowe, in his
minute attached to the telegram:

The moment has passed when it might have been possible to enlist French support in an effort to hold back Russia. . . . The point that matters is whether Germany is or is not absolutely determined to have this war now. . . . There is still a chance that she can be made to hesitate if she can be induced to apprehend that the war will find England by the side of France and Russia. . . . If the moment either Austria or Russia begin to mobilize, [the British] Government give orders to put our whole fleet on an immediate war footing this may conceivably make Germany realize the seriousness of the danger . . . . It would be right, supposing this decision could be taken now, to inform the French and Russian Governments of it.

[Minute by Sir Edward Grey: I think it is premature to make any statements to France and Russia yet.] *

On the same day His Majesty the tsar was so gracious as to write in his own hand in the journal of the council of ministers, deciding in favor of mobilization, "Agreed." Two days, July 24 and 25, settled the fate of Europe.

The die was cast, but the statesmen were slow to realize it. The kaiser received the text of the Serbian reply on July 28, approved it, and wrote "Naturally, as a result, no more cause for war exists," totally ignorant that on the same day Austria was to declare war on Serbia.

On July 31 the French ambassador asked Sir Edward Grey if a meeting of the British cabinet could be called to clear up the position of England at this critical stage. Grey's answer was that "the Cabinet would certainly be summoned as soon as there was some new development, but at the present moment the only answer I could give was that we could not undertake any definite engagement."

The new development came the next day, August 1, 1914. It was the declaration of war by Germany on Russia.

The Russian War Plan
Samsonov's Disaster

Of all the news I heard, the Russian defeat at Tannenberg was the most appalling. General Samsonov was dead, and his army

* G. P. Gooch and H. Temperley, eds., *British Documents on the Origins of the War, 1898–1914* (London, 1926), 11: 81–82.

existed no more. The story of his defeat has been recounted by Russian and foreign historians in a very unsatisfactory way. He has been made solely responsible for the destruction of his army. That was by no means the case. The responsibility of a man stands in direct proportion to the power entrusted to him and to the amount of initiative left to his discretion. Samsonov was practically deprived of both from the moment he assumed command of his army. He was treated as a mere pawn by the supreme command, and his every movement was prescribed and controlled by General Ia. G. Zhilinskii, the commander of the entire Russian front against Germany.

To understand the situation, it is necessary to be acquainted with the plan of the Russian campaign, the idea for which originated with the French. The enormous territory of Russia, its insufficient means of communication, and the inadequate organization of supplies caused the Russian army to be slow to mobilize and even slower to move. The original idea of the Russian general staff was that the Germans would be the first to cross into Russian territory. Here they would be hampered by the difficulties of transport, and the Russians would have ample time to concentrate their troops, to offer defensive combat, and finally to assume the offensive in full force.

Taking Russia as a separate unit, this conception was perfect and well suited to the sluggish mentality of the Russian military chiefs and the slow progress of the unwieldy Russian armies. But the idea of beginning the war with a retreat and passive resistance did not fit into a plan of concerted action with the French ally.

After the conclusion of the Franco-Russian alliance, the French general staff stated that Germany would obviously strike with all her might at France first, hoping that the French army would be obliged to accept a decisive battle within the short distance between Paris and the German border. Then Germany would turn against Russia, which would be deprived of the help of the French, beset by the German invasion.

The views of the French general staff were strictly correct and had to be taken into consideration. The Russian generals agreed in principle, but the necessary preparations for a rapid advance into Germany, in order to invade her simultaneously with her attack on France, were not completed.

The Russian commander in chief, Grand Duke Nicholas, was an enthusiastic man, fond of parades, maneuvers, and all the peacetime displays of military activity, but with a very slight knowledge of strategy and tactics and no understanding at all of the complicated handling and moving of huge armies, with their long trains of horse-drawn carts carrying provisions and munitions. In short, he was prone to give orders without paying much thought to the physical conditions of their execution. The grand duke gave his word of honor to the French that fifteen days after the declaration of war the Russian armies would enter Germany, and he ordered Zhilinskii to execute his promise.

Two armies, the stronger consisting of five army corps under Samsonov and the other with a large contingent of cavalry under Rennenkampf, were massed at once for the invasion of East Prussia. A third army, still in process of formation, was to move on Posen, in Prussian Poland.

Samsonov, who was on leave in the Crimea, had been suddenly ordered to go to the front and assume the command of an army whose chiefs and actual condition were unknown to him. He was given no time to prepare a plan of operations. In a mad rush the army had to cover on foot the last stages on the Russian territory, and they arrived at the German border hungry, thirsty, and exhausted. One army corps had no baggage at all and had to receive food from another corps.

The idea of creating a diversion by attracting to the east part of the German forces pressing the French was excellent. It came as a surprise and threw the German generals into complete confusion. Von Pritwitz, the commander in chief of the eastern front, declared in a panic that he had to abandon the whole of East Prussia, and he was quickly replaced by Hindenburg. Even the chief of the German general staff, Moltke, lost his presence of mind.

Then the Russian tragedy began. The movement of the Russian troops was nothing more than a diversion and had to be conducted as such. But the initial success of the advance of Samsonov and Rennenkampf produced such an impression on the unbalanced mind of the grand duke that he imagined all of Prussia stood open before him. According to the conception of the grand duke, the German army grappling with the French and English was mired in France, and the Russian armies had only to seize the opportunity and march straight on Berlin, hardly meeting any resistance. Consequently, he ordered Zhilinskii to speed the Russian advance regardless of any considerations.

Once the Russian army entered farther into enemy territory,

conditions became critical. East Prussia, along the northern frontier of what was then Russian Poland, comprises a belt of forests intersected by numerous lakes and swamps. The roads were good but narrow, not intended for the passage of hundreds of thousands of men on foot followed by an endless train of horse carts with the paraphernalia of an army on the march. The scouting service and cavalry reconnaissance proved defective. The Germans made rare appearances and immediately withdrew, leaving the Russians in absolute ignorance of the number and tactical disposition of the highly mobile enemy troops, which had at their disposal both railway transport and trucks. The German railways, with a different gauge, could not be used by the Russians.

As the Russian army progressed, its flanks became exposed, and soon the rear also would be threatened. Samsonov, with all his bravery, was not presumptuous or ambitious. A thoroughly honest man, he realized his responsibility toward his soldiers and would on no account jeopardize their safety in order to get promotion or please his superiors. He reported to Zhilinskii that he could not advance further without ascertaining the number and disposition of the enemy troops he had to engage.

In answer, he received from Zhilinskii a flood of peremptory, senseless, abusive telegrams and telephone calls. Samsonov was told that there were no enemy troops before him, that he was a coward, an unheard-of-expression toward an army commander, and that he should move forward at full speed.

Not content with that and breaking all military regulations, Zhilinskii started to telegraph orders to the chiefs of staff of the army corps under Samsonov, with copies to him, virtually depriving him of the direction of the operations. Samsonov could not resign, facing the enemy, and he was not recalled. His corps moved without his orders, according to the command of a superior chief. When the vanguard of the doomed army emerged from the forest belt and entered open country, Samsonov received the information that his left flank was being attacked. Then a second German army poured in on his right flank, supposed to be protected by Rennenkampf, who had in the meantime received orders to move away from Samsonov in a northwestern direction to Koenigsberg, of all places. The Germans closed the ring. The Russian troops fell into indescribable confusion, their resistance collapsed, and Samsonov shot himself.

Incidentally, Samsonov's defeat was the cause of the ruin of the whole German war plan, the origin of which is curiously related to that of World War I. The idea of the plan and of the war were products of the personal initiative of Kaiser Wilhelm. The famous German chancellor, Bismarck, abhorred the very prospect of a simultaneous war with France and Russia. That was enough to spur Wilhelm II to adopt an opposite policy. He dismissed Bismarck and ordered his chief of staff, General Schlieffen, to prepare a plan of campaign against both nations. After that the kaiser walked about contentedly, with the war plan in his pocket, for nearly twenty-five years. He would have continued his peaceful promenade to the end of his days had not the Austrians and the Russians inadvertently pushed him into action.

Unfortunately for the kaiser, Schlieffen had died in the meantime, and his successor Moltke tried to improve the plan. Moltke not only spoiled the plan but failed to execute even his newly revised version. Schlieffen had intended to pass south of Paris. Once the capital was cut off from the rest of France, the moral effect would be about the same as if it were taken. Instead Moltke led his army north of Paris, which produced the opposite result of stiffening the French resistance.

Schlieffen had rightly calculated that the French would at once throw all their available forces to oppose the German invasion. That was just what he needed. The distance from Paris to the frontier being very short, he would be able to meet the main French army a few days after crossing the border. As his reserve brigades were to march together with the troops of the first line, he would have a temporary superiority of numbers over the French and a good chance to inflict a decisive defeat, which would effectively check French resistance for a while. All the German commanders took the neutrality of England for granted. The invasion of Belgium and France was proceeding according to the plan when news was received of the Russian advance into east Prussia. Moltke entirely lost his nerve, took two army corps from the army in France, disorganizing both the army and the plan, and sent these corps to the Russian front on the eve of the battle of the Marne. Consequently, the blow on the Marne failed, and the confused German generals retreated. The month allotted in the plan for the conquest of France ended in a German reverse which could never be redeemed.

Turkey's Entry into the War

After the declaration of war by Germany, the immediate issue facing me was whether Turkey would remain neutral. I wrote to a friend at the embassy in Constantinople. His answer was very vague. The embassies of the Entente supposed that Turkey was hesitating and still undecided, and they used all their efforts to prevent her from joining Germany. As a matter of fact Turkey, on the second day of August, had signed a treaty of alliance with the Central Powers and had asked only for a little time to transport her troops across the Black Sea to the Russian frontier in Asia Minor. Later, however, the Turks began to hesitate. War Minister Enver alone was fully for war. Turkey remained at peace for three whole months, while proceeding with her mobilization.

The beautiful autumn of the Near East had set in. The vineyards around Buja turned from green to red and golden yellow and were full of the fragrance of ripening grapes. One day in November, I took a long walk with my wife and children. Her health had improved, and she watched, smiling, as the children ran after butterflies.

After seeing my family home, I went to the railway station to meet the people coming from Smyrna by a late train. A young Greek approached me and said: "Do you know that you are at war with Turkey?"

"Who said so?"

"The Café Kolonaridis."

It was a large café, the center of Smyrna gossip which had often proved true. I hastened home and found a cavass waiting with a letter from the Italian consul informing me that he had assumed the protection of Russian interests, as Turkey was at war with Russia. I had no information from my embassy. The next morning I moved with my family to Smyrna. The Russian flag was lowered and the badges with the double-headed eagle removed from the caps of the cavasses. A Turkish official told me that I was a prisoner, allowed to remain in my house on parole. He stated that the Russian government had detained the Turkish consuls in Russia, against international law, and in consequence the Russian consuls in Turkey were arrested also. My family was authorized to leave with the English and French consuls.

I had just burned my codes and political archives when a long coded telegram came from the ambassador. I could no longer decipher it and quietly put the useless thing away. My colleagues had been informed the previous day by much shorter cables.

My wife did not want to part with me, but I explained to her that it would be better for us both if she would take the children away from the seat of war. I advised her to go to Athens. Twelve carriages with the departing representatives, their families, and mine rolled away, abandoning the deserted consulates and myself in enemy hands.

Were they really my enemies, these Turks around me? They had always been friendly to me, and they remained unchanged. I received every facility it was in their power to offer me. At the proclamation of martial law a special permit to circulate in the city after sunset was issued to me. My liberty was not restrained in any sense. I wonder if a Russian in Berlin, or for that matter a German in Paris or London, could have enjoyed the same freedom from hostile interference. The Turks had accepted the war as an act of God and showed no hatred toward a foreigner who was in the same plight as they.

I am not a pacifist—quite the contrary—but I could never share the contagion of animosity that spread among the Western nations, Christianity and civilization notwithstanding. As a Russian representative in a Turkish city, I felt personally aggrieved by the rupture with Turkey and was anxious to learn its cause.

A Turkish friend of mine had come from Constantinople. He had been there when war with Russia was declared. It was Bairam, a Turkish festival, and he had called on Talaat Pasha. The grand visier seemed to be far from pleased with the news.

"How did it all happen?" asked my friend.

"Enver says that the Russians fired first."

"Enver lies," exclaimed my friend, and Talaat made no protest.

He was apprehensive that war with England and Russia would endanger the Asian provinces of Turkey, and he preferred to wait until the Germans made good their promise to take Paris. He was from Salonika and was interested in the recovery of his native city. He was more inclined to collaborate with England and Russia than to fight them.

It is curious to note that Lord Kitchener had wanted to be ambassador to Turkey before the war. Maybe he would have been a great success. He was a solid, impressive man, who knew how to deal with Orientals. The ambassadors at Constantinople seemed to be hostile or diffident to Talaat, with the exception of the United States ambassador, Morgenthau, who later broke with Talaat because of the persecution of Armenians, one of the most gruesome episodes of World War I. Talaat needed a strong man on whom he could rely to counterbalance the influence of Enver and the military party. As English field marshal, Kitchener would have been invaluable in Constantinople to oppose the German general, Liman von Sanders. Be that as it may, Constantinople was the only place where Entente diplomacy was completely negated by the Germans.

During a whole fortnight I was totally deprived of news from my family, and I could not stand this uncertainty any longer. I ordered a carriage and went to see the vali.

"What is the matter?" asked the governor-general as he got up from his desk to meet me and shook my hand. "I have given strict orders that you should not be interfered with. Have you any complaint?" He looked questioningly at my disturbed face.

"None whatever," I answered. "I am all right, but I want to leave Smyrna."

The vali laughed. "Why?" he said as we sat down. "Stay here. What's the hurry?" He smiled good-humoredly. But he saw that I was not in a cheerful mood, and he became serious.

"My wife is sick, and she is alone with the children," I answered, speaking to him man to man and making a direct appeal to his sense of humanity. I felt that it would be a poor reason for a European bureaucrat, but a Turk thought differently.

"I see," he said slowly, remaining thoughtful for a few moments. "The only thing I can do is to telegraph the grand visier and ask him as a personal favor to let you go. Talaat Pasha knows you. He may agree."

I thanked Rahmi Bei and went out. War or no war, we felt the same. The next evening I received a note from the Italian consul that the Turkish government authorized my departure. I was the only Russian consul released at that time. To the end of my days I shall remember the Turks.

I landed at Piraeus in Greece and drove to the Grand Hotel at Phaleron. My children saw me and ran down the great staircase at top speed. My wife stood on the upper landing, grasping the handrail and unable to move from emotion.

The next day I called on the legation at Athens. The news I heard was appalling: defeat after defeat. The worst was that Russian soldiers were literally being mowed down by German machine guns. The English and French commanders had been much criticized for their huge losses, but what about the Russian? The pink and flower of the Russian army was annihilated and could not be replaced for a generation. My brother-in-law, General A. A. Michelson, who had been for several years military attaché in Berlin and had an unrivaled knowledge of the German army, was put in command of the Moscow guards and sent to the front. Within the first two months of the war, he was wounded, incapacitated for field service, and his regiment decimated. The other guard regiments fared no better. They were the chief mainstay of the monarchy. The young recruits who later filled their ranks were much less dependable.

Life in Wartime

In Athens the atmosphere was strained. The German minister, Count Wilhelm von Mirbach, was making good progress with his propaganda against the Allies. A strong current of public opinion was drawing King Constantine I of Greece away from Russia. Constantine was the first Greek prince since the fall of Byzantium to be baptized at birth according to the rites of the Greek Orthodox Church and was named in honor of the first and last emperors of Constantinople. Fantastic as it seemed, the Greeks hoped he would reestablish their ancient empire in all its glory. They were ready to join the Allies in the war, provided their troops be permitted to enter Constantinople. This was denied. The pro-Allied cabinet of E. Venizelos fell, and Greece remained neutral.

I received instructions to stay on the theater of war in the eastern Mediterreanean in the expectation of the opening of the Dardanelles by the Anglo-French fleet. As Russian consul general for western Asia Minor, I had under my jurisdiction all the islands occupied partly by the Italians and partly by the Greeks.

I settled my family at Rhodes for the duration of the war. The island was safe and fairly comfortable, as far as this was possible in a war zone, with the Turkish coast in view and German submarines infesting the sea and threatening our limited food supply. The Italians were extremely hospitable and helpful. I left my wife and children amid pleasant surroundings and went alone to the northern part of the Archipelago to be nearer to the operations against the Dardanelles. The islands occupied by the Greeks were all in favor of the Allies and Venizelos. They gave no help to the German submarines, differing in this respect from the islands and the mainland of Greece proper. After a brief stop at Athens, I proceeded to Mytelene (Lesbos), where Venizelos was staying following his resignation as prime minister of Greece. He had unanimous support on the islands. His main difficulty was on the mainland of Greece.

I leave it to the archaeologists to decide to what degree the Greeks of today resemble their ancestors of classical antiquity. One point is certain: the modern Greeks are just as talkative, changeable, quarrelsome, and fond of politics as at the time of Pericles and Aristides—a difficult people to unite and guide in a given direction.

The population of Mytelene adored Venizelos, and he fully deserved his popularity. Born in Crete, with a name slightly recalling the time when Venice was in possession of that island, he looked like a typical Cretan, physically and morally strong, energetic, patriotic, and thoroughly disinterested in money matters. Venizelos was always modest and unassuming, although acutely intelligent. A successful lawyer, he spent all his fortune for the benefit of his country and remained almost penniless himself.

Straight from the steamer I went to the beautiful villa put at the disposal of Venizelos. He received me standing in a large drawing room. "What is the news from Athens?" he asked.

"The king is dangerously ill."

King Constantine was the great impediment in the career of Venizelos, who was powerless against him.

"What kind of illness?"

"Pleurisy with effusions."

"Who said that?"

I named my authority, an unimpeachable one. Venizelos looked impressed. I thought he was going to whistle, but he restrained himself.

For weeks the king lay between life and death, but he finally recovered. He had a powerful constitution and was attended by excellent German doctors. When King Constantine eventually abdicated, the favorable moment for the intervention of Greece had already passed.

I stayed at Mytelene till October 1915. It then became evident that the Anglo-French expeditionary force would never take the Dardanelles. I sent my report accordingly and left for Rhodes. On the island of Samos I boarded a French destroyer. The captain was eagerly looking for German submarines. We traveled in complete darkness, the water splashing around in the depth of night. But apparently the submarines had a preference for unarmed vessels. We met none.

Soon after, an Italian passenger steamer was sunk by the artillery fire of a German submarine close to Rhodes. I must state that the passengers and the crew were allowed to take to the lifeboats. A small French coast guard vessel was torpedoed in the port of Rhodes. The commander was able to swim ashore, but several of his men were drowned. Many ships were sunk in the Straits of Messina, and Rhodes ran short of food. Somebody asked the governor whether he was going to introduce bread cards. It was considered a good system in Germany and later in Russia. "But you cannot eat cards," said the general.

The Allies were sorely tried by the war. This could be seen from the variety of people who joined the military service. At Rhodes I met J. L. Myers, professor of Greek at Oxford University, an outstanding scholar and an extremely active and delightful man. He was in command of a small boat and was chasing submarines. I invited him to visit the site of a temple of Zeus. As is usually the case with unexcavated ruins, there were only a few heaps of stones to be seen. But Professor Myers immediately picked up a small marble slab with a Phoenician inscription, the first to be discovered at Rhodes. The widely known English author, E. M. Compton Mackenzie, also came to Rhodes on a military errand. He wrote truth rather than fiction about the war.

Italy had mobilized to the last man. Strange troops appeared at Rhodes—native infantry from Tripoli, dark, bare footed, charging at a trot with a guttural war whoop, and the "Arditti," said to be formed of smugglers and gangsters, refractory to the usual military discipline. The latter were armed with daggers and hand grenades and were reputed to be desperate and very brave in attacks on trenches. They wore a distinctive uniform with open collars and never mixed with other people. On the opposite end of the social ladder were Italians with historical names, the portraits of whose ancestors may be seen in the museums and palaces of Italy.

German airplanes sometimes roared high above us. One morning I heard my children scream as an enemy flier circled over the city. Guns started to boom, and little clouds of smoke from exploding shrapnel made white spots in the blue sky. The bombs released by the aviator caused little damage, and the children were more excited than frightened.

In the middle of 1916 a courier came on a French destroyer, bringing me codes and fresh news. He was a typical Russian diplomat, a well-educated, conservative young man with means of his own, who should by all rights have been contented and self-confident. But he was neither. I asked him about life at St. Petersburg, which he had left early in the year. For a while he hesitated, then he answered in one word: "Impossible."

I looked at him. He made a despondent gesture with his hands. "Look," he said. "In the best and most expensive restaurants they openly serve you horse meat." It was just like a diplomat to think first of places where one could get the best food.

"If you try to eat at home, you run short of everything, even cereals. And the prices! You cannot live on your salary. Money itself can procure necessities only with great difficulty. I was thinking of retiring to my estate. There I would have plenty to eat: poultry, dairy products, and the like. But I received orders to carry codes to all embassies, legations, and consulates. I had to embark at Murmansk on the Arctic Ocean on account of the blockade of the Baltic. They even gave me a new kind of torpedo to take to England. That's what they call a diplomat's letterbag. No dynamite, of course —just the shell and the mechanism. As if they had no naval officers to take care of the infernal machine. Well, I took it," he said with a sigh of suppressed exasperation. The torpedo seemed to have been the last straw.

"And what do other people think?" I asked.

"That I do not know," he answered. "But the situation is tense. Everybody is nervous. Last summer I traveled with two old colonels going to the front. We were in the same compartment. They did not know who I was, did not care, and talked freely. 'If I should meet the empress,' said one of them, 'I would shoot her down with my own hands.' The other made no objections."

"You left Russia six months ago?" I asked.

"Yes," he answered, "and conditions must be worse now."

It became evident to me that the Russian government was meeting defeat on both fronts, the internal and the external; but the home situation was the more serious.

The war continued relentlessly, and life under its strained conditions proved too much for the weakest members of my family. My youngest son, four years old, was the first to die, and my wife, who attended him, followed him to the grave. I longed to see my mother and share my grief with her, but I was cut off from Russia. A belated letter informed me that she was comfortably settled in a sea resort on the Baltic. Then another letter from St. Petersburg, saying that she had to leave her villa in a hurry because of the war, then— nothing. I wanted to write, but my hand refused to trace the fatal lines about my double loss.

The Burning of Smyrna

When I returned to Smyrna in October 1919, the Greeks had already taken possession of it. It was not a temporary military occupation like that of Constantinople under an allied force. The Greeks had come to stay for good. It remained to be seen what the Turkish reaction would be. A national Turkish government under the leadership of Mustafa Kemal had been established in Ankara and was planning an advance on Smyrna. It was chiefly a Greek town, but it was the outlet of western Asia Minor, with two long railways stretching far into the interior of the land. *"Izmir dogru* [Right on to Smyrna]" was the slogan of the new regime in Ankara.

Late in 1920 I went to Constantinople. The old Russian embassy was still there. I made inquiries about the movement headed by Kemal. "All the Turks are with him at heart," the first dragoman told me.

For a while all looked quiet. In August 1922 I was in Buja with my children. News came about skirmishes on the southern border of the Greek zone of occupation. A bright Russian youth, a friend of mine, who as a mere boy had joined the army and seen much fighting, came to see me and said: "It looks like a diversion. We may expect some developments on another part of the front."

But the Greek commander in chief expected nothing. He asked for permission to go to Athens and granted leaves to his soldiers. One of them, an aviator, came to visit his sister who lived in Buja. There was much rejoicing, laughter, and happy talk as they sat in their garden around a table. This lasted two or three days, then all became silent in the little cottage. I inquired from my neighbor and received the answer that the soldier had been precipitately recalled to the front. That sounded serious. I went to Smyrna and saw my French colleague, who had a military observer with the Greek army.

"The Greeks are fleeing," he said. "They have lost everything, all their artillery and airplanes. They won't stop. But don't tell it to anybody."

"And what will become of Smyrna?" I asked. The consul only shrugged his shoulders as a mute reply.

I asked another colleague: "Who will protect Smyrna if the city is taken?"

"Not I, certainly not I," answered the British consul quickly.

It became evident to me that Smyrna, stripped bare of any protection, diplomatic or military, would be covered only with the fig leaves of international law. The news was kept secret outside official circles. The Greek authorities decided that after their departure the Christian population was to remain in the city. The quay continued to be crowded with a gay throng, and music played in the movies and cafés. It reminded me of the last days of Pompeii.

A few days later we saw Greek soldiers, sullen and without arms, gliding along the sidewalks and disappearing like shadows. The city became dead with fright. Then a bustle arose again. Refugees came streaming from the interior, filling the streets and public places. The Turkish army was slowly advancing upon the heels of the retreating Greeks. A large semicircle of *chetas* (irregular Turkish bands) was driving the Greeks from the villages and closing in on Smyrna. The chetas moved swiftly, burning the villages, and could be in Smyrna in two or three days.

If you are in a tight spot, ask a Scot what to do. I went to confer with the Reverend R. P. Ashe, Scottish rector of the English church in Buja. He had been a member of the first British mission to central Africa and had received the medal of the Royal Geographical Society for his book on Uganda. Surrounded by his numerous family, respected by all, active, modest, and cheerful, he was a rare example of a Christian in the true sense of this word.

We decided to go together to the American college situated at the railway station of Paradise between Smyrna and Buja to inquire if we could take refuge there in case of need, and we were told we were welcome. The president, Dr. Alexander MacLachlan, said that whatever happened he would stay and keep the American flag flying over the college.

The next day in Buja was gloomy. In the evening I sent the children to bed early and sat alone downstairs, keeping a vigil, when I heard a knock at the door. Who could it be so late? It was a quarter of eleven. What peril was threatening the roof sheltering my children? I flung the door open wildly and saw an aged little lady, the sister of Mr. Ashe.

"There is a special train sent by the consul," she said. "The English colony is requested to leave at once, as the chetas may be here any moment. So I came to tell you to leave also."

She spoke quietly with her usual soft voice, without any trace of fear, nodded gently, and vanished in the darkness. It was strange to see this little figure, so weak and so frail, alone in this night full of danger and menace.

The children were soon dressed, their Russian nurse packed a few things, and we all ran to the station. The platform was full of people, with a single English officer in khaki representing the armed forces of Europe. He motioned the people into the cars, ascertained that all the English and Americans were there, and gave the signal for departure. The passengers sat still. In their hurry some had left behind their spectacles, false teeth, and other necessities, and they looked depressed.

In a few minutes we were at Paradise. Together with the family of an American resident of Buja, I got out and walked to the college. Mr. Ashe and his family were directed to proceed to Smyrna and board an English ship. We entered the large campus. On our left stood the president's house, silent and asleep. It was already about midnight. We knocked. Shutters on the upper floor were opened, and a beam of light fell on the ground.

"Hello," shouted the president, appearing in the open window in his pajamas. Our predicament was explained in a few words. We were admitted, distributed into various rooms, and all became silent again.

The night was restful. I awoke with a sense of security and comfort, which lasted through breakfast but ended in perplexity. We had not had time to take much with us the previous night. I had to go to Buja to fetch my belongings at once, before the beginning of the pillage. I tried not to think what would happen if I should meet the chetas, and I left quickly. The day was splendid. The road looked as peaceful as ever, with not a soul on it. I walked the two miles alone, entered Buja, expecting to find robbers around every corner, but met none. I hired a horse and a cart from my neighbor, packed my trunks, and successfully accomplished a strategic retreat to Paradise with arms and baggage.

Dr. MacLachlan placed at our disposal a furnished cottage at the end of the campus. We took our trunks there and unpacked them while the nurse, Mary, cooked dinner. Afterward I smoked on the porch, and the children played on the campus. Everything looked peaceful, and I thought that we were at the end of our troubles.

In the morning my cavass came. "What is the news?" I asked cheerfully. "Where are the chetas?"

"Look there," he answered, pointing south. A cloud of black smoke was rising above the large and prosperous village of Sevdi Koi, a few miles away. That needed no explanation. Greek refugees started to pour in. They were disarmed and allowed to stay on the campus.

Things rapidly began to get worse. Some Greeks and the Moslem emigrants from Crete, living in a neighboring village, started sniping at each other outside, but quite close to, the college grounds. Stray bullets flew over the campus, but no one was hit. A party of American bluejackets arrived and placed a machine gun at the entrance of the large main building. All the teachers, with their families and mine, assembled there. An attack seemed imminent. That night everyone slept in an empty dormitory, We saw burning houses blazing in the neighborhood.

In the morning a Turkish officer called on the president and brought reassuring news. Mustafa Kemal had arrived in Smyrna, and order would be restored immediately. Newspapers appeared again and described Kemal's triumphant entry. The Turks wept with joy and kissed the ground on which the victorious general had trod. We returned to our cottage.

The next day, as we sat at lunch, we heard shooting again, then the rattling of machine guns with increasing intensity, and finally the heavy thunder of artillery discharges. That was something different from the ordinary skirmishes to which we had become accustomed. Shells began to fly, high up over our heads. They could not be seen. We only heard the vicious shriek of the shell, rising to a crescendo as it approached, then fading away in the distance. A cloud of smoke and dust appeared on the spot where the shell struck the ground.

I went to the nearby cottage of Dr. C. A. Rees, the president's assistant. "There is evidently a battle going on," he said. "I am taking the children to the cellar. Do the same."

We were told subsequently that the stray remainder of a Greek division had opened fire on Smyrna. Kemal answered. We happened to be in the middle of the battle. We were not harmed, for the Greek and Turkish field guns were aimed high, and the shells flew over the college. I saw long lines of Turkish cavalry moving along two convergent roads to encircle the Greek forces, which finally surrendered. The Greeks were no match for Mustafa Kemal. Later I talked with some of Kemal's officers. They said that the great attack on Eski Sheir was planned by Kemal and executed in absolute secrecy. When they were ordered to attack, no one knew that it was going to be a decisive battle. The Greeks were taken by surprise, their commander being absent in Smyrna at that time.

Everything looked quiet, and I decided to go to Smyrna, when Dr. MacLachlan had a nasty accident. He had been told that a house belonging to the college but off the campus grounds was being looted. He hastened there at once, alone, although he had a few bluejackets at the college. It was a risky step, but quite in conformity with his energetic and daring character. He met several armed Turks and was wounded in the leg. A Turkish officer rescued him and conveyed him to the college. He recovered soon.

I thanked Dr. MacLachlan for his hospitality and left with my family and luggage in a truck for Smyrna. As we entered the city, we saw empty houses which had been looted and dead bodies still lying in the street. The children were frightened, and I was glad when we reached the consulate. All was in order there.

I was told that a village close to Smyrna was to be burned and went to see the Turkish commander. He said ironically that the village would not be burned. It proved true, but the village was quite empty, as all the inhabitants were Greeks and had left it.

The next day about noon I heard that there were fires in the city. People started to flock to the streets leading to the quay. I was soon informed that the fire was spreading with incredible rapidity and that all the consulates were being evacuated. The consuls boarded destroyers. I had no place to go and remained in the consulate, which stood on the quay.

About midnight the fire came so close that our house was threatened. I took the children and went out into the street. I felt abandoned. No government, no country, no shelter—only the glare of the approaching conflagration, which could mean the end of us all. For a few moments I stood in front of the consulate clasping the hands of my children. I had to make a decision. But what decision, and where to go? Almost mechanically I looked around.

The street leading to the center of the town was barred by French sailors who were helping evacuate the Catholic establishments. I wanted to take that street, but a sailor pointed his revolver at my breast.

"Shoot," I said. The sailor rapidly put his gun back in the holster.

Only the quay remained open to me, but it was crowded with thousands of people. The embankment had no wall, and people risked being pushed into the sea. Later on, the sea was full of floating corpses.

I tried hard to think. I had to be quick and cool. There was little time left, as the conflagration was rapidly approaching. I realized that as soon as the fire reached the houses next to us and the flames started to lick the crowd, there would be a general stampede. To get away from the crowd was my first thought. About two blocks down the quay was brightly illuminated, for the houses on it had already begun to burn. But the quay was empty there, as people kept away from the fire. I decided to reach this empty space and headed straight for the flames.

Our progress was slow, as we had to move through a dense crowd that stood paralyzed with fear. I was walking first, holding the hand of my daughter, who dragged the two small boys. In back of them was the nurse, and last of all a Russian Greek. Sometimes we stopped, and I had to ask people to let us pass. They stood huddled like sheep, mute with terror, but they allowed me to go forward. It seemed an eternity until we reached the end of the two blocks. Several times the thought flashed in my mind that our effort was useless and that we should all perish, but I repulsed this idea and struggled ahead. Finally we reached the open space. I stopped and looked around. Thank God, all my family was there, the children clinging to my clothes and to each other.

A few houses to our left on the quay were still spared by the flames. Farther down all was burning, with tongues of fire stretching across the quay straight to the sea and barring the way. Separate flashes scattered by the current of air floated and disappeared above the water. We could not remain here, as I clearly heard the roar of the approaching fire. Could we pass through the solid wall of houses still untouched by the conflagration and reach the parallel street back of them? I met the eyes of the Greek and saw the same thought in them.

"I know a way out," he said. "Come along."

He walked to a café and opened a door. We passed through the deserted hall, then entered a door and found ourselves on the parallel street. It was still intact, although the fire was roaring close by and the street smelled strongly of petroleum. We walked a few paces and met a Turkish officer. I asked him if we could pass.

"Yes, go straight," he answered and quickly vanished around the corner. There was no time to lose, or we would be trapped by the advancing fire. We hastened our steps and entered a larger street. An automobile flashed by.

"Mr. Jacobs," I shouted. The car stopped. It was E. O. Jacobs of the YMCA.

I doubt that the work of the YMCA people during the fire of Smyrna has been fully acknowledged. They spent all night in the burning city and many days more. Their activity was little short of miraculous. Jacobs took us all in his car to the Turkish quarter, far out of reach of the fire. We stopped on the large plaza in front of the *konak* (government building).

"Stay in the car till morning," said Mr. Jacobs. "You will be safe." He gave us his car and an American sailor as a chauffeur. "I'll see you later."

"And you?" I asked.

"Don't worry about me," he grinned and disappeared in the darkness.

We spent a night of horror in the car. We heard continuous firing and the dull sound of explosions. As I heard later, Armenians had assembled in their cathedral and fought desperately there. The plaza filled with refugees. Turkish soldiers were bringing prisoners. There were cries in the darkness along the seashore and the rattling of revolver shots. We saw two men conducted to the military barracks, their hands bound behind them. One was walking stoically, resigned to his fate. The other was mad with fear. His knees were shaking, and he uttered hysterical cries. I thought he would die of anguish before reaching the place of execution.

In the morning Jacobs appeared again and took us to the quay, close to my consulate, which was still burning. I saw flames dancing like red demons in the windows of the upper floor. An American launch took us to a steamer, and we sailed for Piraeus. As I looked back, Smyrna was an ocean of fire, with pillars of black smoke rising here and there. The steamer passed the fort at the entrance of the gulf. Smyrna vanished behind a cape, and the glorious Ionian sea spread before us, smiling and indifferent under a luminous sky.

Index